Pros and Cons

Pros and Cons

A DEBATER'S HANDBOOK

18th Edition

Edited by

TREVOR SATHER

LONDON AND NEW YORK

First edition by J.B. Askew, published in 1896

Eighteenth edition published 1999
by Routledge
2 Park Square, Milton Park, Abingdon,
Oxon OX14 4RN
Reprinted 1999, 2000, 2004, 2005 (three times),
2006 (twice), 2007 (twice), 2008

*Routledge is an imprint of the Taylor & Francis
Group, an informa business*

© 1999 Routledge

Typeset in Bembo and Franklin Gothic by
Keystroke, Jacaranda Lodge, Wolverhampton

Printed and bound in Great Britain by
TJ International Ltd, Padstow, Cornwall

British Library Cataloguing in Publication Data
A catalogue record for this book is available from
the British Library

*Library of Congress Cataloguing in Publication
Data*
A catalogue record for this book has been
requested

ISBN10: 0-415-19547-0 (hbk)
ISBN10: 0-415-19548-9 (pbk)

ISBN13: 978-0-415-19547-8 (hbk)
ISBN13: 978-0-415-19548-5 (pbk)

CONTENTS

[C] Politics and Economics: National   69

[D] Politics and Economics: International   97

[E] Moral and Religious   **133**

[F] Education, Culture and Sport   **177**

[G] Law and Crime   213

[H] Health, Science and Technology   243

EDITORIAL TEAM

General Editor: Trevor Sather, Head, Centre for International Debate and Communication Training, English-Speaking Union

Assistant Editor: Thomas Dixon, PhD Student, King's College, Cambridge

Contributors:

Alastair Endersby, Head of History, Newstead Wood School for Girls, Kent
Dan Neidle, Trainee Solicitor, Clifford Chance, London
Bobby Webster, Student of English, Trinity College, Cambridge

FOREWORD

When a politician says that he or she wants to open up a 'debate' on this or that burning question of the day the interested citizen should immediately be on their guard. For this is political code for not wanting any kind of real discussion at all. What is meant instead is that we should accept the politician's definition of both problem and answer in terms that the politician wants, and then 'debate' within those parameters. The agenda is thus set; the questions naturally follow on; and so do the consequential policies.

But reasoned argument with no such limits is the stuff of democracy. We need to keep alive a more genuine conception of debate. Of course politicians will wrestle with us to set the agenda and confine the terms of the argument, but citizens need to be wise to their wiles. This means they must be equipped to judge when argument is being guided on to predictable tramlines, supported with insufficient evidence and resting on flimsy core assumptions. They need, in short, to be familiar with and competent in the art of debate themselves.

This book and the debating tradition which it seeks to nurture are thus not just pleasant diversions – although engaging in good argument is very good fun. The art of debate is one of the props on which we build our democracy and capacity to argue our way to the best solutions. In this revised edition it is intriguing how the terms of debate of so many subjects have moved on, even while the subjects themselves remain hardy perennials. But we should expect no other. Times change. Issues change. But what is enduring is our need to debate. I welcome this book and wish everyone associated with it, especially young debaters, every success.

Will Hutton
11 November 1998

PREFACE

The English-Speaking Union and Debating

The English-Speaking Union is an independent, non-political, educational charity with members throughout the UK, the US and some forty-one other countries. Its purpose is to promote international understanding and human achievement through the widening use of English as the language of our global village. The ESU has played a prominent part in debating since shortly after the Second World War, when it lent its support to the tours of America organised by Oxford and Cambridge Universities. Soon it became responsible for administering the tours – opened up to all British universities – and selecting the very best student debaters to go on them: names such as Patrick Mayhew, Brian Walden, Leon Brittan or Michael Howard.

Nowadays, the ESU administers a wide variety of public speaking and debating competitions designed to promote the effective use of spoken English in British universities and schools. In 1995 it set up the Centre for International Debate and Communication Training to co-ordinate the activities and undertake new projects to address the lack of public speaking teaching in the national curriculum. The Centre runs the John Smith Memorial Mace (the national debating competition for British and Irish universities), the national Schools Debating and Public Speaking Competitions, the International Public Speaking Competition, the Universities Mooting Competition and a programme of workshops through the UK and in countries such as Argentina and Portugal. It selects and coaches the England team for the World Schools Debating Championships, and in 1998 hosted those championships in London. All of these activities are seen as part of a coherent whole: an effort to instil into as many people as possible the confidence to speak fluently in public.

About This Book

This is a book of arguments. It is intended for beginner (or lazy) debaters who are helped by suggestions of arguments for and against a variety of controversial topics. First written in 1896, it has undergone seventeen revisions in order to cope with the growing or diminishing relevance of different issues. As the preface to the previous edition pointed out in 1985, each new version bears little resemblance to its predecessor and that is again the case today. We say goodbye to certain topics included previously – feeling that it was too late to debate calling off the Channel Tunnel project, for example – and have added several more; but the bulk of the change has come in the emphasis placed upon and language used to describe perennial favourites. The attitudes towards feminism, gay rights and in particular socialism, for example, have all evolved as Britain has moved away from the radical polarisation of Thatcherite times and towards a greater consensus of liberal capitalism. The eighteenth edition of *Pros and Cons* has therefore updated old topics to fit this modern context.

Examples and Arguments

Examples can be the first to tire and become clichés. No persuasive speech should seek to argue solely by using examples; instead they should be used to support arguments and make them clearer in the minds of the audience – and that is all we have tried to do here. However, the examples used are selective, only temporarily up to date, and in many cases only alluded to rather than explained. Debaters are therefore strongly warned to research their own – to make sure, for example, that laws have not been repealed, governments overthrown, projects abandoned and so on. Nor, for that matter, should the arguments be relied on as being comprehensive; in each case we hope to have given enough on which to base a decent debate, but some will always be missed, and new areas of discussion will arise. It is, in short, a danger to rely on *Pros and Cons* and assume that you are fully prepared for debate!

In our choice of topics we have tried to pick most of those commonly debated at the moment that are likely to remain largely the same for a few years at least. This restriction means that many notable controversies have been omitted, owing to our belief that rapid developments in those areas in recent years may well continue: hence we offer no treatment of Bosnia, Palestine and Israel or Northern Ireland.

About the Editorial Team, and Thanks

All of those involved in the preparation of this edition take part in debating as competitors, adjudicators, coaches and trainers. Trevor Sather is Head of the ESU Centre, responsible for its public speaking and debating programmes and workshops. Co-editor Thomas Dixon is a PhD student at King's College, Cambridge, and a senior member of the Cambridge debating team. Together, as teenagers, they were debating partners and won their first competition relying solely on the seventeenth edition of *Pros and Cons* – despite the warning above.

Two people must be singled out for their extensive research. Alastair Endersby, Head of History at Newstead Wood School for Girls, was Coach of the England Schools Team which won the World Championships in Australia in 1996. Dan Neidle, a solicitor, was Runner-Up at the World Universities Debating Championships in 1997 and on the British Debate Team which toured the US later that year.

Thanks are also due to Denise Rea, the development editor at Routledge, for the opportunity and her patience; Richard Chambers, former Head of the Centre, for initiating the project; Will Hutton; Bobby Webster; Jonathan Hills; Stuart Kirk; and Niki Mardas.

HOW TO DEBATE

THE ART OF DEBATING FOR BEGINNERS OF ANY AGE

Styles and formats of debate differ considerably around the world. 'Policy debate' in the US, for example, is seen very much as an educational discipline, with far more emphasis put on research and content than on rhetorical ability. Enormous amounts of information are delivered at great speed which, at the highest level, only trained judges can follow. In Australia the technique is paramount, with strict requirements of timing, structure, and logical progression of speeches. Britain, where debate was fostered in the heckling bear-pit of the House of Commons, has always enjoyed a different style, where swaying the crowd is the most important thing. Humour, rhetoric and use of striking analogies take precedence over the inconvenience of examples and well-organised argument. Of course, the best debaters in any country will combine all of these skills, which can loosely be summarised as content, strategy and style.

The Rules

The style of debate described here is common in British schools and on the American 'parliamentary' debate circuit, with two speakers per team and two teams per debate. A format involving four teams in a debate, used in British universities, is also described below.

Each speaker is allowed one main speech, seven minutes in length, after which a floor debate is conducted in which members of the audience may contribute opinions. To conclude, one speaker on each team offers a four-minute speech summarising their case, with the Opposition team speaking first. The order of speeches is as follows:

First Proposition Speaker
First Opposition Speaker
Second Proposition Speaker

Second Opposition Speaker
FLOOR DEBATE
Opposition Summary Speech
Proposition Summary Speech

The Standing Orders

The Standing Orders are the actual rules of the debate. To enforce them is the job of the **Chairman**, the 'MC' of the debate. As one would expect in the debating world, controversy rages over many of its terms – but the use of 'Mr' or 'Madam' Chairman can be justified if one adopts the theory that he or she has the hand (*manus*) on the Chair, thereby avoiding the clumsiness of the more politically correct 'Mr/Madam Chairperson'.

All debaters, officials and other members of the audience are members of the **House**, who are called to vote on the motion after the debate. The Chairman does not usually cast a vote but may do so in the case of a tie. The proceedings of the House are subject to the ruling and guidance of the Chairman, to whom all speeches should be addressed using the formula 'Mr (*or Madam*) Chairman' or 'Madam (*or Mr*) Speaker'.

Points of information may be made during a main speech, by either speaker on the opposing team. The first and last minutes of the speech are known as 'protected time' and points may not be offered then, nor are they allowed during the summary speeches nor at any time by other members of the House. To offer a point of information, a speaker must stand up and say, 'On a point of information!'. The speaker holding the Floor (i.e. giving the main speech) then has the right to accept or decline the point. If it is declined, the speaker offering the point must sit down at once. Points of information must not exceed fifteen seconds in length. The clock is not stopped while they are delivered.

Points of order concerning the procedure of the debate are exceptional, but can be made at any time and by any member of the House, if the Standing Orders are being contravened. They must be addressed to the Chairman who will ask for the clock to be stopped while the point is being considered. The Chairman may then rule on the point or act in consultation with adjudicators. A Chairman may also warn and has the discretion to take action against any member of the House who acts in a discourteous manner, harasses the speaker holding the Floor, or obstructs the debate in any way.

Timing

A common model for these debates allows seven minutes for the main speeches and four minutes for the summary speeches. The Chairman should arrange for an audible signal (a bell or a knock) to be given at the end of the first minute of a main speech and another at the end of the sixth minute, between which points of information may be offered. A double bell or knock will sound at the end of seven minutes, after which the speaker should conclude as quickly as possible. If the speaker continues, the Chairman has the discretion to ask him or her to stop immediately.

The Floor Debate

The floor debate is a significant feature of British school and university debating, allowing members of the audience to react to the debate so far. Points may be made in favour of the motion, against it or in abstention, and should be kept short to allow others the chance to speak. All points must be made to the Chair.

The main speakers in the debate do not offer points during the floor debate or reply immediately to any raised. The summary speeches, however, should deal with significant arguments raised.

Summary Speeches

The job of a summary speaker is to review the debate. New arguments should not be introduced, although new examples to illustrate arguments that have been discussed before may be. A single knock or bell should sound after three minutes, and a double signal after four.

Tips for Debaters

If you are taking part in a debating competition, the judges will usually be given three criteria on which to judge you – Content, Strategy and Style or similar categories – and even if you are only trying to sway an audience, it is these three qualities that will make them want to believe you. Most important of all, however, is to remember the key difference between public speaking and debating – in the latter, you must be flexible and respond to the arguments the other team is making. Anyone who reads out a pre-prepared speech or memorises one word for word, without altering it to react to previous speeches, is not debating.

Preparing for the Debate

Seven minutes can seem like a long time if you have nothing to say. Your first task, then, is to research the motion you are given, even those topics on which you are an expert. It is likely that somewhere on the Internet, in an encyclopaedia or in a newspaper you will find a piece of evidence, such as a statistic or little-known fact, that could devastate an argument of your opponents. Reading *Pros and Cons* does not count as thorough research!

Try to think how you would argue the other side of the motion, that is, as if you were your own opponents. Once you have listed their arguments, make sure you have answers to them. But be careful of pre-empting them and bringing up arguments for their side before they have used them – as you may just be giving them ideas that they would not otherwise have thought of. It is useful to have a list of opposition arguments and counter-arguments on the table in front of you during the debate. Then, when your opponents do introduce those arguments, you can quickly make a point of information or start working the reply into your speech.

No talented debater writes out a speech word for word, even to memorise and discard it. Using a system of notes allows you many benefits. You will find it easier to look the audience in the eye; you will deliver your speech more naturally and fluently; and you will be able to add rebuttal arguments to the relevant parts of your speech as you think of them. For example:

Instead of writing this out . . .	**. . . try making notes like this.**
There are many reasons why we should implement a 15% import tax on bananas being brought into Britain. First, the countries producing bananas are clearly making far too much money for their own good – for example Atlantis or Sparta – and we should penalise their greed.	Advocate: 15% import tax on bananas Why? 1 **International benefits** Penalise rich and greedy banana growers – e.g. Atlantis, Sparta
Second, this banana tax would raise £15 million because there are currently 100 million bananas imported every year, sold at £1 each. The £15 million could easily be used to fund a new Academy for Non-Organic Insect Development.	2 **Increased revenue** 100m imported = £15m in revenue – to fund Academy of Non-Org. Insect Dev.
Third, the Ministry for Raising Banana Tax has employed 27 people since 1994 without ever doing anything useful, so this would justify its existence.	3 **Resources already available** Justify salaries at Ministry of Rais. Ban. Tax – 27 employees since 1994

Structuring your Speech

A debating speech delivers a great deal of information to the audience and to the adjudicators. Sadly, most humans do not have a very long attention span and it is unlikely that they will take in all the information unless you make it easy for them. This means **structuring** your speech. You should not have more than three or four different arguments in your speech – and even if you have only one argument, you should look at only three or four case-studies to support it. No-one will remember your points if you have seventeen of them.

Divide your speech into sections. Signpost each section. Make sure each has an introduction and a summary all of its own. In effect, you are giving a running commentary on yourself, describing what position in your own speech you have reached:

> '**Next I am going to expand on my second point, which is** what we could do with the money raised by a banana tax. Let's consider the figures. We currently import 100 million bananas a year and sell them for £1 each. If we put a 15% sales tax on, we would raise another £15 million. This in turn is the exact cost of setting up an Academy for Non-Organic Insect Development. **So my second point is this: the banana tax would bring clear benefits to insect research**. Now, point number three . . . '

In other words, keep drumming your points in by repeating them constantly. Make sure you summarise all your arguments at the end of the speech. Of course, this structure applies to the team as a whole. The first speaker should mention briefly the points that the second speaker will make, and the second will remind us of arguments used by the first:

> 'I will be talking about bananas and pears, while my partner, Robin, will go on in his/her speech to discuss the wider implications of the existence of fruit.'

Timing is very important in the context of structure. If you have three points of roughly equal importance, make sure you spend equal time on them! Be very careful not to spend so much time on your first point that you are forced to cram your other two into your last minute.

Finally, although you may have lots of different points to make, do not forget that they all tie into one guiding principle which you are trying to prove (or disprove): the motion. After every argument or example, remind the audience how this shows that the motion is true (or false).

Thinking on your Feet

Remember that the ability to think quickly and deal with unforeseen arguments is what differentiates debating from public speaking. There are two major areas where you need to think on your feet.

Points of Information

Both speakers should make and accept points of information. It is the only way to prove that you are on top of your material and not simply reading out a speech that someone else could have prepared. Offering points, even if they are not accepted, shows you are interested and active in the debate; accepting them shows you are confident of your arguments. A team that does neither of these is not debating.

When offering a point, you should stand up and say 'On a point of information!'. If you are not accepted, sit down again. If you are, you may make a simple point of no longer than fifteen seconds – do not try to make a mini-speech. You are best advised to offer a fact that disproves what the other speaker is saying, to point out a contradiction in his or her argument, or to ask for further information. Your point should be relevant to the current topic of discussion.

There is a real knack to accepting points of information which comes through practice. Do not take points in mid-sentence, or when you are unsure of what you are saying and could come unstuck. Do not take two in quick succession, and do not take too many. It is easy to be distracted and diminish the impact of your own speech. You should aim to take two or three in a seven-minute speech, at natural pauses. But remember: you should reply to them as soon as they are made: interruptions cannot just be ignored!

Rebuttal

You are also required to address the arguments that the other team has come up with. Even if you find yourself agreeing with a point, you must find some way of undermining it so that it is less appealing to the audience or judges. Question its relevance, point out how it is inconsistent with something else they were saying, or simply disprove it.

There are different ways of fitting rebuttal into your speech. One way is to spend the first few minutes addressing the major points of your opponents, before going on to your main constructive material. You might choose just to seize on several unconnected statements your opponents have made, especially if they can be made to look ridiculous out of context. This is known as **scattergun** rebuttal.

Another method is to **sort the rebuttal** into your speech. For example, if you are planning on covering three different areas – perhaps the economic, social and international benefits of a certain plan – then rebut their economic points during your economic section and so on. This will show adjudicators that you have identified the key arguments and seen how they all fit together.

Stylistic Tips

In competitions, what you say is usually more important than how you say it. But audiences can be swayed by persuasive style, and the ideal speaker will combine all qualities.

First, are you **appealing to listen to?** Make sure you modulate your speech, varying your tone at important points, even changing your volume and speed. An audience will tune out from a speech delivered at the same level throughout its duration. Be prepared to speak more slowly than normal, and to use pauses, especially before important points. And try not to use 'ums' and 'ers' when you hesitate – turn hesitations into pauses, too.

Next, consider your **body language**. Some people have mannerisms that can irritate audiences and distract from what you are saying. Examples of bad body language include putting your hand over your mouth, jangling coins in your pocket, walking back and forth too much or scratching body parts! Good body language is a comfortable stance and the use of gestures to emphasise what you are saying, not to distract from it. Most important of all is eye contact with the audience, which becomes very easy if you are using notes rather than a written speech.

All audiences appreciate **humour**, although some adjudicators will appreciate only a certain type. Debating is not stand-up comedy, and jokes should not be at the expense of content – that is, irrelevant to the debate – and certainly not offensive towards your opponent. Ridicule the arguments, not the people.

Think carefully, also, about what sorts of **rhetoric** you use. In particular do not feel obliged to over-use the traditional vocabulary of debating: 'worthy', 'honourable', 'eloquent' and so on. Modern audiences are scornful of clichés and you will tend to be more convincing if you speak in your own natural dialect.

Some people wonder what difference an **accent** makes. The answer is: none. 'Received pronunciation' is neither a benefit nor a burden in debating; many of history's finest debaters had strong regional accents or speech impediments.

Finally, there is nothing worse for your style than a dry mouth. Make sure you have a glass of water available during your speech, and do not be afraid to use it.

The Roles of the Speakers

First Proposition Speaker

It is the role of the 'first Prop' to **define** the motion, to describe exactly what the basis for debate will be. This means you must first, explain any ambiguous words, second, set any limits to the debate and third, interpret the motion as a whole and state exactly what contention you are going to try and prove. Some things to think about are:

This House would censor the Internet
What exactly do we mean when we say 'Internet' – the Web, e-mail or anything transmitted by modem? What sort of things should we aim to censor? And who for? What is censorship? And who is going to do it? A valid definition would be: 'The British government should make it illegal for any written or pictorial material to be sent or posted on the World Wide Web that is pornographic or racist.'

This House would respect its elders
Who is this House? And who are its elders? Is respect a vague feeling towards someone, or does it require a definite action? In this situation it is acceptable (although not mandatory) to tie the motion in to a specific issue, in order to provide a focused debate. A valid definition would be: 'The vast majority of people who

have made major beneficial differences to society were over the age of 50.' An equally good definition would be: 'The British government should continue to provide guaranteed welfare for the elderly and abandon plans to privatise the state pension.' Vague motions of this sort which beg specific topics to be substituted are very common on the British university circuit but less so – although not unheard of – in school debates.

Although it is generally accepted that the Proposition may define the motion in any way it chooses, intelligent and straightforward definitions are expected. In particular, a good definition must be fair to the Opposition and give its members an equal case to argue back. If, for example, the proposers of the motion 'This House would break a bad law' defined 'bad law' as being 'a law that it is impossible to observe, such as a law against breathing', then such a law must *by definition* be broken and the Opposition has nothing to argue. This is a **truistic** definition and would result in the Proposition losing the debate.

On the other hand, motions are taken as being general principles rather than statements of absolute truth. In other words, if you are arguing that 'the United Nations is impotent', you only have to show that in the **vast majority** of cases this principle is true rather than **in every single case**. There are always one or two small exceptions to anything, but the Opposition should not win this debate unless it shows that the UN has had a *major* area of success.

After the definition, the first proposer should say how the case will be split between the two speakers, and then go on to prove his or her half.

First Opposition Speaker

The job of the first Opp speaker is to rebut the arguments of the Proposition (perhaps by highlighting inconsistencies or weaknesses) and to explain why there is a difference between the two sides. This speaker is the first to isolate exactly what the debate will be about, by saying which part of the Proposition's case his or her side will agree with and which it chooses to dispute. He or she will then go on to explain the structure of the Opposition case, and to prove his or her points.

Here you must be prepared to be flexible, as you may need to react to a slightly unusual or unexpected definition. You should accept any definition by the Proposition unless it presents an unreasonable or clearly irrelevant interpretation of the motion, or is truistic and does not leave you a side to argue. In these cases you may **challenge** the definition by stating your reasons for rejecting it and introducing an alternative interpretation. The second Prop speaker must adopt your definition unless he or she can prove that his or her team's is valid.

It must be emphasised that **definitional debates are generally not good ones**. The best debates involve an interesting and fair proposition which the first Opposition speaker accepts.

Second Proposition and Opposition Speakers

The second speakers on each team should divide their time between rebutting points made by their opponents and continuing with their side of the argument. At the end of a second speech, a brief summary of the whole argument of your side should be given.

Summary Speeches

Either speaker on the team may make the summary speech, after the floor debate. It is intended to review the major issues of the debate and to leave a lasting impression on the minds of the audience or adjudicators that is favourable to your side. A summary speaker has been compared with 'a biased news reporter', going over the various arguments that have already been made but implying that your side has won them all.

It is important to concentrate on the major areas of difference between the two sides, rather than on trivial points or areas of agreement. Your job is to remind the audience 'exactly where we disagreed in this debate', and then to prove why your arguments in these areas are superior. You are therefore looking at the debate as a whole rather than simply reviewing points one by one.

New arguments should not be introduced into summary speeches. You are reviewing the debate that has already happened, not starting a new one. However, if major arguments have been raised in a floor debate, you should also incorporate those into your speech.

Other Styles of Debate

The most common format of debate in the UK is known as British **parliamentary** style, and this involves four teams of two people all taking part in one debate, with two teams on each side. In order to win the debate you must agree with the other team on your side, but argue that side better than they do. Four speakers sit down each side of a table, facing each other, with the Chairman at the end – similar to the layout of the House of Commons. The order of speeches is: 1 Prop; 1 Opp; 2 Prop; 2 Opp; 3 Prop; 3 Opp; 4 Prop; 4 Opp. There are no summary speeches. Points of information may be made by any of the opposing speakers.

Debating societies wishing to encourage many audience members to take part might like to try a **hat debate**. Suggestions of different motions are taken from the Floor and put in a hat. Two volunteers who will speak in the first debate are given one motion at random, and allocated sides by the flip of a coin. They are given ten minutes to prepare, say, a four-minute speech each. Then, just before they begin debating, the Chairman selects another two volunteers and gives them a motion to prepare while the first debate is taking place. This can be repeated several times.

Or, for individual speakers, you might prefer a **balloon debate**. Pick about five or six people, each of whom chooses a famous historical or contemporary individual to impersonate. They take part in a role-play scenario, set in a hot air balloon which is rapidly sinking. One of them must be thrown overboard in order to save the others – but which? Each participant makes a speech saying why *he* or *she* should be allowed to stay in the debate. The audience votes, and the losers are disqualified from the debate.

SECTION A

Philosophical/Political Theory

Anarchism

Pros

[1]   Anarchism aims for a classless society but, unlike communism, rejects a strong controlling state. Anarchism fights for human freedom by opposing all forms of hierarchical organisation and control – these are inherently repressive. It does not argue for complete disorder but advocates local co-operation and universal pacifism.

[2]   Anarchists recognise that even so-called democracies are essentially repressive institutions in which an educated, privileged elite of politicians and civil servants imposes its will on the mass of people. Anarchists want to live in a non-hierarchical, *natural* world of free association in which individual expression is paramount and all the paraphernalia of voting, government, taxation, laws and police are done away with.

[3]   While anarchism may not achieve its aim of universal non-hierarchical living, it is still an important voice of dissent, highlighting the injustices done to minorities, animals and the environment. Many anarchists are truly self-sufficient, living off the land, making their own clothes and bartering with each other. Such people include the 'new age travellers' and radical environmentalists who opt out of traditional hierarchies altogether for a natural, pacifist lifestyle.

Cons

[1]   While it may be possible to live in a state of complete anarchy it is not desirable to do so. All the greatest achievements in science, technology and the arts have only been possible through human society and co-operation. This requires a degree of social organisation and structure. As populations increase, so the degree of hierarchy and government needs to increase. Far from being repressive, democratic government is a way to prevent powerful or fanatical minorities creating tyrannical regimes.

[2]   The answer to the problem of undemocratic democracies is reform, not anarchy. Democracies can be made more representative through devolution, proportional representation and increased use of the referendum. In any case, 'free association' between people (perhaps local co-operation in agriculture or learning or trade), where successful, will be continued and eventually formalised in its optimal form. An anarchic 'state of nature' will inevitably evolve through the formalisation of co-operation on larger scales into something like the societies we now have. Anarchism, then, is a pointlessly retrograde act – a state of anarchy can never last.

[3]   Anarchism is often used as a political rationalisation of acts of terrorism and civil disobedience in the name of 'animal rights' or 'ecology'. These acts should be seen for what they are – self-indulgent and anti-social acts passed off as an expression

Possible motions:
This House would rage against the machine.
This House would drop out.
This House says 'Anarchy rules'.

Related topics:
Civil Disobedience
Democracy
Legislation v. Individual Freedom
Terrorism (Justifiable)

of 'anarchist' morality. A true anarchist would not eat, wear or use anything created by those who are part of the organised state. As long as these terrorists and eco-warriors use the fruits of the labour of the members of the hierarchical society they seek to subvert, they are acting hypocritically. At any rate, their acts of vandalism and violence belie their professed pacifism.

Capitalism v. Socialism

Pros

[1]   The fundamental basis of human life, and of the natural world as a whole, is competition. Human nature is fundamentally selfish and competitive, and capitalism recognises that by letting the most successful individuals flourish through hard work and success in an open competitive market. Capitalism is an economic and social version of the 'survival of the fittest'.

[2]   Capitalism gives supreme autonomy to individuals and accords them protection for their property. Hard work should be rewarded with material gain, not penalised with punitive taxes.

[3]   The endeavours of the entrepreneur, the landowner or the capitalist in fact benefit not only those individuals but all those millions who work under them. Individuals who bring in investment from abroad and create successful enterprises are already benefiting the community at large by creating wealth, employment,

Cons

[1]   The natural and human worlds are characterised by co-operation as much as by competition. In nature, species flourish through the practice of 'reciprocal altruism' – mutual helping behaviour. Groups rather than individuals are the unit of selection. Socialism recognises these facts and proposes an equal co-operative society rather than an unnaturally harsh, individualist and competitive one.

[2]   The capitalist belief in the autonomy of the individual is a myth. We are all dependent first on our parents and more broadly on the education, resources, services, industry, technology and agriculture of fellow members of society. An 'autonomous individual' would not survive more than a few days. We are all reliant on and responsible for each other.

[3]   As in nature, so in society, favourable variations and adaptations are the work of *chance*. Such chance advantages as

better working conditions and an improved quality of life – they should not be required to do so a second time through redistribution of their private wealth.

[4] A socialist system encourages laziness and welfare dependency. A capitalist system encourages enterprise and progress. People see that hard work and ingenuity are rewarded and thus they are motivated. In a socialist system where the state provides for all, there is no motivation to work hard, and the elimination of the market halts the processes of competition and selection.

[5] Free competition is the only way to protect against monopolies. State-owned and -run monopolies, in the absence of competition, become inefficient, wasteful, and bureaucratic, and supply bad overpriced services to the consumer.

[6] The nation state has had its day. Nations will form into ever broader economic and political alliances (e.g. the US, the EU). In these circumstances it does not make sense to force individuals to share their wealth among a virtually non-existent 'nation', or among a large conglomerate of nations which is so culturally, politically and economically diverse as to make the socialist idea that all are part of one 'community' look ridiculous. The real economic unit is not the state, nor the confederation, but the *individual*.

a good education, an in-born intelligence or sense for business, or success in the lottery of the market-place, do not mark out an individual as anything more than lucky or in the right place at the right time. It is society at large (*using* particular individuals) that creates commercial and industrial success and it is society at large that should benefit. Therefore wealthy individuals should be taxed at a high rate and their wealth redistributed through the welfare system.

[4] One does not need to be a capitalist or individualist to believe in progress. Historically, the forms of socialism employed by the Soviet Union produced immense scientific and technological progress. A socialist system does not entail providing more than minimal welfare support for those truly in need. Flexible socialist systems do not therefore do away with the attraction of paid employment over welfare.

[5] Large-scale industries (such as a state-run health or education service) are more efficient than smaller ones through economies of scale. There is also a 'third way' compatible with socialist ideology, which allows some competition while still retaining ultimate state control of important services.

[6] The nation state has not had its day but is in a process of transition. There is currently a dual process of change both towards nationalism and a guarding of national cultural identity (as in the nations of Eastern Europe) and a simultaneous movement towards transnational alliances (e.g. the EU). In the future there will still be loyalty to a national society

Possible motions:

This House believes that the community is more important than the individual.

This House believes there is no such thing as society.

This House believes in enterprise.

This House believes in the survival of the fittest.

Related topics:

Democracy

Ideology v. Pragmatism

Legislation v. Individual Freedom

Marxism

Privatisation

Welfare State

National Health Service (Privatisation of)

Pensions (Ending State Provision of)

Salary Capping

Taxation (Direct, Abolition of)

Trade Unions (Modernisation of)

Workfare

Democracy (Imposition of)

Private Schools

Tuition Fees for University Students

and also a broader communitarianism that will be potentially global. These developments open new horizons for socialism, they do not mean its end.

Censorship by the State

This is one of the most common topics, underpinning many civil rights issues, media debates, and efforts of the state to regulate new technological developments. 'Censorship' is an ambiguous term but the debate is better if the Proposition takes it as it is commonly accepted, as the banning of certain texts, images, films, etc. Defining censorship simply as regulation or indeed as 'any law' makes it too easy for the Proposition to win.

Pros

[1]   Freedom of speech is never an absolute right but an aspiration. It ceases to be a right when it causes harm to

Cons

[1]   Censorship is wrong in principle. However violently we may disagree with a person's point of view or mode of

others – we all recognise the value of, for example, legislating against incitement to racial hatred. Therefore it is not the case that censorship is wrong in principle.

[2] Certain types of literature or visual image have been conclusively linked to crime. Excessive sex and violence in film and television has been shown (especially in studies in the US) to contribute to a tendency towards similar behaviour in spectators. There is no excuse for this and such images must be sacrificed, no matter what their artistic merit.

[3] We also accept forms of state censorship in the practice of giving 'certificates' to films, videos and some computer games so that children below a certain age are not exposed to inappropriate scenes of sex or violence. We should entrust the state, as our moral guardians, with the regulation of material such as this, as well as material on the Internet, in order to provide consistent moral protection for all our children. Sex and violence in magazines and on television should be made as inaccessible to children as possible – pornographic magazines should only be available to adults with ID, and explicit TV programmes should only be shown late at night.

[4] We need state censorship in the case of hardcore pornography in particular. Children as well as young men and women need to be protected from exploitation by pornographers. And society at large should be protected from the seedy, unhealthy, repressive and objectifying attitudes to women and sex perpetuated by pornography.

expression, they must be free to express themselves in a free and civilised society. Censorship such as legislation against incitement to racial hatred drives racists and others underground and thus entrenches and ghettoises that section of the community rather than drawing its members into open and rational debate.

[2] In fact, the link between sex and violence on screen and in real life is far from conclusive. To look at it from another angle, those individuals who *already have tendencies* to violence are likely to watch violent 'video nasties', just as those with a predilection for rape are likely to use pornography. The two are therefore connected but the individual's personality is formed first.

[3] Such forms of state regulation are notoriously ineffectual. Children of all ages can obtain access to '18 certificate' videos and games and adult Internet sites if they really want to. In the end the only effective protection of children from inappropriate material must come from the parent. And this protection is not a form of state censorship but of individual parental choice and control. That is the appropriate location for such decisions.

[4] Again, people will get hold of pornography if they want it. Censorship will not change the number of people who use pornography. It is down to the parent and the community to bring up children with healthy attitudes – not down to the state to make ineffectual legislation about what sort of images should be published. In the end pornographic pictures and films will not have a truly harmful effect on a well-balanced

[5]   We need state censorship to protect public figures from unacceptable intrusions by the gutter press. State legislation on privacy would be a good example of legitimate censorship. Already courts can place injunctions on newspapers to prevent them from publishing material likely to put an individual in danger (e.g. the location of a suspected paedophile or a criminal who has been released after serving a prison term). These forms of censorship are right and necessary.

mind. Pornography only has insidious effects on those who are unbalanced for other reasons or have been abused. Child pornography is a red herring – it is already illegal, breaking existing laws on age of consent, and we do not need extra censorship laws to attack it.

[5]   In principle, newspapers should not be 'gagged' in this way. If a mob is determined to find the location of a criminal then it will do so without the help of the press, and the individual in question will in any case be able to seek protection or a secret identity through the police. As for privacy laws – public figures accept that their lives become public property when they enter the public sphere. They also have recourse through libel and defamation laws. These laws, along with self-regulation, and not state *censorship*, are the ways to regulate the media.

Possible motions:

This House believes there is no place for censorship in a democracy.
This House would censor.
This House fears a free press.

Related topics:

Legislation v. Individual Freedom
Broadcasting (Ending Public Control of)
Pornography
Privacy of Public Figures
Internet (Censorship of)

Civil Disobedience

Pros

[1]   Democratic governments which are elected only every four to five years do not provide true or adequate representation of public interests. Once a government is elected, it may entirely ignore the will of the electorate until its term is finished. Therefore civil disobedience (e.g. the student riots of 1968 in Paris; the miners' strike in Britain in the 1980s; the 'Poll Tax riots' and the non-payment of Poll Tax

Cons

[1]   In fact, democratic means are much broader than a general election every few years. The election of local representatives takes place regularly. MPs in Britain are available for 'surgery' with their constituents every week and will always respond to letters and bring matters of concern to the attention of ministers. Given this direct democratic access to government, through letter-writing and

in Britain in 1990; occupations of construction sites by roads protesters at Manchester Airport and the Newbury bypass) is necessary as an effective method for the people's voice to be heard even in democratic countries – as a last resort.

[2] Historically, civil disobedience has triumphed over insidious regimes and forms of prejudice where other methods have failed, e.g. the movements orchestrated in India by Gandhi and in America by Martin Luther King. More recently the riots and looting in Indonesia in 1998 protested against a corrupt and undemocratic regime. Peaceful protests by minorities in undemocratic countries are often banned or quashed, or they can fail to bring about change. None the less civil disobedience movements can be entirely peaceful (e.g. Gandhi).

[3] Civil disobedience involving public confrontation with authority is often the only way to bring an issue to wider public and international attention. This tactic was successfully employed by the 'suffragettes' of the early women's movement, and also by supporters of nuclear disarmament, from the philosopher Bertrand Russell, who was arrested for civil disobedience several times in the cause of pacifism, to the women of Greenham Common in the 1980s (the last cruise missiles were withdrawn from the base in 1991). The student protests in Tiananmen Square in 1989 (and their brutal crushing by the authorities) brought the human rights abuses of the Chinese regime to the forefront of international attention and concern more effectively than anything else before or since.

lobbying, there is no need for civil disobedience.

[2] Peaceful protest is quite possible, even in an undemocratic society, without resorting to civil disobedience. A point can be made quite well without coming into confrontation with police, trespassing or causing disturbance and damage to people or property. The racist attacks on the Chinese in Indonesia in 1998 illustrate how civil disobedience, however worthy the cause, too often descends into a breakdown of law and order and legitimates all sorts of other crimes.

[3] There is no excuse for provoking violent confrontations with police, rioting, looting or trespassing. Such actions result in assaults, injuries and sometimes in deaths (e.g. during the miners' strike, and during the looting and riots in Indonesia in 1998, which started as a pro-democracy demonstration). Animal rights campaigners and anti-abortion campaigners have been particularly violent in the past. This is too high a price to pay for media attention – such groups should use peaceful and lawful methods to make their point.

Possible motions:

This House supports civil disobedience.

This House believes the end justifies the means.

This House would break the law in the cause of justice.

Related topics:

Anarchism

Democracy

Ends v. Means

Pacifism

Terrorism (Justifiable)

Democracy

In Western democracies we frequently forget that there are other types of political system and that ours may not necessarily be the best. In debates set in democracies, e.g. that 'leaders should listen more to their people', the Proposition must do more than *assume* that 'democracy is a good thing' – this is an assertion that needs to be justified.

Pros

[1]   A country should be governed by representatives, chosen by every (adult) member of society, who are answerable to and removable by the people. This way a minority, wealthy, land-owning, military or educated elite will not be allowed disproportionate power. This ideal of the liberal democratic society was established by the French and American Revolutions and is endorsed as the ideal method of government around the world.

[2]   Certainly, modern democracies could be made more truly democratic, and this is happening through increased use of referendum (especially in Switzerland and also in France and Britain – e.g. on Scottish and Welsh devolution, the Northern Ireland settlement, and questions of European integration) and proportional representation (e.g. in the Scottish parliament and the Welsh assembly). Democracy is brought closer to the people by devolving power to local government. People also have a direct voice through access to representatives throughout their term of office (in Britain, through MPs' weekly 'surgeries').

[3]   Decisions must be made according to the will of the people. People should be as well informed as possible by the politicians, scientists, economists and the media in order to make those decisions –

Cons

[1]   Modern 'democracies' (unlike Athenian democracy in which the whole population met to make decisions) are a sham. Such a system is impossible except on a very small scale. For a large country, decisive and effective leadership and government is incompatible with true democracy. Therefore we have supposedly democratic systems in which the people have a say every four to five years but have no real input into important decisions. There is nothing wrong with this – an educated minority *should* be entrusted with power and leadership – but it is not 'democratic'.

[2]   These measures are mere tokens – rhetorical gestures required to keep the people happy and satisfy proponents of democracy. But the truth is still that real power is isolated within an elite of politicians and civil servants. It is the political parties which decide who will stand for election and who will be allocated the 'safe seats', thereby effectively, undemocratically, determining the constitution of the House of Commons. In Britain we have a powerful unelected second chamber (the House of Lords) that functions effectively through the *appointment* of leading industrialists, scientists, academics, politicians and civil servants. Referenda and elections are a harmless gesture in the direction of

but it is their will that counts. In a liberal democracy the press provides informed, independent analysis on which the public can base opinions.

Possible motions:

This House believes in democracy.

This House believes that democracy is a sham.

Related topics:

Capitalism v. Socialism

Civil Disobedience

Marxism

Coalition Government v. Party Government

House of Lords (Abolition of)

Monarchy v. Presidency

Proportional Representation

Referenda (Increased Use of)

Voting (Compulsory)

Affirmative Action

Democracy (Imposition of)

Terrorism (Justifiable)

Terrorists (Negotiation with)

High Art v. Low Art

Judges (Election of)

populism but do not change the fact that real democracy is an unattainable and undesirable system.

[3]   It is the media, the spin doctors and the politicians who determine the 'will of the people'. People do not have a 'democratic will' that comes out of thin air. The opinions of the mass of people are moulded by the partial and biased information fed to them by the gutter press, and control of the press is where real power lies – with the educated, intelligent and successful members of society, and there is nothing wrong with that.

Ends v. Means

Pros

[1]   The end always justifies the means. Our morality should be a 'consequentialist' one – we should judge an action on the higher good (or bad) that it brings about as its consequence. If I can save a hundred innocent children from dying by murdering one, then I should do so. This is a more pragmatic and long-term view of morality.

Cons

[1]   The end does not justify the means. We must have firm moral rules that we stick to as closely as possible. Regardless of what an act brings about, if it is wrong then it is wrong. If I can save a hundred innocent children by murdering one – however those strange circumstances might arise! – I should not, as it is always wrong to kill innocents. Pragmatism compromises moral integrity.

[2]   In politics it is acceptable to be somewhat secretive, undemocratic or corrupt if the end is a recognised good. For example, the shipment of arms to Sierra Leone from Britain in 1998 was (probably) done with deliberate secrecy and in contravention of a UN arms embargo, but helped to reinstate a democratically elected leader to power and overthrow the leaders of the military coup. So the breaking of international law was justified by the end – the restoration of democracy.

[3]   In war the end (justice) justifies the means (killing). No-one thinks war is an ideal solution but, for example, in 1939 there was no option left but to declare war on Germany to halt its aggressive territorial expansion. Justice and the protection of nations' sovereignty (and, had it been known earlier, the prevention of the Holocaust) were ends that justified the means of war.

[4]   When democratic routes of protest are unavailable under repressive regimes, violent and unlawful protest – even terrorism – is justifiable as the means to the end of democracy. Violent protest is the only way to get enough international attention and support for the cause.

[5]   If the greatest good for the greatest number can be attained by taxing the rich at 90 per cent or by forcing landowners to share out their land and wealth among poorer members of society then, however unfair it is on them, it is right to do so. It is also right to give women and ethnic minorities preferential treatment in the job market until equality is achieved. In the pursuit of economic and political equality, the end justifies the means.

[2]   To allow the flouting of international (or domestic) law by politicians at whim is to go down a slippery slope to corrupt government and despotism. The whole point of our legal system is to have a morality and set of rules that are above subjective personal judgements of what is a good or a bad thing. Governments must stick to the rules and achieve whatever good results they seek by legal means. The price of such pragmatism – dishonest government – is too high.

[3]   First, war, unlike corruption in the previous example, is not something that is always inherently wrong. Killing in war is not immoral in the way in which killing in general is. Second, however, the ends in the case of the Second World War did not justify either the bombing of hundreds of thousands of civilians (especially in Dresden by the Allies) or the dropping of nuclear bombs on Nagasaki and Hiroshima. Bombing civilians and using nuclear weapons – however desirable was the defeat of Germany and Japan – is always and everywhere wrong.

[4]   There are always other ways of campaigning against injustice. In the case of overthrowing unjust regimes (e.g. South Africa, Indonesia) it was always ultimately international economic and political pressure that succeeded. If the international community fails to act without the inhabitants first resorting to violence then that is a failing of the international community that should be rectified – but not a justification for rioting, looting and killing, which are always wrong.

[5]   Punitive taxes and the absolute redistribution of wealth are merely wrong

Possible motions:

This House believes the end justifies the means.

This House believes in the greatest good for the greatest number.

Related topics:

Civil Disobedience
Ideology v. Pragmatism
Pacifism
Bill of Rights
Voting (Compulsory)
Affirmative Action
Democracy (Imposition of)
Dictators (Assassination of)
Sanctions (Use of)
Terrorism (Justifiable)
Terrorists (Negotiation with)
Abortion on Demand
Animal Experimentation and Vivisection
   (Banning of)
Euthanasia
Homosexuals (Outing of)
Corporal Punishment
Capital Punishment
Child Curfews
Zero Tolerance
Eugenics: IVF and Genetic Screening
Genetic Engineering
Global Warming (More Action on)
Internet (Censorship of)
Nuclear Energy
Science: a Menace to Civilisation?

and unfair. Social justice is not attained by reducing all to the lowest common denominator. And jobs should always be offered on the merit and worth of the candidate – privileging a candidate on grounds other than merit and suitability is always wrong. 'The greatest good for the greatest number' is not an excuse for injustices being perpetrated.

Ideology v. Pragmatism

Many debates involve this clash in some form or other. The best debates have ideological and practical arguments on both sides, but it is often the case that one side will rely more on principle and one more on practical benefits. The following is merely a simplified version to illustrate the foundations of this basic debate.

Pros

[1]   Morality comprises of principles that have evolved over time as the best way to order a society: e.g. the principle that we should not kill another person, that we should help those less fortunate than ourselves, that the role of the doctor is always to preserve life, and so on. In forming specific policies it is our job to apply these principles to particular situations. It is by the rational and systematic application of a set of principles that a society's laws and policies are coherent and defensible. The pragmatist sacrifices that coherence and consistency in abandoning specific principles.

[2]   The pragmatist is being dishonest. He must appeal to certain principles in deciding what *is* the greatest good for the greatest number. His refusal to make those principles explicit simply reveals that he has an ever-shifting, ungrounded set of values, some of which are contradictory, to which he is tacitly appealing in an underhand way – e.g. the principle that individual autonomy overrides the moral authority of religion, the principle that individual sexual freedom is a greater good than social condemnation of promiscuity, the principle that social condemnation of violent behaviour is a greater good than individual freedom to defend oneself. The ideologist is merely being more honest and open than the pragmatist about his or her values and principles. The ideologist also resists the idea that all values are utterly relative to a specific time and culture and that there are no enduring moral principles.

[3]   Ideology is essential to give a lead

Cons

[1]   Morality is not an abstract thing containing specific timeless principles, but is an *ad hoc* enterprise, making decisions and policies 'on the hoof' to secure tangible practical results or benefits. Pragmatism itself rests on just one general guiding principle, rather than on a set of specifics – the 'utilitarian' principle (advocated by Jeremy Bentham and other progressive social reformers of the eighteenth and nineteenth centuries) or the 'consequentialist' view of ethics. The utilitarian will adopt the policy that secures the greatest happiness for the greatest number. The consequentialist judges the moral goodness of an action not by the intentions of the agent nor by the action's conformation to a prior moral code but simply by its practical consequences. The ideologist blinds himself or herself to the best and most just practical option by adhering dogmatically to an age-old principle, however inappropriate to the specific case. Examples include the Catholic church's continued condemnation of homosexuality and abortion on the grounds of Biblical principles, the refusal to legalise prostitution on the grounds of Victorian morality, and the refusal to ban handguns in the US on the grounds of the constitutional right to bear arms. The pragmatist sacrifices principles for the sake of practical results.

[2]   The difference between the ideologist and the pragmatist is that the pragmatist does not unnecessarily commit himself to specific principles and policies. Certainly a pragmatist has *some* values – but they are secondary to the underlying belief that the consequences of policies

to society and let it clearly be known what is right and wrong. Principles must be upheld to give moral certainty to society and so that justice is seen to be done – so that each case is seen to be treated in the same fair way. The ideologist stands by what is *right*.

Possible motions:

This House would stick to its principles.

This House believes in right and wrong.

This House is idealistic.

Related topics:

Capitalism v. Socialism

Pacifism

Tradition v. Innovation

Affirmative Action

National Health Service (Privatisation of)

Environment (Links to International Trade and Relations)

Nuclear Weapons (Banning of)

Gays in the Military

Tuition Fees for University Students

Drugs (Legalisation of)

Prostitution (Legalisation of)

and actions are more important than their conformity to a moral code. This means that the pragmatist is more open to changing values and problems in society over time and is more adaptable to change. The pragmatist will weigh up the pros and cons of a situation and decide which policy benefits the most people (where benefit is calculated in terms that are indeed relative to the time and culture in question). For instance, the pragmatist will talk to terrorists even if it is 'morally wrong on principle' (according to the ideologist) if talking might ultimately reduce the amount of death and suffering.

[3] Pragmatism is essential to ensure not logical coherence between rules and policies, but tangible benefits. Principles can be sacrificed for the sake of real natural justice, which does not come by blindly applying set principles. The world is not a morally certain place, and treating all cases and cultures as the same is not fair, it is simply foolish. The pragmatist is realistic in acknowledging the moral messiness of the world. The pragmatist is interested in what *works*.

Legislation v. Individual Freedom

A central issue in most debates about government social policy. How far should politicians intrude into our lives? What are the benefits of letting them? This can be, of course, a classic Left v. Right debate, with socialists supporting an interventionist state because of the benefits it can offer and conservatives valuing their individual freedom above all – as many militia groups in the US resent any legislation affecting them. Some even refuse to accept the authority of the American government.

Pros

[1] Legislation is required to protect society at large. In electing representatives

Cons

[1] Legislation is required to constrain and punish those who act to reduce our

we democratically mandate them to draw up the rules by which we all should live. Basic civil liberties must be curtailed to ensure the safety of others, as with banning handguns or imposing a speed limit on drivers. Individual rights and freedoms must be balanced by duties to society.

[2]   The state must also legislate to protect its citizens from self-imposed damage. It is the responsibility of an elected government to research the dangers of certain practices or substances and constrain the freedoms of its members for their own safety. Hard drugs, alcohol and tobacco for the young, violent sports and sado-masochistic violence should all be regulated or banned for this reason.

[3]   A further role of the state is to provide children with certain basic opportunities and protections. We allow the state to take it upon itself to make certain of these compulsory in order to protect children from ill-informed decisions they may make themselves, or from irresponsible parents. In the past parents would curtail children's schooling to utilise them as labour to bring in family income. In preventing this, the state curtails freedoms for the good of the individual children and for the long-term benefits to society of an educated and healthy population.

[4]   We also owe to our animal cousins a duty of care that should be enforced by state legislation, by banning blood sports and vivisection.

[5]   Legislation must be seen as indirectly constructive as well as limiting. If the state is expected to provide services,

individual freedoms, for example those violent criminals who threaten our freedom from fear and attack. Its role is to *protect* our freedoms, not to curtail them. 'Society' is merely a collection of individuals who must be treated as morally responsible agents, allowed to make moral choices for themselves and to speak freely. Crimes should be punished but personal moral choice must not be infringed.

[2]   The libertarian principle is that people can do whatever they wish, as long as it does not harm others – and this must mean that they are allowed to hurt themselves. If consenting adults wish to indulge in sado-masochism, bare-knuckle boxing, or driving without a seat belt (which endangers no-one other than themselves) then there is no reason for the state to prevent them. The role of the state is, at most, to provide information about the risks of such activities.

[3]   The case is not the same with children, who do need to be protected and guided prior to full intellectual and moral maturity. However, the principle still applies that the freedom of independent morally mature individuals is paramount. The state has gone too far in making educational and medical opportunities *compulsory*. The parent is naturally, biologically, responsible for the care of the child. If parents wish to educate their child at home or not at all, or have religious objections to medical interferences with their child, then as parents their views must prevail – those of certain Christian beliefs object to blood transfusions, and however harsh it seems, it must be their right to prescribe the same for their family.

for example – surely a good thing – then it must raise money through taxation to do so. Individuals cannot club together to build roads for their local area; a central government must have the role and power to create a social and environmental infrastructure for the country.

Possible motions:

This House needs a nanny state.

This House would put society first.

This House would legislate, not liberate.

Related topics:

Anarchism

Ideology v. Pragmatism

Welfare State

Voting (Compulsory)

National ID Cards

National Service ((Re-) Introduction of)

Salary Capping (Mandatory)

Population Control

Blood Sports (Abolition of)

Privacy of Public Figures

Mandatory Retirement Age

School Sport (Compulsory)

School Uniform

Child Curfews

Drugs (Legalisation of)

Handguns (Ownership of)

Prohibition of Alcohol

Internet (Censorship of)

Smoking (Banning of)

[4]   As superior animals at the top of the food chain and the most successful species in the history of evolution we have a natural right to use animals for our own ends. Governments should represent the interest of the individuals to whom they are answerable, not the supposed 'rights' of lower species.

[5]   Obviously the government should have some role in providing essential services (roads, public transport, national defence and so on) – but these should be kept to a minimum as should taxation. Individuals can contribute to non-essential services (arts programmes, scholarships, etc.) as they wish and give to the charities of their choice.

Marxism

Pros

[1]   Marxism proposes that, as history develops, feudalism gives rise to capitalism, then socialism, and finally the ideal classless society is realised. Lenin and Stalin were not true to the Marxist ideals but were corrupted by power. But the Marxist dream of an egalitarian classless society is one we should still strive for.

[2]   Even if the classless society is still a far-off dream, we can endorse the Marxist analysis of the 'class struggle', and can see that the working classes should rise up against the exploitative capitalists to demand redistribution of wealth and the ownership of the means of production by the workers. The capitalists are not giving this up voluntarily.

[3]   We should endorse the Marxist view that there is no really individual property and that we are all dependent on society at large for our livelihood and security. Therefore all property is property of the whole people, and should be redistributed in an egalitarian way. The autonomy of the individual is a myth.

[4]   Marxist socialism requires strong government, 'enlightened dictatorship', and a strictly planned and controlled economy working in the interest of the whole community with emphasis on science, technology and industry (as in the Soviet 'five-year plans'). The state is all-powerful, but working in the interests of all the people. This is an ideal model for an enlightened classless society. There is

Cons

[1]   History has taught unequivocally that Marx and Engels were simply mistaken. It was not the most capitalist countries (Britain, Germany, the US) that became socialist by revolution but Russia, which was less advanced. The regimes of Lenin and Stalin (and Mao, in China) made it clear that a 'classless society' is not the result of these forms of socialism. Instead the 'first among equals' are inevitably corrupted into despotism by the power that they have over the masses.

[2]   Marxist analysis of the 'class struggle' is outdated and unrealistic. In a modern capitalist state everyone can be a shareholder and can receive dividends from the company they work for or own a share in, no matter how modest their income. There is no longer an owner–worker divide. And history has shown that gradual change, rather than revolution, has been the most successful route to a fairer and more affluent society.

[3]   Individual enterprise should be rewarded. Marxism and communism fail to recognise the autonomy of the individual and the right of the individual to private property.

[4]   Marxism is undemocratic, unrepresentative and restrictive of economic freedoms. It can never again flourish in a world dominated by liberal democracy, where the power of the state must always be balanced against individual freedoms. In China – one of the last remaining

no *necessary* link between Marxism and despotism or human rights abuses. Indeed Marxist communism can be practised at a devolved level, in local communes or regional 'soviets' as well as at higher levels of government.

communist regimes – moves are inevitably being made towards a capitalist free market economy and, more slowly, towards democracy.

Possible motions:
This House would be communist.
This House would give Marxism another try.

Related topics:
Capitalism v. Socialism
Ideology v. Pragmatism
Privatisation
Welfare State
Monarchy v. Presidency
National Health Service (Privatisation of)
Pensions (Ending State Provision of)
Democracy (Imposition of)
Oxbridge (Abolition of)
Private Schools

Pacifism

In one of the most famous debates ever at the Oxford Union, the motion 'This House will in no circumstances fight for its King and Country', was passed in 1933 by 275 votes to 153. It sparked off a national controversy in the press, and Winston Churchill denounced it as 'that abject, squalid, shameless avowal' and 'this ever shameful motion'. It is rumoured that the vote gave Adolf Hitler confidence that Great Britain would not militarily oppose his expansion in Europe.

Pros

[1]   Great moral and religious leaders (Jesus, Buddha, Gandhi) have been pacifists and taught, rightly, that violence always begets violence – 'those that live by the sword die by the sword'. The only hope for human harmony is the rejection of all violence, even in self-defence.

Cons

[1]   In practice, world religions (especially Islam and Christianity) have believed in holy wars and crusades as a part of their role. Pacifism is simply an unrealistic and idealistic belief. There are times when force (for example uprising against an unjust regime or rioting)

[2]   Pacifists such as the 'conscientious objectors' of the two world wars (some of whom were executed for their refusal to fight) have always served an invaluable role questioning the prevailing territorial militarism of the majority. Pacifists say there is always another way. The carnage of the First World War and the Vietnam War in particular is now seen by many as appallingly futile and wasteful of human life.

[3]   In the extreme cases where war seems to be inevitable (perhaps the Second World War) pacifists can continue to campaign against the many cruelties and excesses of war (the maltreatment and torture of prisoners of war, the bombing of civilians, the use of nuclear, chemical and biological weapons).

[4]   There are no true victors from a war. Issues are rarely settled by a war but persist afterwards at the cost of millions of lives. There are still territorial and national disputes and civil wars in Eastern Europe and the Balkans (Bosnia, Serbia, the former Yugoslavia) despite the world wars and countless supposed settlements. War in these cases is futile and the UN should do more to enforce peace in these areas.

or even war (e.g. in the face of Hitler's aggression) are the only remaining options. What use are pacifists then?

[2]   Pacifism was a luxury that most could not afford during the world wars. There was a job to be done to maintain international justice and prevent the expansion of an aggressor. In those circumstances it is morally wrong to sit back and do nothing.

[3]   Opposition to the excesses of war and contraventions of the Geneva Convention are not the preserve of the pacifist. The true pacifist rejects the use of war outright.

[4]   Often disputes can persist after wars but often also some resolution is achieved (e.g. the Second World War, or the Gulf War – as a result of which Saddam Hussein withdrew from Kuwait). Violent conflict is a last resort but is shown by evolutionary biology to be an inevitable fact of nature and by history to be an inevitable fact of international relations. Nations should determine their own settlements and boundaries and this, regrettably, sometimes involves the use of force.

Possible motions:
This House would not fight for its country.
This House rejects all forms of violence.

Related topics:
Ends v. Means
National Service ((Re-) Introduction of)
Armaments (Limitation of Conventional)

Dictators (Assassination of)
Nuclear Weapons (Banning of)
Terrorism (Justifiable)
United Nations (Standing Army for)
Contact Sports (Abolition of)
Corporal Punishment
Capital Punishment
Handguns (Ownership of)

Privatisation

Pros

[1]   In Britain, both New Labour and Conservative are now committed to the virtues of private ownership and competition in a free market. The New Labour Party has abandoned 'Clause 4' of its constitution which expressed a commitment to public ownership of 'the means of production, distribution and exchange'.

[2]   Private businesses in a free market are in competition and must therefore seek to attract customers by reducing prices and improving services. This contrasts with the old nationalised (state-owned and -run) industries such as British Coal and British Steel, which were perceived as inefficient and uncompetitive. Privatisation also allows companies to raise money in the City instead of only from the Treasury.

[3]   Privatisation gives ordinary people a chance to be 'stakeholders' in the nation's economy by owning shares in services and industries. Privatised industries and services are answerable to shareholders. Having a real financial stake in a company will give people a direct interest and a say in the running of national services.

[4]   'Fund-holding' medical centres and 'grant-maintained' schools were introduced by the Conservatives as a way to introduce competition into the welfare state and give schools and doctors purchasing power in an open market, and to reduce the inefficiency of centrally administered funds.

Cons

[1]   There is more to providing a good service than ruthless efficiency, free market economics and the drive to make profits. The vulnerable sectors of society will always suffer from privatisation. People in isolated villages will have their unprofitable public transport scrapped. Treating elderly patients will not represent an efficient targeting of medical resources. Public ownership ensures that health, education and the utilities are run with a conscience. Furthermore, there is a 'Third Way' that invites private investment in particular projects (e.g. the overhaul of the fabric of the London Underground system, hospital and school meals) while retaining overall state control of fundamental services.

[2]   It is misleading to identify privatisation with deregulation. Monopolies can be ended through deregulation without the government giving up its control of a state-owned and/or state-run element within an open market. A state-run service operating within an open market, drawing finance from the private sector and giving ordinary people a chance to invest, is the ideal of the 'Third Way' mentioned above. Neither is it true that privatisation always brings improved service and increased efficiency. There has been much opposition to privatisation in cases such as water and train companies in Britain that have not improved services and yet have provided huge salaries and bonuses for 'fat cat' directors.

[5]   The welfare state is in crisis. The rate of spending on welfare is increasing more rapidly than overall economic growth. This is an untenable position that requires private sector investment as the remedy. It will be necessary for people to be obliged to take out private health-care insurance and private pension funds whenever they can afford to do so, especially as the population ages with the extension of life expectancy.

[6]   It is right that hard work and indi-vidual enterprise should be rewarded, and that part of that reward should be the opportunity to pay for superior health-care and education. Hard work should not be punished by high, redistributive taxes, taking money from the rich to pay for the ideal of free universal welfare for the rest. Those who use private sector education, health and pensions continue to pay tax and finance public services that they do not use. In other words, they are already repaying their debt to society, without increasing taxation.

Possible motion:
This House welcomes privatisation.

Related topics:
Capitalism v. Socialism
Marxism
Welfare State
Broadcasting (Ending Public Control of)
National Health Service (Privatisation of)
Pensions (Ending State Provision of)
Trade Unions (Modernisation of)
Arts Funding by State (Abolition of)
Private Schools
Sport (Commercialisation of)
Tuition Fees for University Students

[3]   It is a fantasy to suppose that private individuals who are shareholders or stake-holders exercise any power over privatised industries. The only way to guarantee answerability to the *people* is for utilities and services to be run by the government, which is truly open to influence through the democratic processes.

[4]   Giving funds to individual schools, surgeries and hospitals has several un-desirable consequences: doctors and teachers end up spending much of their valuable time engaged in paperwork, expensive resources cannot be afforded out of an individual annual budget, so large-scale investment or expensive sorts of medical treatment will not be available to some under this system, depending on the *local* demands on resources that year in their area. A state-owned and -run health service will always be able to offer treatments universally regardless of local differences.

[5]   People have until now always paid for public services through taxation and there is no reason why they should not continue to do so simply through an increase in taxation (as proposed by the Liberal Democrats in Britain).

[6]   Private healthcare and education take up much more than their share of resources and expertise. The best teachers and doctors are 'poached' and hence unavailable to the less well-off who rely on the state sector. Hence privatisation of education and healthcare further deepens the class divide between those who can and those who cannot afford them. Those who become rich by enterprise and hard work rely directly and indirectly on the rest of society for their education,

opportunities and wealth. Society can only function by 'reciprocal altruism' – those who succeed must help those who do not (in this case by paying large amounts of tax to fund public services).

Tradition v. Innovation

Many debates will end up polarising into one between the case for traditional values and the case for innovation and change. Tradition or innovation are sometimes argued for as good things *in themselves*, and at other times argued for as means to an end. Below are some sample arguments.

Pros

[1]   We need a sense of continuity with the past in order to benefit from the insight and wisdom of past generations and learn about the ethos from which contemporary morality, politics and culture have emerged. Respect for tradition and authority is of itself a good thing because it is essential for social continuity and the preservation of moral stability. Moral relativism is a doctrine that, as we have seen already, leads to moral degeneracy and the break-up of society and the family.

[2]   Uncontrolled technological advances are particularly dangerous. Books, drawing and the theatre are being replaced by electronic forms of entertainment (CDs, computer games, videos, the Internet) that are intellectually bankrupt and morally insidious. Children are growing up with a shallow lust for violence and no higher sentiments of truth or morality. Traditional sorts of education and entertainment should be reinstated in an attempt to rebuild some of the moral fabric of society.

Cons

[1]   Innovation and diversification are of themselves good things. They reject the authoritarianism of traditionalists, who use old religious and moral views to oppress groups such as homosexuals and women, and to attack positive innovations such as the advent of political correctness simply on the grounds that it is new. Innovative thinking allows us to redefine, for example, 'family values' or 'sexual ethics' in a modern way that breaks free from the constraints of traditional ideas. Innovation recognises the value of diverse approaches (from many different religions, cultures and minority groups) providing cultural pluralism and acknowledging moral relativism.

[2]   Children have never been saints – new technologies have had no significant effect on them. Many (most) still grow up to be morally respectable, law-abiding and worthy citizens. As for new technologies, they should be encouraged as ways for children to learn about history, science, literature, religion and other cultures in a new, dynamic and exciting way

[3]   In medicine unrestrained advances have also been disastrous. Enthusiasm for the 'wonder drug' of Thalidomide, for example, led to thousands of children being born deformed. Science and medicine (especially in the area of human reproduction, embryo research, cloning etc.) should be kept in check by traditional moral and religious teachings about the absolute sanctity of human life and the warning against 'playing God'. Science cannot answer moral questions about the status of foetuses or the morality of cloning.

[4]   The first-past-the-post electoral system, the monarchy and the House of Lords in Britain are great traditional institutions that have served the nation proudly for many centuries. It would be foolish and sacrilegious to destroy them on a superficial and ill-thought-out modernising whim.

Possible motions:

This House believes in traditions.
This House regrets the rise of modern technology.
This House would respect its elders.
This House looks to the past, not the future.

Related topics:

Ends v. Means
House of Lords (Abolition of)
Classics (Latin and Greek) in Education
High Art v. Low Art
Museums (Entrance Fees to)
Oxbridge (Abolition of)
Alternative Medicine
Science: a Menace to Civilisation?

on the Internet and with multi-media CD-ROMs.

[3]   In medicine and science we have learned from our mistakes. Science and medicine now use even more rigorous testing procedures. It is irresponsible to argue against innovations (e.g. in genetic engineering) that could save millions of lives on the grounds of scare stories and traditionalism. As for the sanctity of life and 'playing God', these raise questions – which science can often answer – such as when sentient human life begins. And when science alone is not enough, new pluralist ethics, drawing on secular humanism as well as different religions, should replace outdated theological views.

[4]   Tradition should be sacrificed in the interest of modern values of equality, democracy and accountability. We should innovate in the name of democracy, introducing proportional representation, presidency and an elected second chamber.

Welfare State

Pros

[1] Society should provide free education (arguably including university education), healthcare, unemployment and
sickness benefits, and old age pensions
for all. These are fundamental rights in
a humane society (and the yardstick of
a civilised society is sometimes said to be
how well it looks after its pensioners).
The welfare state, as defined in the 1942
Beveridge Report, should be universal
and free for all.

[2] State-owned and -run welfare
services are the property of the nation
and therefore should be available to all.
They are a physical manifestation of
the responsibility of society to each of its
members. Everyone pays tax and National
Insurance, and so everyone should receive
free welfare.

[3] In the interest of equality there
should be no private education, health
services or pensions. The state should
have a monopoly on the welfare state
in order to ensure truly efficient welfare
– through economies of scale and centralisation – which is also egalitarian.
The best resources can be distributed
within the public system rather than
being creamed off for the elite who
can afford private schools and private
healthcare.

[4] It is a myth that we can no longer
afford universal welfare – this is a smoke-
screen for ideological objections. In fact,

Cons

[1] State welfare should be provided
not as a matter of course but only in cases
of extreme need. The welfare state should
function only as a safety net. Even in
communist countries and in postwar
Britain, where there was great enthusiasm
for these ideas, economic realities have
made free welfare for all an unrealisable
dream.

[2] Society is responsible to all its
members, but equally its members should
not all receive welfare if they can afford
private healthcare, education and pensions. All state benefits should be means
tested so that only the truly needy receive
them.

[3] It is right that those who are hard-
working and successful should be able to
buy superior education and healthcare,
which are not rights but luxuries or privileges to be earned. Privatisation of
healthcare, education and pensions means
competition on the free market and
therefore better and cheaper services.

[4] The cost of the welfare state is rising more rapidly than the rate of overall
economic growth. In the case of many
new and expensive drugs and medical
techniques it is simply impractical to
expect the state to pay for all. Private
investment and private health insurance
are the only sensible way forward.

economies in capitalist countries are constantly growing year on year and so an increasing welfare bill is not an insurmountable problem.

Possible motions:

This House would not means test state benefits.

This House believes in welfare for all.

This House believes that the welfare state is a right, not a safety net.

Related topics:

Capitalism v. Socialism

Marxism

Privatisation

National Health Service (Privatisation of)

Pensions (Ending State Provision of)

Taxation (Direct, Abolition of)

Workfare

Beggars (Giving Money to)

Arts Funding by the State (Abolition of)

Mandatory Retirement Age

Private Schools

Tuition Fees for University Students

SECTION B

Constitutional/Governance

Bill of Rights

There are three crucial questions at issue here. First, to what extent do people actually have inalienable or fundamental 'rights'? Second, if they do have such rights from birth, what are they, and who decides what they are? Third, is it necessary for each nation to write down the rights of its citizens in a constitutional document – a 'bill of rights' – in the way in which the US has done?

Pros

[1]   There are certain inalienable rights that no transient majority, whether in parliament or country, should be able to override. Indeed this principle of 'reciprocity' underpins liberal democracies – one can be in the majority one day, and the minority another – and it is thus in everybody's interest that minority rights be protected. In many countries (e.g. the US, Germany) there is a codified bill of rights that parliament either cannot change, or requires an overwhelming majority to change. But Britain's current constitution is driven by the doctrine of 'parliamentary supremacy' – parliament can pass whatever law it likes, trampling on individual freedom if it so wishes. And Britain's 'winner takes all' electoral system effectively gives a prime minister unchecked power.

[2]   It is easy to exaggerate the difficulties of framing a bill of rights. Dozens of nations have solved this problem. Of course there will be difficulties – but controversy is a ubiquitous feature of political life.

[3]   In Britain we have seen too many governments abuse their freedom. Margaret Thatcher removed the right to join a trade union at GCHQ and freedom

Cons

[1]   Unfortunately there is no absolute concept of what is a 'right' – the question of how to define 'rights' is one that has divided philosophers for centuries. There can never be any political consensus on the matter. For example: is being allowed to have an abortion a right, or do unborn children have rights? Is there a right to own a firearm? Should people have a right to a job? At what age do children acquire the full range of rights of adults? The list is endless. Thus any bill of rights adopted would either be mired in political controversy or watered down and rendered bland and ineffectual.

[2]   The above problems are compounded by the question of which rights take priority over others; to take but the most obvious example, the right to free speech and the right to privacy inevitably conflict. The legal arguments employed to resolve these difficulties remove the very element of certainty a bill of rights aims to protect.

[3]   For a bill of rights to be able to withstand the will of parliament, it must be difficult, if not impossible, for future parliaments to amend it. Herein lies yet another problem – for as our rather transient concept of rights changes through

of speech from Sinn Féin. John Major removed the freedom of assembly from demonstrators and the right to silence from suspected criminals. Nor are these isolated incidents – and a bill of rights is the only way to prevent their recurrence.

[4]   Most of the criticisms made – unelected judges and an ossified bill of rights – are really criticisms of the American system. If the rights are drawn as simply as possible, the scope for judicial intervention is significantly reduced. For example, the European Charter of Human Rights has been the subject of extensive legislation, none of which has extended the Charter into territory more properly the preserve of politics.

the decades, so the bill of rights will remain as a fossilised reminder of past values. So our American cousins are stuck with a constitution that was progressive in the eighteenth century but is downright dangerous today.

[4]   All of the problems raised above are inevitably reduced to legal questions to be resolved by some form of supreme constitutional court. Thus are essentially political questions potentially placed in the hands of unelected and unaccountable judges. (Most judges in the US are elected, but Supreme Court Judges are appointed.) And of course the judges must remain unaccountable and unrepresentative, or majority opinion will triumph, albeit indirectly, and the purpose of the bill of rights is negated.

Possible motions:
This House demands a bill of rights.
This House would codify its rights.

Related topics:
Civil Disobedience
Written Constitution

Churches in Politics

In an increasingly secular world, does the Church still have anything left to say about social and political issues, or should it be confined to the realm of private spirituality? And if it does have anything to say about political matters, will anybody listen? Or is it the case that in a multi-cultural society only democratically elected politicians should have the authority to shape social and economic policy?

Pros

[1]   Religion and politics cannot be compartmentalised. The idea that there is a clear line between religion and politics is recent in origin and wholly artificial.

Cons

[1]   Politics and religion are separate spheres of life. Religious leaders can minister to people's private moral and spiritual needs and politicians should be

From the Hebrew prophets, through Jesus to Mohammed, religious leaders have always linked spiritual progress with social change. The fight against poverty, disease, social injustice and economic inequalities as practised and preached by Jesus, for example, is an explicitly political agenda. It is right that churches should continue to take political stands. There is no such thing as 'private' morality or religion – these are inherently social phenomena.

[2]　Religion has had a progressive role in society through history and retains it today. The first attack on the divine right of kings can be found in the Book of Kings in the Bible. Slavery was first prohibited by Jewish religious leaders 2,500 years before Lord Wilberforce. From Martin Luther King to the Beveridge Report, it has been religion that has inspired society's betterment.

[3]　Religious leaders do not rely on the support of companies, organisations or political parties. In times of political consensus, we need such people to defend those in society who have no voice. Religious leaders can fulfil a unique role as genuine critics of the abuses and diseases of the secular world – a position that no secular figure could take without being accused of hypocrisy. This is the traditional role that was played by Biblical prophets such as Jeremiah and Hosea.

[4]　In our multi-cultural and multi-faith world, the leaders of many different faiths (rather than just Christian leaders) should be encouraged to take part in the political system – for example by taking seats in the House of Lords.

left to deal with broader social and political matters. Church attendances are plummeting. Standards of private morality are at an all-time low. These are the priorities that religious leaders should be tackling, leaving debates about health service reform, the social security system, defence spending and international aid to the politicians who are elected to make decisions on these matters.

[2]　The encroachment of religion into politics is inherently dangerous in the modern world. The accountability of political leaders is essential to avoid corruption and self-interest – yet religious leaders can by their very nature never be accountable. It is true that in the past religion and politics were inextricably linked, but that is no longer the case. In the modern democratic world there are secular political mechanisms to ensure representation for the poor and under-privileged without religion interfering.

[3]　The potential political power of religious leaders is vast. For this reason alone, they are open to hijacking by political extremists. The extremes and certainties of religion have no place in a political life that must be about compromise and pragmatism. Democratically unaccountable religious leaders straying into politics too often can be responsible for whipping up public outcry by peddling their extreme and zealous views (e.g. against homosexual marriages, in favour of the death penalty or against nuclear weapons). Religious leaders should restrict themselves to preaching to their flocks about religion and morality.

[4]　When Britain had a single religion,

Possible motions:

This House believes that religion is and should be a political force.

This House believes that religion and politics should mix.

Related topics:

Disestablishment of the Church of England

Monarchy v. Presidency

Sunday Entertainment and Shopping (Restricting)

Islam (Fear of)

God (Existence of)

Religious Teaching in Schools

the Christian faith, it made sense for religious leaders to make political statements, but now they will necessarily be partial and unrepresentative because we do not live in a Christian society but in a multi-faith community. Bishops should be removed from the House of Lords and religious leaders should accept that they are no longer credible political figures.

Coalition Government v. Party Government

Pros

[1]   Most countries are governed by coalitions, alliances of political parties that share out power. This can be contrasted with the 'strong' party systems of Britain and the US, where one party is in power by itself at any one time. Coalitions are more democratic, as they naturally represent more strands of opinion.

[2]   The British and US political parties may appear monolithic, but they are in actuality themselves coalitions. For example, the Republicans are an uneasy mix of fundamentalist Christians and libertarians, while the British Labour Party spans the spectrum from Trotskyists to monetarists and the Tories are fundamentally split over their approach to European integration. The view that the political parties are monolithic deceives the electorate. The problems of coalition politics

Cons

[1]   Countries run by coalition governments are renowned for their instability, lack of democracy and Byzantine politics. Throughout Europe, the power-brokers behind coalition governments are the small parties that hold the balance of power. Yes, it is far from ideal that a party with 40 per cent of the vote can control a government, but it is even less ideal for parties with 15 per cent or even 5 per cent of the vote to decide who governs.

[2]   Good government requires the making of decisions that are unpopular in the short term. Coalition governments find this difficult, as a period of unpopularity may prompt their coalition 'partners' to jump ship and form a government with opposition parties. Thus coalitions can lead to a dishonest populism.

are just as common in 'strong' party politics, but the electorate does not get to see
what is going on. So coalition is in reality
a necessary feature of both the alternative
systems.

[3]   By its very nature, 'winner takes all'
politics results in much of the population
backing losers, and hence being unrepresentative. A coalition government can in
many ways be considered a microcosm
of the electorate as a whole, rather than
merely representing one vested interest.
The ease with which alliances can shift
promotes rather than hinders democracy,
as government will change with the
popular mood.

[3]   Government by coalition makes it
difficult to hold political parties to
account. In Britain and (to a lesser extent)
in the US, the governing party will be
judged against its manifesto promises.
The parties governing as a coalition must
amalgamate their manifestos – no-one
can then expect a particular party to do
what it promised. This has happened
time and time again in France, where
the manifestos of the winning Gaullists
or Socialists are utterly impracticable and
never have the slightest chance of being
implemented.

Possible motions:
This House believes in government by
    coalition.
This House values co-operation above leader-
    ship.
This House demands fully representative
    government.

Related topics:
Democracy
Ideology v. Pragmatism
Proportional Representation
Referenda (Increased Use of)
Regional Government

Devolution of Scotland and Wales

A bill for the creation of Scottish and Welsh assemblies was introduced in 1976 but
rejected by referenda in Scotland and Wales in 1979. Devolution of Scotland and
Wales was one of the manifesto pledges of Tony Blair's 'New Labour' Party, which
was elected into government with a landslide majority in May 1997. Referenda
on devolution in Scotland and Wales were among the first visible acts of the new
government, both taking place in September 1997. The result of the referenda was
a 'Yes' to devolution in both cases, although only by an incredibly narrow majority
in Wales. As a result there will be a Welsh assembly and a Scottish parliament. In
a second question on the Scottish referendum the voters were asked whether the

proposed new parliament should have tax-raising powers. The answer given by the voters to this question was also 'Yes'. The Welsh assembly will not have tax-raising powers. The question remains: Was devolution of powers to Scottish and Welsh assemblies a mistake or will it prove to be the correct decision?

Pros

[1]   There is much to Scotland and Wales that is different from England – in Scotland's case even a different legal system. The peoples of Scotland and Wales have different problems and different political priorities. Maintaining the United Kingdom while recognising these differences is only possible by the devolution of power. All over Europe, there are partially self-governing regions within countries, the most successful examples perhaps being Catalonia in Spain, the German 'Länder' system and the Swiss federation of quasi-autonomous 'Cantons'.

[2]   In the past the balance of political and economic power in the United Kingdom has been overwhelmingly weighted towards Westminster, London and the south-east of England. This is unrepresentative and unfair. It is a basic principle of democracy that decisions should always be taken at the lowest possible level. There are some areas of government, such as defence, education and health policy, that are best handled nationally. Others, such as planning and traffic schemes, should be the province of local councils. But many decisions, from transport policy to education, are more efficiently and democratically dealt with at the intermediate regional level. It is this sort of intermediate regional government that is appropriate to Scotland and Wales.

Cons

[1]   Cultural identity and political autonomy are totally different matters. It is nonsense to say that national identity can only be maintained through political structures. Scottish and Welsh identity is as strong as ever it was. Indeed, much of what we now consider as traditional Scottish culture (from haggis to kilts) dates from the nineteenth century – a time when Scotland was very much part of the United Kingdom. Other regions of Britain, from Liverpool to Cornwall, have a strong local identity despite having far less political autonomy than Scotland.

[2]   Cynicism and distrust of politicians is at an all-time high. Devolution will create yet another tier of expensively maintained politicians, giving handouts to their own constituencies. If we want real empowerment of communities, we should devolve power all the way down to local councils rather than creating a totalitarianism of the regions. An intermediate level of regional government is an unsatisfactory and unnecessary halfway house.

[3]   The referenda, especially the one for the Welsh assembly, did not provide convincing majorities at all. In both cases the turnout was low (60 per cent in Scotland and 50 per cent in Wales) and in the case of Wales only 50.3 per cent of those who voted said 'Yes' to devolution – the narrowest of possible majorities. As

[3] The referenda of 1997 showed conclusively that the people of Scotland and Wales wanted devolution. In Scotland 74 per cent of the votes cast were 'Yes' votes. There is clearly, as the late John Smith said, a 'firm and settled' view in favour of devolution among the populations of the countries concerned. To defy that view is to defy democracy, and bottle up resentment that can only lead to the break-up of the United Kingdom.

[4] Devolution is a balanced and stable arrangement that provides just the right compromise between those who argue for complete independence of Scotland and Wales, and those who would have Westminster strictly control both those countries. Without devolution, dissatisfaction with the status quo would find its outlet in calls for outright independence. Devolution is the ideal middle way staving off the views from both extremes.

Possible motion:

This House has no regrets about devolution.

Related topics:

Proportional Representation
Regional Government
Commonwealth (Abolition of)

a result, in neither case did more than 50 per cent of those eligible to vote actually vote 'Yes'. In 1979 both countries said 'No', in 1997 they very marginally said 'Yes'. These are not firm and settled expressions of the will of the people of Scotland and Wales. We should have required two significant 'Yes' votes five or ten years apart to establish a truly settled view for such a major constitutional change.

[4] Devolution should be opposed because it inevitably leads to the break-up of the Union. The boundaries between powers devolved to the regions and powers retained at Westminster will be fiercely contested. Every power retained will be resented, every power devolved one more step down the slippery slope. There is also the infamous 'West Lothian question' (so named because it was first raised by the West Lothian Labour MP Tam Dalyell) – why should Scottish MPs have a say at Westminster when English MPs have no say over decisions made in the Scottish parliament? Devolution seems to give Wales and Scotland twice as much power and representation as England and an unfair say in English matters. The only solution to this problem is complete independence for all the countries of the Union.

Disestablishment of the Church of England

Currently in Britain the Church of England is 'established'. This means that Anglican Christianity is the official religion of Great Britain. The monarch is head of the Church of England. In addition, senior bishops of the Church of England can sit in the House of Lords. There have been increasing calls for the disestablishment of the Church of England – the ending of its privileged status as official religion of Britain – from many quarters, both within and outside the Church itself.

Pros

[1]   The case against the establishment of the Church of England is simple – it is an embarrassing anachronism. It fails to reflect our largely secular-multicultural society. In Britain today, believers are a minority, Christians an even smaller minority, and Church of England worshippers a tiny fraction of the population. To provide such a minority with a legally and constitutionally privileged position is bizarre. The secularisation of the past two centuries and the rise of an atheistic and scientific world view make all forms of traditional religion irrelevant. Moral issues are discussed by philosophers, scientists and bio-ethicists – there is no need for the superstitious angle provided by religions.

[2]   Establishment is not just philosophically objectionable, but embodies religious discrimination in practice. The monarch has to swear an oath of allegiance to uphold the Church of England. Bishops sit in the House of Lords – no other religious leaders do. More perniciously, the heir to the throne cannot marry a Catholic, and the prime minister cannot be a Catholic. These medieval hangovers contribute to a Catholic sense of victimisation, particularly in Northern Ireland. To end this religious discrimination, the Church of England should lose its secular privileges and be disestablished.

[3]   Ironically, establishment has actually been dangerous for the Church of England in recent times as its ties to the state have prevented it from speaking out. Margaret Thatcher's damning of the 'Faith in the City' report produced by the

Cons

[1]   The Church of England has been central to British history for four hundred years and still plays a vital role. Historically Christianity has been fully engaged with secular laws, wars and social policies. The separation of Church and state is a development of the past century or two. It is right that moral and spiritual leaders should be involved in political decision making. It cannot be denied that religion is still vitally important for a great many people. The Christianity represented by the Church of England is not an exclusivist religion – there are few of other faiths who view it with hostility. Indeed, Muslim and Jewish leaders oppose disestablishment.

[2]   These are academic niceties of symbolic importance only. Attacking establishment can accomplish little in practice, and ignores the real problems of prejudice and religious mistrust. Disestablishment would send out a strong signal that there is no place for religion in modern society. Instead of taking away the secular and political role of the Church of England, all major religions should be given some degree of representation in parliament and by the royal family. Leaders of other religions should be given a place in the House of Lords, and Charles, Prince of Wales, has already stated that he sees himself as 'Defender of Faith' in a multi-cultural Britain rather than 'Defender of the (Christian) faith'. Religious discrimination can be ended by making the establishment multi-faith rather than no-faith.

[3]   So-called secular societies have not

Church of England in the 1980s, and the meddling of parliament in the debate over the ordination of women show the danger that can result from this.

Possible motions:
This House calls for the disestablishment of the Church of England.
This House believes that religion and politics do not mix.

Related topics:
Churches in Politics
Monarchy v. Presidency
Religious Teaching in Schools

proved a success. Stalinist Russia's suppression of religion resulted in the revival of superstition on an unprecedented scale. The constitutional separation of church and state in the US sits uneasily with vulgar and extreme expressions of fundamentalism.

Eighteen-year-old MPs

Pros

[1]   In Britain currently you have to be at least 21 years old to stand for Parliament. This used to be in line with the minimum voting age. Now that the voting age has been reduced from 21 to 18 there is no logical reason to prevent those aged 18-20 standing for parliament. Eighteen-year-olds can marry and they pay taxes. So, 18-year-olds are fully fledged members of society. If the democratic system is designed to reflect the views of those aged 18 and above (the electorate) then it is only proper that 18-year-olds should be allowed to be representatives. It is ageist and discriminatory to exclude them from that role. It implies that they are second-class citizens.

[2]   Being an MP (or representative) is not the same as being a business person

Cons

[1]   It is misleading to present standing for parliament and voting in an election as comparable democratic functions. Being an MP, unlike simply voting for one, requires a level of life experience and maturity that an 18-year-old cannot possibly possess. Many complex issues and different groups need to be understood and represented. A democratically elected assembly is required to *represent* the views and interests of the electorate but not to *resemble* that electorate in every detail of demography, such as age.

[2]   The electorate of a constituency cannot be expected to trust an 18-year-old to fulfil such a demanding role. Eighteen-year-olds with little or no life- or work-experience are not given highly responsible jobs in industry and

or even a political leader. An elected representative merely needs to present an open and articulate channel of communication for those he or she represents. Intelligence, listening skills, openness, integrity and articulacy are all skills that can be well developed by the age of 18.

[3]   Elected assemblies are too often stuffy, pompous and out of touch with the public, especially with the needs and interests of the young. Allowing 18-year-olds to be democratic representatives will give a voice to those concerns and do something to bring the democratic process closer to real people.

[4]   Young people are well known for being idealistic and this is a great strength in an ever more cynical political world. Eighteen-year-olds could bring dynamism, idealism and values to bear in the political system.

[5]   Students in schools, colleges and universities are already involved in politics and representation at a high level through student unions. Through these organisations 18-year-olds could have accumulated much relevant knowledge and experience, campaigning on educational, social and environmental issues. We should consider re-introducing university MPs who would give students a real voice in parliament. There are already many MPs who, in effect, represent a limited interest group such as the trade unions or a particular industry (tobacco, cars, arms) associated with their constituency. University MPs would be similar to these other MPs.

commerce, nor should they be in politics. This is recognised in the US where members of the House of Representatives must be at least 25 years old, and Senators must be at least 30.

[3]   There is no significant sense in which 18-year-olds are more 'in touch' with reality than 21-year-olds (or, perhaps, 61-year-olds). This is just ageist rhetoric. And, in fact, the sort of 18-year-old who wanted to become an MP would most likely be a precocious and pompous young person not in touch with youth culture at all.

[4]   First, it is ageist to suggest that people in their thirties, forties or fifties cannot be idealistic or dynamic. Second, there cannot be a significant difference in degree of idealism between an 18-year-old and a 21-year-old. Third, it is questionable whether wide-eyed naive idealism is truly an attractive trait in a representative when the alternative is idealism balanced with pragmatism and informed by worldly experience and deep thought.

[5]   The narrow range of issues that concerns student unions (mainly education and its funding) is not sufficient experience for the broad issues and challenges of being an MP. The sort of people who would want to be MPs at the age of 18 would most likely want to go to university – this would not be compatible with the huge demands on time and commitment of being an MP. For these reasons the idea of university MPs is untenable. If there are other 'single issue' MPs in parliament then they are failing in their job as representatives of all interests

Possible motions:

This House would allow 18-year-olds to be
MPs.

This House would give the young a voice.

Related topics:

Term Limits for MPs
Voting Age (Reduction of)
Mandatory Retirement Age
School-leaving Age

in their constituency and should not be
seen as examples of good MPs. Eighteen-
year-olds in general, and university MPs in
particular, would have too little experience and too narrow a range of expertise,
interests and concerns.

House of Lords, Abolition of

At the time of writing the Labour government under Tony Blair has declared its
intention to reform the House of Lords, at least by removing the voting rights of
hereditary peers. We have therefore left out another debate, on 'Reforming the House
of Lords'; but it will be interesting to debate the success of Blair's reforms when they
come into effect.

Pros

[1]   The rationale for a second chamber
(the bicameral system) comes from
centuries-old political philosophy and
a time when parliaments were so unrepresentative that they had to be held in
check. In a modern democracy, checks
and balances are supplied by the people
themselves rather than massed ranks
of politicians. Rather than fiddle with
the way the House of Lords works, it
would be much simpler and more effective to abolish it outright. There is no
need to have two chambers in a democratic parliamentary system. Norway, for
example, has a single-chamber parliament,
the Storting; Israel's parliament, the
Knesset, is also a single-chamber legislature. Other countries with single-chamber
elected legislatures include Albania,

Cons

[1]   The reason why almost every major
democracy has a second chamber is that
the overwhelming will of the populace
can be ignored by a government with
a suitably large majority in a unicameral
(or 'single-chamber') parliament. Even
Britain's bizarre and unrepresentative
House of Lords prevented some of the
worst excesses of Thatcherism and has
stood up against some of the policies
pushed through by Tony Blair's massive
Commons majority (e.g. tuition fees for
students). Rather than abolish the House
of Lords, we should reform it. Options for
a reformed second chamber include a
fully elected second chamber (like the US
Senate).

[2]   So-called 'gridlock' is in fact a

Bulgaria, Denmark, Portugal, Egypt and Bangladesh.

[2]   If the second chamber is not to be a carbon copy of the first, it must be elected by a different system and at a different time. All successful governments go through periods of unpopularity – and it is likely that elections for the second chamber would occur in one of these periods. This is a formula for US-style 'gridlock', where the second chamber (in the US, the Senate) stymies the policies of the elected government (in the US, the House of Representatives).

[3]   Abolishing the House of Lords would send a message to the electorate that its political system had been democratically reformed and rejuvenated. Even if a second chamber were elected, the old image of a fusty chamber full of unaccountable, sleepy, drunk or senile old men and women would persist in public consciousness as long as there was a House of Lords. Abolishing the House of Lords would restore public confidence in the democratic system.

[4]   We need to make a clean break with the anti-meritocratic rule of the privileged and the 'old boy network' of past political eras. Abolition of the House of Lords is the most important step in this new political age.

proper manifestation of representative democracy. No fleeting majority in a first chamber – reflecting temporary swings in opinion polls – should have absolute power. The balance provided by a second chamber (elected or otherwise) is to be welcomed, as is the disruption of the programme of the majority party in the first chamber that the second chamber can bring about – a parliamentary embodiment of popular dissent. In Britain and the US it is almost always only a minority of the electorate (around 40 per cent) that votes for the ruling party. A unicameral parliament is the first step towards a one-party state and totalitarianism.

[3]   Public confidence in the system is of *some* importance, but simply to bow to alleged public stereotypes and prejudices in a matter of such constitutional importance would be to give in to the worst kind of populism and gesture politics. A reformed House of Lords with appointed peers and no voting rights for hereditary peers, perhaps even with a changed name ('The Second Chamber', 'The Senior House', 'The Senate') could recapture public confidence.

[4]   Every new age (wrongly) believes it has invented meritocracy and fair and open government. The whole democratic system exists to fight against the concentration of power in any one group. That is why the existence of a second chamber is so important. Our ideal should be reform that is still in continuity with the great democratic traditions of our parliament rather than a petulant and melodramatic destruction of a central element of it.

Monarchy v. Presidency

Britain is one of the oldest surviving hereditary monarchies. Several other European countries are monarchies (Denmark, Sweden, Norway, the Netherlands and Spain) along with a few countries further afield (such as Morocco and Lesotho in Africa and Bhutan in Asia). Arab sheikhs and the Japanese emperor are also hereditary rulers. Historically, a partially elected parliament was seen as a mechanism to check the power of the monarch. As centuries passed, more and more real power passed to parliaments and away from monarchs, in some cases through violent revolution (as in France and Russia). In other cases, such as Britain or the Netherlands, the process was more gradual and the monarch has simply been left with only ceremonial duties and nominal powers. Is there any point in maintaining this institution or is an elected president the only appropriate head of state in the modern world?

Pros

[1]   It is the genius of the British con-stitution to make apparently untenable institutions such as the monarchy and the House of Lords work and provide stability in each new era. There is value in tradition, particularly when it has served our country so well. The monarchy holds Britain together in times of national dis-aster (e.g. the Blitz or the death of Diana) and unites the nation in times of peace. The monarch symbolises the nation and its heritage not only for Britons but also for the nations of the Commonwealth who still recognise the British monarch as the symbolic head of their egalitarian and modern association.

[2]   The monarch symbolises the United Kingdom as no elected politician

Cons

[1]   Britain's hereditary monarchy is a ludicrous anachronism. The divine right of kings may have been acceptable nine hundred or even one or two hundred years ago, but it has no place in today's egalitarian and secular society. The Queen has unmerited political influence that few members of parliament can dream of (e.g. weekly meetings with the prime minister). The Queen represents every-thing that was bad about the Britain of the past – the empire, the class system and unearned wealth and power. In today's multi-cultural society, the idea of a mon-arch who must be a white Anglo-Saxon Christian is quite untenable.

[2]   The British prime minister has more personal power than any other

ever could. Every opinion poll shows she has the support of at least three-quarters of the population. No politician in history has matched that degree of sustained popularity. Any candidates for a presidency would need to seek the backing of one or more parties – and hence be dragged into the political fray, as has happened in Ireland. With public respect for politicians at an all-time low, surely we should welcome heads of state who stand above petty party politics. Paradoxically, it is the unelected nature of the monarchy which ensures its independence and its popularity.

[3]   'Crown' property does not belong to the Queen or to the monarchy, it belongs to the nation. Very little of the land, houses and property ascribed to the Queen is kept from the public. In fact the royal family generates a vast amount of money for Britain through the trade in tourism which it attracts. Without a monarch, Buckingham Palace would lose its mystique as would ceremonies such as the Changing of the Guard.

Possible motions:

This House would be a citizen, not a subject.
This House would rather have a president than a monarch.

Related topics:

Democracy
Tradition v. Innovation
Disestablishment of the Church of England
House of Lords (Abolition of)

democratic leader. The American president has to contend with an often hostile House and Senate, while the French president is checked by a parliament and prime minister. But a British premier has automatic parliamentary support. This lack of 'checks and balances' is caused by an unelected head of state who has no political role. By replacing the monarch with an elected president we could fill this democratic deficit. The fact that a president would have political allegiance of one sort or another would not be a bad thing. If presidential and parliamentary elections were staggered, the president would normally not be allied to the ruling party, thus providing a welcome democratic balance. The experience of Ireland has been that an elected head of state can have a political affiliation but still fulfil a relatively neutral and statesmanlike role.

[3]   The Queen is the richest woman in the world. The monarchy costs the exchequer £30 million every year. More significantly, the Crown is the largest landowner in the country; if sold off, the receipts could be used to fund massive investment into our infrastructure – schools, hospitals and public transport. It is unacceptable to see economic inequality and deprivation persist at the same time as one particular family continues to enjoy extremes of wealth by the mere fact of its ancestry.

Party Funding by the State

Pros

[1]   Many political scandals in Britain and America have been caused by the quest for funding of political parties and candidates. A notable example came in 1997 when the Labour government argued for an exemption for Formula One motor racing from the Europe-wide ban on tobacco advertising in sporting events. It later emerged that the head of Formula One, Bernie Ecclestone, had donated £1 million to the Labour Party. When politicians are forced to compete for cash, they place themselves in hock to lobbyists and interest groups (such as the arms, alcohol and tobacco industries) and the weak or dishonest will break the law. If private political donations were banned and replaced with state funding, perhaps proportionate to average opinion poll rating, these problems would not arise.

[2]   The necessity for a plentiful source of funding for a political campaign prevents new parties without wealthy contacts and supporters from breaking into the mainstream and gives an unfair advantage to parties with business support, which will usually be the established parties. State funding provides a level playing field and encourages the formation of new parties.

[3]   Freedom of speech cannot be used to justify millionaires buying votes. Democracy is under threat from millionaires with money to spend and parties with politicians to sell. The costs of state funding are trifling compared with

Cons

[1]   State funding controls actually foster and encourage corruption by their complexity and lack of transparency. French politics is engulfed by funding scandals, despite limited state funding. Campaign spending limits in British local elections are totally ignored and unenforced. In practice, private individuals and groups who wish to make donations, perhaps with half a mind to influence future legislation, will always find ways of doing so, for example by making donations to funds set up by politicians ostensibly, for example, for 'research' purposes.

[2]   When there are many other calls on the public purse, it is absurd to suggest that the state should be throwing money at politicians. Why should our taxes go to parties which are not in power and which we may well not support? And if parties are removed from the necessity to raise funds from their membership, they lose any obligation to serve their membership and become centralised and unrepresentative. It is also likely that state money being provided for any party with a modest degree of support (say a minimum of 5 per cent or 10 per cent) would give encouragement to extremist parties and possibly even end up giving state money to racist and nationalist political parties.

[3]   Freedom of speech and political belief are pivotal in a democracy. Banning private donations to political parties removes this freedom from the individual, and places vital decisions in the hands

national budgets, and the potential savings in terms of democracy are far-reaching.

Possible motions:

This House believes that the state should fund political parties.

This House would ban all private donations to political parties.

Related topics:

Democracy

Politicians' Outside Interests (Banning of)

of unelected bureaucrats on funding committees. Bernie Ecclestone, for example, claimed that he simply admired Tony Blair and his New Labour Party's opposition to punitive taxes and so wanted to help finance its advertising. It should be the right of any individual to make such a decision.

Politicians' Outside Interests, Banning of

Pros

[1]   Politicians are elected to serve their constituents full time, and for this they are well paid. When members of parliament continue their past employment or accept new directorships or posts as consultants, they are short-changing and insulting their constituents, who expect their MP to be working solely for them.

[2]   Britain should not be ruled by 'pressure group politics', where the most important decisions are made by small interest groups which influence the most important MPs. This subverts natural democracy where all MPs represent their constituency and the people who elected them.

[3]   It is impossible to police outside interests. We can never know precisely what an MP has promised to do in exchange for money, even if that money is declared in the Register of Members'

Cons

[1]   The recent trend for politics to be populated by career politicians is deplorable. Few 'normal' people would enter politics if they had to abandon their previous life, especially as the salaries of MPs, once expenses and researchers' fees are deducted, are actually very small. It is far better to allow outside interests and attract, for example, experienced businesspeople or lawyers to parliament.

[2]   MPs are elected to represent the population of the UK, which must include interest groups as well as geographical constituencies. They will always represent the special interests of vocal groups of constituents with particular grievances (e.g. cases of alleged miscarriages of justice) but that need not totally exclude representing broader interest groups. An MP's own constituents must always be his or her first concern but need not be the only concern.

Interests. The only solution is outright abolition.

[4] It is wrong in principle for any individual or group to be able to buy political power and influence. Even if lobby groups are allowed to influence politicians, they should not be allowed *financial* arrangements with them. Otherwise only the wealthy groups paying the most (major corporations selling tobacco, arms, cars, etc.) would be able to win legislation in their favour; smaller, poorer factions (e.g. animal rights defenders) would have no say. If money is removed from the equation, then each opinion has a more equal chance of being heard.

Possible motions:
This House would ban MPs from having outside interests.
This House believes that MPs should represent their constituents, not lobby groups.

Related topics:
Capitalism v. Socialism
Ideology v. Pragmatism
Party Funding by the State
Trade Unions (Modernisation of)
Privacy of Public Figures
Sport (Commercialisation of)

[3] Political lobbying is acceptable so long as politicians declare their paymasters. It is not the fact that finance is involved at all that is objectionable – a politician's job is to persuade the government to pass legislation, so why should they not profit from doing their job? – but the fact that, if the arrangement is concealed, their motives are unclear. Declaration of outside interests is sufficient – they need not be banned.

[4] Politicians do not have the time to listen to every opinion and weigh them up against each other. By the very nature of capitalism some groups will wield more power and may be able to influence parliament directly; but there are many other methods which smaller parties can use to make themselves heard. These include petitions, use of the media, direct action and so on.

Proportional Representation

In recent years in Britain the Liberal Democratic Party in particular has argued for reform of the electoral system. It favours a system of proportional representation (PR), such as that used for elections to the European parliament and to the Scottish and Welsh assemblies, in which the proportion of MPs a party gains is the same as the proportion of the population that voted for that party. The present 'first past the post' system means that most governing parties need to receive only around 40 per cent of the vote to have a decent majority in the House of Commons. In 1997 Tony Blair promised to set up an 'electoral commission' to consider the question of switching to a PR system for the Westminster parliament, but indicated that he was opposed to such a switch.

Pros

[1]   Britain's current electoral system is winner-takes-all, 'first past the post' democracy. Whichever single candidate gains the most votes wins the constituency, and votes for the other parties are ignored, even if the winner only won by a couple of votes. Thus parties with a slight lead in the country can get a vastly disproportionate majority in Parliament. Small parties are not represented at all. For example, in the 1997 general election, Labour won less than 45 per cent of the popular vote but 64 per cent of the seats in parliament. The Liberal Democrats' 17 per cent of the vote gave them around 7 per cent of the seats. And the Referendum Party's 2.5 per cent gave them no MPs at all, as happened with the Green Party's 15 per cent in the 1990 elections for the European parliament. This cannot be fair. Introducing PR is the way to end this unfairness.

[2]   It is right that we should be governed by coalitions, since in reality there is no majority opinion on most issues. The art of social harmony and fair government is the ability to reach compromises. This is the most mature and civilised way to govern. 'Strength of government' seen another way is simply the minority steamrolling their views through over the majority.

[3]   MPs often get elected with a

Cons

[1]   All electoral systems are unfair in one way or another. PR creates governments that are at the mercy of the whims of tiny parties with negligible electoral support. Such small parties can hold larger parties to ransom if it is their support that makes the difference between a coalition government maintaining an overall majority or losing it. PR leads to instability and disproportionate power for small parties.

[2]   PR creates weak coalition governments, as in Italy where the Communist Party, despite a low level of support, frequently holds considerable sway by offering to form coalitions with larger parties and thus form a majority government. Elections there are far more frequent than in Britain, for example, because the coalition governments that PR produces are weak and unstable and frequently collapse. No system is perfect, but the current one at least guarantees some continuity and strength of government over a sufficient period of time to instigate a legislative programme.

[3]   Systems that count a voter's second choice force political parties to bargain for each other's second place recommendations. Back-room dealings like this do not aid democracy. Second, would the public be happy to be ruled by a party that was everyone's second choice – as,

minority of the vote. In 1997, the Liberal Democrats won Tweeddale with 31 per cent of the vote; seats won with under 35 per cent of the vote were by no means uncommon. So the people's so-called representatives normally represent only a minority of their constituents.

[4] In 'safe' seats, there is hardly any incentive for people to vote. In seats in the north west where Labour regularly wins 80 per cent of the vote, it is often said that a root vegetable with a red rosette would be elected. People feel their vote is wasted, since the result is a foregone conclusion. With a PR system everyone's vote counts even if they are in the minority in their particular constituency.

for example, the Liberal Democrats could well be in Britain?

[4] Many of the systems proposed are hugely complex. If the public does not understand the political system then results can seem arbitrary and accountability is lost. The uncertainty and confusion this creates can cause disillusion with the democratic process. The transparency of the 'first past the post' system is one of its many virtues.

Possible motions:
This House believes in proportional representation.
This House believes that the 'first past the post' system is undemocratic.

Related topics:
Democracy
Coalition Government v. Party Government
Devolution of Scotland and Wales
Referenda (Increased Use of)
Regional Government

Referenda, Increased Use of

Pros

[1] The first democracy, in ancient Athens, did not rely on elected politicians and parliaments. Instead, the citizens met in a square to debate and vote on every issue of policy. Modern democracy and the size of the modern electorate have removed this participative element from day-to-day politics. We should return to this direct form of democracy. For example, setting a minimum turnout of 50 per

Cons

[1] Government involves more than individual decisions. There has to be an underlying strategy, one that is not blown with the wind from day to day. Government by constant referenda does not allow this. California holds dozens of referenda every year. The reams of paper voters have to read through result in widespread apathy, low turnouts and consequently freakish results.

cent and requiring a 70 per cent or higher majority of those voting for a decision to be made would guard against freakish results being produced by small numbers of voters. Referenda might work particularly well at the level of local government, making transport, environmental and planning decisions.

[2]   Modern technology gives us the power to return to the Athenian ideal. It is now entirely practicable for every major policy decision to be made by referenda via the Internet.

[3]   Britain's essentially two-party system often falls out of touch with the public. There are many issues where the will of the public is simply ignored because both parties agree – from drugs to capital punishment. Genuine democracy would circumvent the parties' prejudices and put power back in the hands of the people.

[4]   When important constitutional decisions need to be made concerning matters such as greater involvement in the European Union, the devolution of Scotland and Wales, and the 'Good Friday Agreement' in Northern Ireland in 1998, matters are so significant as to demand the direct say of the people – in some, but not all cases, representatives cannot be entrusted with total power but must bow to the direct decision of the people. This should happen more often than it currently does on important issues such as reform of the House of Lords, privacy laws, party funding, electoral reform, crime and punishment and allocation of lottery grants. Switzerland provides a model of an effective direct democracy in which referenda are frequently held to determine policy decisions.

[2]   The vast majority of people are not interested in politics on a day-to-day basis. Government by constant referenda would become government by the politically obsessed – government by zealots and extremists. A system based on Internet access would be elitist and privilege the rich and technologically educated over those without the equipment or know-how to vote via the Internet.

[3]   The phrasing of the question to be asked in any referendum has a significant impact on the result. The timing can also be crucial. The politicians who control the wording and timing are retaining significant power, and in a way that is insidiously unaccountable. So, in fact, referendum results are often simply manipulated by the media machines of the political parties involved. Furthermore, it is a strength of the first-past-the-post democratic system that government is not just a version of mob rule. Capital punishment has not been reintroduced in Britain despite much popular support because the question is settled by elected representatives with a higher than average amount of information, experience and intellectual ability at their disposal. Using referenda may be more superficially democratic but will lead to mob rule as opposed to enlightened government. 'Real' democracy is not necessarily a good thing.

[4]   It is already the case that referenda are used for important constitutional issues, which is appropriate. But they should not be used for anything else. Elected representatives must be trusted with other decisions. It is they, especially ministers and civil servants, who have the

Possible motions:

This House calls for more use of the referendum.

This House believes that true democracy is
direct democracy.

Related topics:

Democracy

Devolution of Scotland and Wales

Voting (Compulsory)

Written Constitution

time, information, expertise and authority
to make well-informed decisions. There
is no need for any increased use of
referenda.

Regional Government

Do we need a level of government between local councils and Westminster?
This debate occupies a position on the domestic scene equivalent to that of the
'United States of Europe' debate on the international stage. In both cases, the goal
of local autonomy is brought into tension with the goal of collective unity and
identity.

Pros

[1] Modern democracies have
developed in a way that has resulted in
excessive power accruing to central
government. Central government decides,
for example, how to share out public
spending between education, health,
police, defence and so on. We have
grown accustomed to this but it is
essentially undemocratic. The ideal of
democracy – government by the people –
is best attained by increased regional
government. This brings power and
decisions closer to 'real people' rather
than seeing power centralised in the
hands of a few politicians.

[2] Some decisions are truly national
– e.g. defence policy, contributions to

Cons

[1] It is necessary to have a strong
centralised government so that important
decisions can be taken on behalf of
the nation by one publicly visible and
democratically accountable executive.
Democracy is not about government *by*
the people but government *on behalf of*
the people, in a way that is *answerable*
to the people. A nation retains its unity
and coherence by having a single policy
on important matters of domestic as well
as foreign policy.

[2] In a country the size of the US,
differences in laws about speed limits and
so on cause relatively few problems. In a
country the size of England, the difficulties of enforcing varying speed limits

and role in trans-national economic and political alliances and organisations (e.g. the UN, NATO, the EU, NAFTA) – but most decisions could be taken at a more local level (as happens in the Cantons of Switzerland, for example, and, to some extent, in the different states of the US). For example, laws on the minimum age for driving, drinking, smoking, having sex or marrying, speed limits and so on can be decided on a region to region basis. More major decisions on taxation and spending can also be devolved so that regions set their own priorities. Regional legislatures could decide, for example, what law and order policy to follow for the special problems of their region, or tailor the curriculum in schools in a way supported by the inhabitants of the region.

[3]   This process of regionalisation has already happened to some extent with the devolution of Scotland. It should be extended to the regions of England, Wales and Northern Ireland too. Thus areas in the west and north of England would no longer have to feel that they were being unfairly subjected to the decisions of a London-centred legislature, and could raise some of their own taxes for their own priorities.

[4]   In the modern world federalism is the preferred and successful mode of government. The US and the EU are the two most influential and successful examples. The way such power blocs work is to combine regionalisation with centralisation in the right balance. Centralisation alone (e.g. Hitler's Germany, Stalin's Russia, Thatcher's Britain) leads to unacceptable social injustice, economic

or minimum drinking ages between neighbouring regions would be more considerable. But, more importantly, decisions about education, health and police *must* be made nationally in the interests of equality. There must be a national curriculum so that a GCSE, A-level or other qualification means the same thing throughout the country so that all have the same qualification and the same opportunities with employers throughout the country. Health spending must be the same throughout the country, unless (as has started to happen with fund-holding GPs and hospital trusts) what medical treatment you can have will depend on which region you live in and the drugs and treatments your region has decided it will pay for. Wage settlements for public sector employees (teachers, doctors, the police force) must be the same nationally for the sake of equality. Policing must be nationally consistent. Devolving decisions about taxation and spending would make Britain a confederation rather than a nation. In the interests of national unity and coherence, further regionalisation must be opposed.

[3]   The example of Scotland illustrates perfectly the point that regionalisation and devolution are the first steps down the slippery slope to complete independence. It is important for a nation to keep fiscal policy in particular centralised so as to remain truly a nation.

[4]   Nationhood is defined by culture, not by politics and economics. Britain can join in an economic alliance with the rest of the European Union, and even grant some powers to Brussels as part of that alliance. But sovereignty and

inequality and unaccountability of government. Regionalisation for all but the most central and truly (trans-)national decisions is the way forward. The nation state is a romantic ideal of the past. Cultural and linguistic boundaries are rapidly being broken down (especially by information technology). Power should devolve to the lowest level – to regional communities of people who genuinely identify themselves around local issues and local traditions.

national identity are separate historical and cultural aspects of the nation that are independent of political and economic strategies. Regionalisation will break down the traditional cultural identity of a nation. Whatever powers may be granted to supra-national organisations (e.g. to determine trading conditions or lay down universal rights), or devolved to regional councils (e.g. local transport policy, planning decisions), the central focus of power and government must remain the nation state.

Possible motions:
This House believes in the devolution of power.
This House would decentralise government.
This House demands greater regional government.

Related topics:
Devolution of Scotland and Wales
Proportional Representation
United States of Europe

Term Limits for MPs

This debate, along with the debates about 18-year-old MPs and a mandatory retirement age, addresses the question of whether we need to take any action to counteract the perceived dominance of older and more established figures, particularly in political life. It also raises the question of whether politics should be perceived as a career in itself. At present there is no limit to the number of terms in office that an MP can serve, whether as a back-bencher, a minister, or even as prime minister. Margaret Thatcher won three consecutive terms as prime minister (the last of which she did not complete, having been deposed in 1990 by her own party in favour of John Major). In the US an individual may only serve as president for a maximum of two terms.

Pros

[1] A regrettable trend in recent years has been the development of the

Cons

[1] This is a perfectly valid view – but it is not valid to force this view onto the

'professional politician'. Politics should be a brief interlude in a career, not a career in itself. Limiting members of parliament to a set number of terms (two or even one) would therefore be healthy for democracy.

[2] Young people are diving into student politics, emerging as full-time political organisers and resurfacing as parliamentary candidates a few years later without every having done a 'real job'. This produces bland politicians with no experience of the real world. Term limits would mean that people would be more inclined to accumulate experience before entering the political system for their one chance as an elected representative.

[3] Once elected, politicians enjoy a significant 'incumbency factor'. The publicity their post affords them and the apparatus available to them provide a significant advantage to them and a disadvantage to their opponents; this is unfair and undemocratic.

[4] Like introducing a mandatory retirement age, limiting the amount of time a person can serve as an MP will create regular openings for young talented people at the bottom end of the scale. Term limits would increase the number of younger and more energetic representatives and relax the stranglehold on power enjoyed by the career politician by virtue simply of his or her age. In practice an experienced MP is never deselected in favour of a younger candidate, however out of touch he or she has become, and this perpetuates an ageing and ageist House of Commons. Legislation must be passed to force local parties to select new

political system. If people want to prevent someone standing two or three times, they can vote against them. And if we want to re-elect a veteran MP, we should be able to. To attempt to remove elected representatives by legal means is undemocratic.

[2] Term limits create 'lame duck' politicians in their last term who know they will never face the electorate again. This has the double disadvantage of reducing their moral authority and eliminating their motivation to keep in touch with their public. Term limits would produce less effective representatives. As for the argument that career politicians are ineffective because they start when they are too young, we agree – it is on this side of the debate that we affirm the value of experience. This problem is not addressed by term limits, but by having a higher minimum age for MPs (perhaps 30 years old, the lower limit to be a US senator).

[3] In a system where politicians are under unprecedented pressure both from the executive and from lobbyists, in-experienced neophytes are ill-equipped to cope. Experienced legislators benefit both their constituents and parliament. Term limits would effectively abolish the experienced politician at considerable loss to the nation. Even more power would then be concentrated in the hands of unelected civil servants and functionaries.

[4] It is ageist to assume that younger MPs will be more dynamic and talented, and it is foolish to throw away the experience and skills of older MPs. It is down to the political parties to select

candidates, say every ten years, to counteract the current inequitable system.

Possible motions:

This House would limit the term of MPs.

This House regrets the rise of the career politician.

This House favours youth over experience in its politicians.

Related topics:

Tradition v. Innovation

Eighteen-year-old MPs

their candidates and down to them to decide whether to value youth over experience or vice versa. This is not a decision that should be forced upon them by legislation.

Voting, Compulsory

The only major democracy in which voting is compulsory is Australia (voting is also compulsory in the tiny Pacific island state of Nauru, which has a population of around 10,000). In Australia, failure to vote is punishable by fines or even by imprisonment.

Pros

[1]   Turnout in British elections is distressingly low. In the 1998 local elections it averaged 30 per cent, and in some areas under 20 per cent. Even in the 1997 general election, almost 30 per cent of the population did not vote. Voting is compulsory in other countries such as Australia, and failure to comply can result in fines or even imprisonment. We should adopt the same system to secure greater democratic involvement of the population. Proxy voting and postal voting will be available for those who cannot physically get to the polling station – voting by the Internet could also be arranged.

[2]   Low participation rates are doubly dangerous. They mean our politicians are

Cons

[1]   There are many reasons why people do not vote. Up to 10 per cent of the population is not on the electoral register at any one time. Many people cannot get away from work, or find someone to look after their children. Some cannot physically get to a polling booth, others are simply not interested in politics. None of these motivations can be affected by forcing people to vote – those who cannot will continue not to, and those who are not interested will vote randomly or for fringe candidates.

[2]   Abstention from voting is a democratic right. There is a long and noble tradition of political abstention, from Dr Johnson to David Owen. To deny the right to abstain in a vote is as dictatorial

not representative of the population as a whole. Since the poor and disadvantaged are far less likely to vote than any other socio-economic group, they can safely be ignored by mainstream politicians. The only way to break this cycle is mandatory voting.

[3] Liberal democracy relies upon a balance of rights. The above argument shows that our democracy is endangered through a lack of participation in elections. The resolution of such a crisis may in a small way restrict some personal liberties, but it is in the interests of society as a whole. We compel people to wear seatbelts and to serve on juries and we should not be afraid to do the same in the case of voting. Besides, anyone wishing to register an abstention can do so by spoiling the ballot paper, or leaving it unmarked.

[4] Especially after the suffering of and sacrifices made by suffragettes and others in the campaign for universal suffrage, we owe it to our ancestors and to history to exercise our democratic right to vote. If people are so apathetic that they will not do this freely, we must make it compulsory.

Possible motions:
This House would make voting compulsory.
This House believes it is a crime not to vote.
This House believes that voting is a duty.

Related topics:
Democracy
Legislation v. Individual Freedom
Democracy (Imposition of)

as to deny the right to support or oppose it. Just as the right to free speech is complemented by the right to silence, so the right to vote is balanced by the right of abstention. Refraining from the democratic process is a democratic statement of disenchantment. Forcing those who are disenchanted with politics in general to go and spoil a paper is a pointless waste of resources. Their right to register dissatisfaction should not be taken away by politicians who want to hide the fact of their unpopularity and irrelevance in society.

[3] The 'balance of rights' arguments cannot be used to infringe an individual's liberty. How would this system be enforced? If those who refused to vote also refused to pay fines, presumably we would gaol them. Creating political prisoners can hardly help the democratic process. The analogy with jury service does not hold since we do not *need* people to vote in order for an important social institution to function (in the way that we *do* need a jury to turn up for the justice system to function). Elections do not need a 100 per cent, or even an 80 per cent, turnout in order to fulfil their function. The analogy with seatbelts does not hold since not voting does not endanger the life of self or others.

[4] Suffragettes and other suffrage campaigners sought to make voting a right rather than a privilege, but they did not seek to make it a *duty*. Campaigners for equality for blacks, homosexuals or women have ensured that they have *access* to higher education, political power and the professions, but these groups are not now *forced* to attend university, stand for

parliament or become a lawyer or a soldier. Similarly it is wrong to confuse the importance of having the *right* to vote with a repressive system of *forced* voting.

Voting Age, Reduction of

Pros

[1]   In society today young people reach social and intellectual maturity at a younger age than ever before. By the time compulsory schooling ends at the age of 16, young people are well informed and mature enough to vote.

[2]   Not only can young people leave school and get a job at 16, they can also have sex and get married. It is absurd for a married person with a job and children not to be recognised as an adult who can vote. Voting is an important decision, but so is getting married. Such a person is a full adult member of society and should be treated as such.

[3]   Because of the advances in information technology over recent decades, teenagers are now more aware of political issues than ever before. The broadcast media in particular ensure that everyone, including 16-year-olds, is familiar with the issues of the day. There is no need to wait for young people to be 18 in order for them to have a fuller understanding of politics.

[4]   Even if one takes a pessimistic view of the ability of some 16-year-old school-leavers to make a well-informed and well-thought-out democratic decision, it

Cons

[1]   It is not true that young people are more mature than ever in today's society. They masquerade as adults by mimicking traditionally adult behaviours (drinking, smoking, using drugs, having sex, swearing, fighting) at younger and younger ages, but that does not make them mature. If anything, the voting age should be raised to give these immature would-be adults a longer time *actually* to grow up and mature *intellectually*.

[2]   It is perfectly acceptable for different 'rites of passage' to occur at different ages. The ages for leaving school, being allowed to have sex, smoke, drive, drink and vote are staggered over three years (16, 17, 18). This reflects the considered decisions of a series of governments about the appropriate age for very different activities. Voting is a responsible act that requires more than a year or two of adult experience of life and politics. The age for voting should stay at 18 or, be raised to 21 − as indeed should the age for marriage, another momentously important decision that should not be made by adolescents.

[3]   On the contrary, the rise of broadcast media and information technology has led to a ridiculously simplistic and superficial political world emerging − a

is not clear that the passage of two years will make any real difference to such people. Many people are politically unsophisticated or disinterested in politics, but there is not a significant difference between the ages of 16 and 18. The same proportion of 16-year-olds as of 18-year-olds will be apathetic, disinterested or ill informed. The extra two years without a vote is a case of arbitrary discrimination.

[5]   In any case, voters are not required to be fully informed or highly intellectual – such a requirement would be elitist and anti-democratic. Sixteen-year-olds are, in most other respects, adult members of society.

Possible motion:

This House would reduce the voting age to 16.

Related topics:

Tradition v. Innovation
Eighteen-year-old MPs
Voting (Compulsory)
School-leaving Age
Child Curfews

world in which real political argumentation has been replaced by the 'soundbite'. This is a reason to demand that the voter be *older* and be wiser to the tricks of the media spin-doctor. A 16-year-old voter would be putty in the hands of media managers.

[4]   There is a significant difference between the levels of analysis of which a 16-year-old and an 18-year-old are capable. Sixteen-year-olds are still children mentally. Ideally the voting age would be 21, to allow fuller mental development.

[5]   Voters have a duty to inform themselves and be competent participants in the process of politics and democracy. Voting should not be made available to all but should be restricted to those who qualify. This would not be an elitist measure but would simply ensure that a bare minimum of competence in understanding political ideas was attained. Something analogous to the driving test should be introduced for 18- (or 21-) year-olds, which they must pass before they can vote. It is a sentimental misunderstanding of democracy to think that anyone at all should be given a say. We do not let just anyone drive on our roads without maturity or instruction, and we should not let just anyone determine who we are governed by without maturity or instruction.

Written Constitution

The 'constitution' of a country is the set of fundamental laws that lay down the system of government and define the relations of the executive, the legislature and the judiciary. Almost all countries have a written constitution, of which the oldest is the American constitution of 1787. (The Bill of Rights is a set of ten amendments incorporated into that constitution in 1791.) The United Kingdom is the exception in having only a 'virtual constitution'. That is to say that the constitution is not written down in a document anywhere but has emerged over the centuries as the result of various different agreements, laws and precedents. Important laws that are part of this 'virtual constitution' are Magna Carta of 1215, the Habeas Corpus Act of 1689, the Parliament Acts of 1911 and 1949 and the Reform Acts passed between 1832 and 1928 to extend the electorate. An organisation called 'Charter 88' was set up in 1988 by a group who were concerned with what they perceived as the autocratic way in which Margaret Thatcher passed unpopular legislation with small Commons majorities and on a minority vote from the electorate as a whole. Charter 88 argues that a written constitution would safeguard the liberty of the individual against the excesses of an 'elective dictatorship'. The massive majority of the Labour government elected in 1997 and the 'presidential' or 'dictatorial' style of Tony Blair led to renewed concerns about the excess of power put into the hands of elected politicians.

Pros

[1]   In countries with a written constitution, the parliament cannot pass laws infringing on the rights of citizens. If it does, the courts can declare the laws illegal. For example, segregation in the United States was ruled unconstitutional by the Supreme Court despite several state assemblies supporting it. Without a written constitution for the judiciary to appeal to, the power of parliament is ultimate and this means that there is no constitutional way for unjust and unpopular laws such as the Conservatives' Poll Tax legislation of 1990, or the ban on beef on the bone and the banning of handguns by the Labour government in 1997, to be deleted from the statute book. A written constitution provides a check on parliamentary power.

[2]   Britain is one of only two democracies in the world without a written constitution (the other, Israel, has spent fifty years failing to agree on one). And since British law is made by governments

Cons

[1]   This is a theoretical argument that ignores the facts. The countries with written constitutions have been just as reprobate in their assaults on individual rights as those countries without. The constitution of the US was said to allow for slavery and segregation, and today it fails to stop the death penalty – the ultimate expression of the state's oppression of the individual. In practice, Britain has a very good human rights record – much better than most countries that have written constitutions. Nigeria and Iraq both have written constitutions.

[2]   Written constitutions are ruled upon by judges, who, in Britain, are unelected and who tend to be pro-establishment, if not reactionary. If society is minded to oppress minority rights, the chances are that judges will also be so minded, and interpret a constitution accordingly – just as segregation was said by successive US Supreme Courts to be constitutional. It is less desirable to place more power in the

with minority public support (generally around 40 per cent), it is all the more vital that that minority is not given unimpeded power. Charter 88 was founded in response to the particular excesses of Thatcherism, but a written constitution, including a bill of rights, is needed to guard against all future autocratic parliaments of whatever political leaning.

[3]   Liberal democracy relies on the 'rule of law', first enshrined in Magna Carta in 1215 in England to guard individual rights against the excesses of the monarchy and royal officials. Thus the idea was established that the powers of government must themselves be subject to law. But the British parliament is subject to no authority beyond its control of itself. This is philosophically repugnant and politically dangerous. A written constitution would remedy this situation.

hands of judges (whether unelected or elected) than it is to place it in the hands of elected representatives.

[3]   Of course Britain does have a constitution, albeit an unwritten and hence subtle one. British history has shown that the convoluted interaction between precedent, convention and the wrath of a vengeful electorate at the ballot box is a more effective check on politicians than any legalistic written formulations.

Possible motion:
This House demands a written constitution.

Related topics:
Legislation v. Individual Freedom
Bill of Rights

SECTION C

Politics and Economics: National

Affirmative Action

Affirmative action is the concerted use of legislation or policy to favour minority groups over others, in an effort to redress previous discrimination against them. It may include mandatory hiring or selection quotas, all-'minority' short-lists, extra funding for education/training projects to promote 'minority' candidates, and so on. The Proposition does not have to offer a specific affirmative action proposal but to do so may produce a better debate.

Pros

[1] The race, gender or sexual preference of an individual should not affect the potential to succeed on his or her own merits. The mix of people in jobs, higher education, political office and so on should be very close to the proportions of each group in the nation as a whole. This has not been the case in the past and concerted steps must be taken to redress the balance – to create a 'level playing field'.

[2] Affirmative action can overcome traditional prejudice by bringing to the fore the qualities of a group which is discriminated against. The appointment of Colin Powell as the US Army's first black chief of staff in the early 1990s, and the Labour Party's promotion of female candidates in winnable seats were very effective in changing attitudes; this will continue until prejudice is no longer current and fair hiring practices are the norm.

[3] Having beneficiaries of affirmative action on the 'inside' (of companies, governments, etc.) will shake up recruitment procedures and working conditions, ensuring that informal and unspoken codes of behaviour which discriminate

Cons

[1] Every type of person has equality of opportunity but only those who deserve a position on merit should win it. We live in a meritocracy where employers, universities, and so on should choose the best person for the best position, irrespective of background. To do anything else is inequitable.

[2] In fact, prejudice can be increased, as other groups resent the new privileges of affirmative action beneficiaries, with the suspicion that newly selected or promoted individuals did not make it on merit but through government patronage. This is made worse when selection procedures are transparent, as in university examinations where test scores may reveal that individuals with better qualifications are rejected in favour of the less able. Such accusations led to the dismantling of many university affirmative action programmes in the US, for instance at the University of California (where, incidentally, many Asian-Americans from wealthy backgrounds took advantage of measures designed to help black and Hispanic students). After the 1997 elections in Britain, the principle of affirmative action suffered from the alleged shortcomings of 'Blair's Babes', the huge influx of young

against minorities are no longer acceptable.

[4] The legacy of past discrimination exists even where there is no prejudicial treatment today – although university selection or, say, the legal profession is open to all, many may be handicapped by poor education or low expectations. Only pro-active government action can be successful in bridging this gap.

[5] Affirmative action may be liable to charges of tokenism at first, if candidates are chosen purely on the basis of race, gender, and so on, when merit alone would not have got them selected. But this is to miss the long-term point – having more women in parliament or blacks in the senior ranks of the army, of whatever calibre, will raise expectations and encourage people from the group in question that the doors are open to them. Eventually the quality of the intake will rise, and at that point affirmative action will have been successful and can be phased out.

Possible motions:
This House supports affirmative action.
This House would introduce hiring quotas.

Related topics:
Ends v. Means
Legislation v. Individual Freedom
Feminism (Devaluation of Parenthood by)
Gays in the Military
Political Correctness
Oxbridge (Abolition of)
Judges (Election of)

female MPs; it is not racist or sexist to be worried that people in positions of authority are not up to the job.

[3] Again, this is simply not true in practice. People winning their places through affirmative action are not welcomed by those who have won theirs on merit; instead, divisions are hardened, cliques formed and suspicion intensified. Even on the inside the former will rapidly find themselves excluded.

[4] Past wrongs are no justification for reverse discrimination. Women gained the vote in Britain on an equal basis in 1928, and slavery was abolished in the US in 1865 – so why should their descendants still be privileged? Why make white males pay for past wrongs in which they had no complicity? Also, we must give the current meritocracy time to work; the reason why there are so many white males in senior management is because universities in the 1950s and 1960s were dominated by the same group – but when today's undergraduates are middle-aged, we will find a very different make-up in senior positions.

[5] The whole idea is nothing more than tokenism, if candidates are selected to make a point rather than to do a job. Not only does this devalue the principles of affirmative action but it can also handicap its beneficiaries, as excluded groups become used to patronage and less motivated to succeed on their own. More simply, why should you work hard at school if you will get a place at university anyway?

Broadcasting, Ending Public Control of

This is an example of a debate over the role of the state in a free society. The Proposition could include specific plans such as privatising the BBC and/or funding it through advertising and commercial sponsorship, with an end to government interference in its management and programming.

Pros

[1] The nature and power of broadcasting mean that it ought not to be subject to governmental control, for fear of bias and censorship, and the suppression of minority opinion. French TV and radio under General de Gaulle were notably hindered by state control, and even the BBC has been subject to numerous attempts by Ministers to censor programmes. Its board of governors is appointed by the government.

[2] Too much of the money paid to the BBC for television licences is spent on radio and TV programmes of little interest to most, while government interference leads to religious programming and party political broadcasts instead of popular shows. Even ITV is forced to maintain its mid-evening news, constantly disrupting feature films. Throwing radio and television open to the market will ensure that the audience gets the programmes it wants.

[3] The BBC licence fee is a regressive poll tax which equals a higher proportion of a poor family's income than of a rich family's. The poor family has little choice whether to pay it – unlike the rich, these people have little access to other leisure pursuits.

Cons

[1] Broadcasting is the most powerful method of conveying educational and political messages to the public, and it cannot be left without regulation to private control. Some form of public control is necessary to guarantee high standards and impartiality. Otherwise broadcasting may end up as the tail that wagged the dog, as in Italy where Silvio Berlusconi was able to promote his own political ambitions through his dominance of Italian media. Many in Britain and elsewhere are suspicious of the agenda of Rupert Murdoch, the dominant figure behind Sky and Fox television networks. Public control can ensure fair access for all political parties, especially at election time.

[2] Broadcasting is not like other businesses and the free market is not the place for it. The BBC safeguards and transmits national culture and encourages excellence. The television and radio schedules, and government interference, combine to make sure that all tastes are catered for across a broad spectrum of the public – including minority groups and the very young – rather than showing only programmes that are certain to win high viewing figures. It is also free (after the licence fee), while privatised television hides costs such as pay-per-view

[4]   Allowing the free market to operate fully in television and radio will also
strengthen our ability to compete in the
global market place and to remain abreast
of developments in satellite, cable, digital
and high-definition TV and interactive
programming via the Internet.

[5]   Free sports broadcasting for all, as
guaranteed by the government's 'listing' of
certain events, is a fine idea in principle.
But it penalises the sporting organisations
(the TCCB, the FA, etc.) by reducing
their ability to earn revenue in a free
market. If this means that English cricket
is significantly poorer, then its players
and coaches will be less well paid, and
facilities will suffer, with a detrimental
effect on its ability to compete internationally. The rude health of English
football, by contrast, coincided with its
exclusive deal with Sky Television and the
revenue which that brought.

Possible motions:
This House would privatise the BBC.
This House believes that the state should have
   no role in broadcasting.

Related topics:
Capitalism v. Socialism
Censorship by the State
National Health Service (Privatisation of)
Arts Funding by State (Abolition of)
Museums (Entrance Fees to)
Sport (Commercialisation of)
Trials (Televised)
Internet (Censorship of)

events and the higher price of goods due
to artificially inflated advertising rates.

[3]   The BBC caters, or attempts to
cater, for all sorts of viewers and it is only
right that everyone should make an equal
contribution towards it. It is certainly not
the job of a television company to worry
about how many leisure pursuits a family
has.

[4]   There is no reason why government interference in broadcasting should
hinder its technological development.
On the contrary, it can help to support
services that would suffer in the free
market, such as the BBC World Service.
It is also important to control technological developments in the airwaves
and prevent chaos from unlimited private
usage, which would disrupt essential
services such as police radio, air traffic
control and telephone communication.

[5]   Public control offers benefits in
the form of guaranteed access to sporting
events such as home Test Matches, the
FA Cup Final, Wimbledon, all of which
have to be shown free on terrestrial television. These events are of great national
importance and their potential as tools
for pay-per-view companies to squeeze
money from obsessed fans is vast.

Calendar Reform

Pros

[1]   Our current calendar, devised by Pope Gregory XIII in 1582, is inconvenient, illogical and prejudicial, and the arbitrary division of the year into months of uneven length could easily be improved upon. The basis of the calendar on a fixed point of AD 1, which refers (probably erroneously) to the year in which Christ was born, is surely offensive to those who do not share the world view of Christianity. Many different calendars exist anyway – the Eastern Orthodox Churches, for example, are split among themselves after some but not all skipped the first thirteen days in October 1923. It would be better to settle on a common fixed point (Year Zero) of meaning to all humanity – for instance, the splitting of the atom, the founding of the United Nations or the launch of the first sputnik.

[2]   There are several logical methods for tidying up the calendar to avoid current irregularities with pay, holidays, etc. A simplistic version would abolish weeks and months altogether and distinguish the date only by number – you could make an appointment for 11am on the 159th. Leap years would end on the 366th.

[3]   Just as the Imperial system gave way to the metric/decimal, it is inevitable that measurement of time will be standardised at some point in the future. There is considerable support already for a change, mainly in two schools of thought – the equal months school

Cons

[1]   All systems of chronology are arbitrary to some extent, and the choice of any fixed point in history on which to base a calendar is utterly so. Christ's birth has immense cultural and historical significance to the entire world, and the Gregorian Calendar has been satisfactorily accepted for four centuries. Months and days all get their names from ancient mythology or cultures (e.g. January from Janus (Roman), Wednesday from Woden (Anglo-Saxon) and Thursday from Thor (Viking)). They are named differently in other languages in any case.

[2]   None of these schemes would be useful unless universally adopted, and this would not be the case – it took even Britain 170 years to accept the Gregorian Calendar. Countries and religions using their own calendars (e.g. China or the Islamic nations) would be equally unlikely to embrace it.

[3]   In fact, the support for calendar reform is very small, consisting of a handful of cranks. Similar schemes have been tried in the past, and failed – for example, the French Revolution Calendar with twelve months of thirty days, plus five extra holidays, which lasted from 1793 to 1806. Russia abolished Saturday and Sunday in favour of a five-day week but has reverted.

[4]   The number 13 is widely unpopular because of superstition. It is also difficult to divide by and impossible to divide into.

(favouring the 'International Fixed Calendar') and the equal quarters school (favouring the 'World Calendar').

[4]   A perpetual calendar would have great advantages in business and accounting. George Eastman, the founder of Kodak, argued passionately against the variation in working days in different months and against the 'Wandering Easter', and advocated an early version of the International Fixed Calendar. This would involve thirteen months of twenty-eight days, with the extra month ('Sol') and an extra day between 28 December and 1 January, called 'Year Day'. Months, quarter-years, and half-years would all be the same length and the need for annual calendar updates would be gone. Kodak has implemented his calendar successfully, and many companies in France pay on the basis of a thirteen-month calendar (with the thirteenth given as a welcome bonus before Christmas).

[5]   Calendar reform has been accepted in the past. The costs of its implementation would be outweighed by the reduction in costs through simplification. Computers should serve our interests, not vice versa.

Neither quarter- nor half-years would consist of a whole number of months. Thirteen monthly balancings, stock-takings and payments would increase the complications.

[5]   It has also failed in the past, as shown above. The costs of replacing calendar systems throughout today's technological world would be enormous, and immensely dangerous – surely the millennium bug shows the problems we can create when we do not plan properly for chronology.

Possible motions:
This House believes it is time for a change.
This House would change the calendar.

Immigration, Relaxation of Laws against

A reasonable Opposition will not wish to ban all immigrants, so this debate is essentially about the scale desirable. Both sides will probably agree that those experiencing genuine persecution for political or religious activities in their own country deserve asylum; a fruitful debate will focus on those whose motivation for immigration is less clear-cut.

Pros

[1]   Current restrictions on immigration are impossible to justify as they victimise

Cons

[1]   In today's world of mass communication, it will rapidly be known which

those fleeing persecution and oppression in their own countries. In theory the UK is open to genuine refugees, but the immigration criteria are so concerned to weed out economic migrants claiming political refugee status that it is made very difficult and humiliating for those in real danger.

[2] Britain is an obvious place of shelter to many: partly as a legacy of empire, partly because of our reputation as home to the mother of all parliaments and to democracy, and partly because we have accepted refugees for centuries (e.g. the French Huguenots in the sixteenth and seventeenth centuries and East European Jews in the late nineteenth century). We should be proud of this heritage and maintain it. Restrictions imposed since the 1960s because of fears about the post-war influx should be lifted now that the fears have proved ill-founded.

[3] Immigrants are important to our economy and culture. Many possess special skills; all bring new ideas and contribute their cultural heritage to our own. Almost all immigrants are very young and by their nature ambitious and dynamic. Such individuals (e.g. Ugandan Asians in the 1970s and Cambodians in the early 1980s) are often prepared to work very hard, building up small businesses and contributing to the economy. They are less likely to rely on the welfare state than those who have grown up taking it for granted.

[4] Current laws are often racist in their underlying assumptions – why are Americans, Australians and Canadians allowed in much more easily than those

countries combine economic prosperity and opportunity with generous social benefits and relaxed economic laws. If we relax our restrictions we will soon become known as an easy target. We must prioritise the opportunities of settlement, offering them first to those whose birthright they are. Genuine refugees must be welcomed but a strict line between the deserving and undeserving must also be maintained.

[2] Times have changed, and Britain is no longer in need of extra labour. In the past immigrants brought specialist skills which we did not have; now we have acquired them, and where we need to acquire more we do so through technology and communication rather than manpower. Britain is no longer a world power at the head of an empire; while we should be proud of our heritage, we must recognise that our role and facilities have changed.

[3] Many migrants place a strain on the welfare state which British subjects have paid for; poor English can make them hard to employ and children may need special schooling for the same reasons. We must also be careful to safeguard our own culture – the US is a melting-pot of cultures but Britain is not. Previous immigrant groups have been integrated slowly over a long period of time. An open–door policy risks losing this organic development and its social cohesion, alienating many existing citizens and raising the dark spectre of racism – as has happened in Israel where the Ethiopian Falashas and Russian immigrants have created strains in what was previously a relatively cohesive state.

from Africa and Asia? A study by the Commission for Racial Equality showed that 1 in 140 visitors from the New Commonwealth and Pakistan were refused entry compared with 1 in 4,100 from the Old (white) Commonwealth.

Possible motions:

This House would relax immigration rules.
This House believes that charity begins at home.

Related topics:

European Union (Expansion of)
United States of Europe

[4]   Our relations with 'western countries' are as equals; many British citizens seek to work in Australia and North America, and relatively few in Africa or Asia. It is also true that countries from the New Commonwealth are generally poorer economically, and their immigrants arrive here for economic reasons – and so must be vetted more carefully.

National Health Service, Privatisation of

The Proposition is unlikely to argue that governments have no responsibility for the health of their citizens and should leave even the poorest to fend for themselves – but they can promote privatised healthcare in which state funding acts only as a safety net for the neediest. The Opposition is broadly defending the status quo – or perhaps calling for a return to the situation in the 1980s before government policy introduced limited market forces into the NHS – of a government-run health service free at the point of use to all citizens.

Pros

[1]   State bureaucracies are notoriously inefficient. Government-run healthcare raises costs (meaning higher taxes), misdirects investment and encourages waste (through unnecessary treatments, overprescription, complacency and overstaffing). A regulated, market framework would avoid these problems, reducing costs and raising standards. This could be achieved by privatising the NHS, replacing current entitlements with personal health insurance, and implementing a

Cons

[1]   Far from being inefficient, the NHS is very successful at keeping costs down – Britain pays a far smaller proportion of its GDP towards healthcare than the US, where private medicine is the norm, or France, where the nationalised health service is less regulated and less managed than ours. It is the quality of management that counts.

[2]   Direct taxation would merely be replaced with compulsory health

government safety net of insurance funding for the poor.

[2]   Taxes should be lowered wherever possible, giving individuals control over their own money. With private healthcare one can choose from different levels of insurance depending on preference and lifestyle.

[3]   The quality of hospitals would undoubtedly improve. With the prospect of long-term profits, private hospitals would invest in new wards and beds, up-to-date technology and new research, as pharmaceutical companies do today.

[4]   Privatisation puts the responsibility for healthcare back on the consumer or citizen. Lower insurance premiums would reward those with healthy lifestyles, encouraging better diets, more exercise and less drinking or smoking. Those with dangerous hobbies (e.g. skydiving) would pay more. At the moment the healthy and safe are effectively subsidising those with self-destructive habits, who use hospitals much more.

Possible motions:

This House would privatise the NHS.

This House believes that good health is a human right.

Related topics:

Capitalism v. Socialism

Ideology v. Pragmatism

Privatisation

Welfare State

Broadcasting (Ending Public Control of)

Pensions (Ending State Provision of)

Taxation (Direct, Abolition of)

Smoking (Banning of)

insurance, as in the US. The ability of the government to create a more equal society by redistributing wealth would also be reduced; the poor are likely to end up paying a considerably higher proportion of their income towards health insurance than the rich. The wealthy would benefit from better treatment, newer technology, more expensive drugs and better qualified doctors. Healthcare is not like other goods and should not be treated as such.

[3]   The Labour government elected in 1997 allowed private sector–public sector partnerships to fund the NHS anyway. Ultimately, however, medical improvements must be paid for in some way and are funded either through increased taxation (which at least is means-tested) or through higher treatment costs and insurance premiums.

[4]   Such lifestyle decisions are not made on purely financial grounds – if they were, no-one would smoke. Giving insurance companies too much flexibility with premium rates would be very dangerous; if the poorest members of society needed most hospital treatment because of poor nutrition, how could their premiums be held down?   The elderly and those with genetic diseases or AIDS could be charged equally heavily. In reality, the government would have to regulate premium rates so extensively that the 'free market' description would be meaningless.

National Identity Cards

The arguments below assume a motion on the introduction of compulsory identity cards. A debate on voluntary identity cards is possible, and the last set of points addresses this.

Pros

[1]   Many forms of crime depend upon individuals claiming to be someone else (e.g. benefit fraud, tax evasion, dealing in stolen goods, terrorism, gaol-breaking, illegal immigration, or lying to police after another crime). At present we have no form of standard identification for domestic use that is widely accepted. Different forms of identification are demanded for different activities. If we had one official and standard form of ID, verification by police would be easier and many crimes would be avoided.

[2]   Britain is unusual in Europe in not requiring identity cards; yet our European neighbours are hardly authoritarian police states. When abroad we willingly carry a passport, while at home almost everyone carries a driving licence. Carrying identification causes no problem to innocent people; it is only criminals who would resist. Encouraging police harassment is a negligible risk: the circumstances under which ID cards would be demanded could be carefully regulated.

[3]   ID cards are useful not only for society but also for the holder. There are many daily transactions where identification is required; currently we are forced to carry a large number of separate cards. In the US, where driving licences bear photos, they are used as identification

Cons

[1]   Identity cards represent a major intrusion by the government into the privacy of the individual, and would greatly increase state control. In order to be effective, card-carrying would have to be compulsory (as with the road tax disc) and failure to produce it would be a crime. This would use up valuable police and court time.

[2]   Britain is very different from continental European countries, lacking their experience of authoritarian government under Napoleon and, in many cases, Fascism. Along with the US, Australia and similar countries, we value our liberties highly and should be wary of any attempts to undermine them. ID cards would allow a considerable degree of police harassment in the name of enforcing the policy, probably targeted at minority groups who are already more likely to be stopped on suspicion of motoring offences. This harassment is a genuine problem in France. Relations between minority groups and police will only grow worse.

[3]   With separate cards we have a choice about whether and when to carry them, and which ones to take out with us. Smart-card technology is so advanced as to be dangerous; we would have no idea what information was contained on

for a wide variety of purposes (proving the owner is old enough to drink, guaranteeing cheques, etc.). Modern smart-card technology would allow one small card to encode a huge range of information, including photographic images, retina and fingerprint records, signature, passport, driving licence, criminal record, bank and credit details and even employee and library/club membership details.

[4]   Given that most people currently carry all their multiple forms of identification in the same wallet or handbag, the problems of losing a single card are unlikely to be worse in practice. In fact, the chance of being impersonated is less, if photo, retina and fingerprint details cannot be detached from the card; at the moment a thief could discard all forms of photo ID, but keep, for example, a credit card and forge the signature.

[5]   Identity cards could be made voluntary, producing many of the benefits of compulsory cards while avoiding most of the issues of civil liberty. Photos could be added to driving licences which nearly everyone carries already.

Possible motions:

This House would introduce a National Identity Card.

This House would remain anonymous.

Related topics:

Legislation v. Individual Freedom

Bill of Rights

Zero Tolerance

our ID cards that could be read by others, and no choice about how much information to declare. Employers and the police could discriminate against us on the basis of hidden facts that we should have the right to keep hidden. The cost of introducing 60 million smart cards and vast numbers of card-reading machines would be enormous. Theft of the cards would become major business, and police are always technologically less advanced than the criminals, as credit card fraud and on-line financial crime suggest.

[4]   The chance of losing all your forms of identification in one go is high and immensely inconvenient – your entire identity would be erased until a new one could be obtained, which would presumably be a strict and lengthy process. If criminals did obtain card-reading technology, they could have access to all parts of your life via a stolen card and impersonation would become much easier.

[5]   Voluntary schemes are likely to be the thin end of the wedge, soliciting public support before proposals to make cards compulsory are tabled. In any case, unfair suspicion would naturally fall on those who chose not to carry them – an infringement on civil liberties. Courts might take 'not carrying a card' into account in the same way that the right to silence is treated. Voluntary in theory would become compulsory in practice if banks, rail companies, airlines and so on demanded cards to be shown as part of transactions. To use driving licences would penalise non-drivers.

National Lottery, Abolition of

A popular topic which often produces lively debates. The Proposition should not just consider what is wrong with the way the Lottery is run in Britain (e.g. profits by the franchise-holders, choice of recipients for lottery funding and so on), as the Opposition could argue that these are issues of regulation. Rather, what is wrong with the principle of a lottery in the first place?

Pros

[1]   Lotteries provide the hope of success for many people, but in practice the chances of winning are extremely low (about 1 in 14 million in Britain). It is statistically sensible to avoid buying a ticket until Friday, as until then your chance of winning is less than your chance of being run over by a car before Saturday's draw. Governments which promote such activity are taking advantage of the gullibility of their citizens – yes, it could be you, but this is really very unlikely.

[2]   Lotteries are nothing more than indirect, regressive taxation, targeted at the poor who are most eager to win the jackpot but least able to afford the tickets. Some 80 per cent of players in Britain are in income groups C, D and E.

[3]   The British lottery is not only regressive but iniquitous; money raised largely from working-class players is redistributed to the middle class who gain disproportionately from cultural projects funded from its profits (e.g. the Royal Opera House, the Millennium Dome, museums). London has been similarly favoured, attracting much more funding than regional projects.

Cons

[1]   The lottery is harmless fun which brings colour into people's lives. It is patronising to assume that players are stupid and expecting to win; they know full well that they are only 'buying a chance', and are happy with that. Every week some individuals do win millions of pounds. We must let people make up their own minds about their own money. It is not the role of the state to manage personal finance.

[2]   The Proposition is equating poverty with stupidity; just because poorer people play the lottery more does not mean that they should not be trusted to do so. No-one likes paying taxes; there is nothing wrong with exploiting alternative ways of funding projects for public benefit, provided that the public is well informed about the destinations of the money. In any case, the shift of government funding, from direct taxation such as income and corporation tax to indirect taxes such as VAT and excise duties, has hit the wallets of the poor to a much greater extent.

[3]   The assumption that working-class people do not benefit from cultural projects is snobbish and ignores the fact that it has often been the high cost of 'elite' culture which prevents most people from

[4]   Lotteries encourage gambling (and the British lottery can be played at 16, two years below the gambling age). This is an addictive activity which governments normally seek to restrict. Players may impoverish themselves and their unwilling families. Scratch-card lottery games are particularly dangerous as they provide an instant possibility of winning, which may encourage losers to buy more cards immediately.

[5]   The claim that lotteries raise money for charity is irresponsible. Direct contributions to charity fall when lotteries are introduced, as happened in Britain in 1994. Many people greatly overestimate the proportion of their ticket price that will go to charity; and they cease to have any control over the choice of charities to which their money goes. Government-appointed bodies may be more inclined to favour certain types of charity (e.g. domestic rather than international) over others.

[6]   National lotteries redirect existing expenditure on gambling, reducing the profits of pools and race betting industries and causing job losses.

[7]   If a lottery is allowed, it should not be run for profit as Camelot has done in Britain. Even its 1 per cent profit equates to almost £70,000 per annum for every employee; it is a licence to print money. Either the government or a non-profit consortium (such as that led by Richard Branson) should administer the lottery, and direct a higher proportion of the income to good causes.

enjoying it. Lottery funding brings many more of these opportunities to the wider public: construction of sports facilities and Millennium projects, youth theatre and music groups and so on. These are of benefit to everyone but not necessary to the survival of the country: so better to raise money for them through optional contributions via the Lottery than through mandatory taxation.

[4]   This is a classic issue of liberty – should we disallow an activity enjoyable to many (e.g. alcohol, football, handguns) simply because a small minority will abuse it or prove unable to cope? We should rather trust the individual right to choose over a paternalist government which takes decisions for us.

[5]   Even if direct contributions to charity fall, the overall amount given to them will still increase. A total of 28 per cent of British lottery income is given to the five Good Causes – arts, sports, charities, heritage, and the Millennium – most of which are community-based projects. Additional publicity is given to these projects through lottery broadcasts on TV, while very often lottery funding for capital projects (e.g. new theatre buildings, community centres, purchase of art treasures) is dependent on the charity raising matching funding, thus encouraging further donations. Charity donations are usually less anyway in the lower income groups which form most of the Lottery's players.

[6]   The Lottery has been highly beneficial in reviving the fortunes of small shops such as newsagents and local Post Offices. It also creates many jobs through

Possible motions:

This House would abolish the National Lottery.

This House believes it could be you.

This House believes that it is immoral to tax stupidity.

This House would nationalise the lottery.

Related topics:

Gambling (Immorality of)

Arts Funding by the State (Abolition of)

Museums (Entrance Fees to)

the new projects it stimulates (the Henley Centre Report predicted that 110,000 jobs would be created under Camelot's franchise). Other types of gambling have benefited anyway from the deregulation of the gambling industry in the mid-1990s which accompanied the creation of the Lottery.

[7]   Camelot was far more successful in raising money for good causes than initial government and independent predictions suggested; it deserves to be rewarded. The franchise-holder suffers the financial consequences should the lottery fail; and removing the motive of personal profit is unlikely to result in such effective management and marketing (the National Lottery game is the UK's most widely recognised consumer brand). The whole history of nationalised industries suggests this.

National Service, (Re-) Introduction of

The Proposition needs to define what it means by 'national service'. In postwar Britain, in several continental countries and Israel today, national service means military service with one of the armed forces. This is a valid debate although some countries (e.g. France and Italy) are currently abandoning the system; but other forms of national service could be considered: public service on environmental projects, working with the homeless, disabled and underprivileged, and so on. A choice between the two could be offered.

Other issues should be considered: at what age should it be compulsory (pre- or post-university, or should there be a choice)? Should it be for men and women (only Israel currently has national service for women)?

Pros

[1]   It is the right of the state to call upon its citizens to serve it in times of need, and democratic governments in

Cons

[1]   There is no clear and present danger to Britain to justify military conscription, and the existence of 'other needs' is

particular have a mandate for such action. No-one would dispute the importance of national service in times of war. Conscription on a permanent basis would keep a 'standing army' ready and trained for times of emergency as well as catering for other needs.

[2]   National service promotes a clear sense of nationhood, integrating individuals from diverse groups and fostering a respect for different cultural and regional traditions. Over a generation this will help to create a more cohesive yet tolerant society, more committed to public life. We can compare older generations in Britain with their more feckless successors, and look to the states of Italy and Israel where national service provides valuable social cohesion.

[3]   National service also provides the young with valuable experience, teaching self-discipline, a sense of purpose and important skills (e.g. driving, IT, administration and personnel management), along with a wider sense of responsibility to the community. In a way they are re-paying their debt to the society which offers them largely free education and welfare benefits throughout their lives.

[4]   National service provides a way to tackle social problems, from the environment to urban deprivation and major disaster relief.

Possible motion:

This House would reintroduce National Service.

disputable. The military does not wish to see the re-introduction of conscription, as it dilutes the professionalism of a standing army, and many of its best instructors waste time training recruits who do not wish to be there. In continental Europe the military is often less keen on national service than its political masters.

[2]   Britain does not have the unrest of Italy and Israel, and such arguments may mask a more dangerous agenda. National service could easily be used for propaganda, not celebrating differences but seeking to eradicate them; the British armed forces do not have a strong reputation for political correctness. Compulsory patriotism is questionable and may be misused by politicians.

[3]   In fact compulsory service is likely to be resented, undermining any possible benefits. A huge bureaucracy would be needed to prevent candidates evading call-up, which would often be easier for prosperous middle-class 'insiders' than for working-class families – as in the US at the time of the Vietnam War. The scheme would cost vast sums even without this bureaucracy. Taxpayers already contribute to the welfare state; there is no need to make them pay this debt twice.

[4]   As with any form of forced labour (e.g. slavery or workfare), leaving such projects to national service recruits will simply ensure they are done badly, with little enthusiasm. Many people are currently paid to undertake the kind of work that non-military national service would involve; their jobs and salaries would be at risk. It might also discourage volunteerism; if the state provides a

Related topics:
Legislation v. Individual Freedom
Pacifism
United Nations (Standing Army for)
Gays in the Military
School-leaving Age
Child Curfews

workforce for such projects, there is no incentive for anyone else to help. Instead, we should encourage a voluntary national service plan, perhaps with lower tuition fees at university for those involved.

Pensions, Ending State Provision of

Like the future of healthcare and unemployment benefits, this issue is made particularly topical by the rapidly escalating costs to developed countries of old-age entitlements (pensions and free medical care). As life expectancy increases, the average age of the population is growing, and in the twenty-first century many more retired citizens will be supported by many fewer taxpayers. Britain does not face as severe a problem financing pensions as do some other countries, but even here the National Insurance system of deducting from one's salary in order to pay for future welfare needs (including healthcare and pensions) is a myth – in fact the money is spent immediately by the government and is not saved for the future.

Pros

[1]   Although civilised societies should provide for their citizens in old age, it does not follow that governments must be involved. Private pension schemes could ensure that everyone planned for and funded his or her own retirement income, reducing the burden on the state and its taxpayers.

[2]   Government bureaucracies seldom provide services as efficient as their private counterparts. A better system would be to force citizens to invest in pension plans, but with considerable freedom as to how this is done. This system is successful in Chile, and personal and corporate pension schemes are growing everywhere. The skill of investment managers to guarantee returns is likely to provide higher pensions than the government can.

Cons

[1]   It is society's duty to care for its elder citizens, and it is the government's duty to ensure that those who cannot look after themselves are catered for. Many people do not earn enough that they would or could contribute voluntarily to a pension scheme; a state-controlled scheme is the only way to ensure they do not become penniless upon retirement.

[2]   The problems of government control existed in nationalised industries, but are not true of the welfare state – pensions, healthcare, education, and so on – since the free market is a poor way of guaranteeing these goods.

[3]   Governments can at least monitor state pension funds and guard against fraud. The exploitation of the Mirror

[3] Private pension schemes are not subject to political interference. This is a risk especially since older people are more likely to vote than the young, and can therefore elect governments who will pay generous pensions while squandering resources for the future. This is especially true in the US where cuts to Medicaid and Medicare are seen as political suicide, since a president doing so risks losing the retired vote.

[4] Privatising pensions ends the 'dependency culture' and gives responsibility back to the individual, who should learn to live with his or her own economic choices and the consequences. Some may choose to invest in pensions, others in their children's education in the expectation that they will repay the gift. It should be a personal choice, and lazy spendthrifts should not benefit from an equal state pension.

Group Pension Fund by Robert Maxwell showed how vulnerable private funds can be to dishonest businessmen. Political interference is a strong possibility anyway; in 1997 the Labour government removed tax advantages from private pension schemes. Governments also have the onus to intervene to prevent private schemes from 'going bust'; this unwritten guarantee encourages private firms to speculate recklessly (e.g. the savings and loan industry in the US in the early 1980s, or Asian banks in the 1990s).

[4] This is a remarkably heartless attitude which would leave those who do not invest wisely, leave investment too late or cannot afford to invest in the first place without the safety net of government support. Self-sufficient individuals can (and do) invest in private pension schemes over and above the National Insurance system, giving them all the freedom they need to create a comfortable retirement.

Possible motion:

This House would privatise the pensions system.

Related topics:

Capitalism v. Socialism
Welfare State
National Health Service (Privatisation of)
Taxation (Direct, Abolition of)
Mandatory Retirement Age

Salary Capping, Mandatory

This debate is about the principle of a maximum salary level, and the Proposition does not have to suggest what that level should be – although it might be more interesting to do so. Benefits in kind and bonuses, such as share options or pension, healthcare and mortgage allowances should also be considered.

Pros

[1]   It is unfair for a few to be paid far more than they could ever spend while many others receive low wages. Economically, there is no need for anyone to receive a salary above, say, £200,000: this will amply guarantee a very comfortable standard of living. The money saved could be put to much better uses, and huge salaries exacerbate social tensions and perpetuate class divisions. Uproar greets every announcement of 'fat cat' bonuses, such as the decision by partners of Goldman Sachs in 1998 to award themselves post-flotation share packages of up to £100 million each. This money should be redistributed more equally.

[2]   A salary cap need not thwart ambition if applied only to salaries – i.e. to employees paid by someone else. Profits derived from the ownership of a business need not be affected, encouraging ambitious and able individuals to create their own companies, with all the economic benefits this provides for society.

[3]   The emphasis upon rewards of employment could be shifted from the purely financial to issues of job satisfaction. Employees are more likely to commit their long-term future to a company, and companies likewise would ensure that their employees are stimulated and given

Cons

[1]   There is no evidence in Britain of social tensions so great that such a massive intrusion into the free market in contracts between employer and employee would be justified. The nature of capitalism is that successful businessmen – who frequently work for years, taking risks and depriving themselves of holidays and family time – are rewarded and incited to succeed even more. Many companies are so large that the sums saved through a salary cap elsewhere would be meaningless – perhaps an extra £1 a week for each ordinary employee or a fractional increase in investment or research budgets.

[2]   This definition of salaries is very limited and creates anomalies. The limited company is not the only form of business; many, such as accountancy, consultancy or law partnerships, are actually owned by their senior practitioners. With a salary cap most of the ablest and most ambitious people would be directed towards such careers, in preference to limited companies; and many businesses would remain wholly owned by their founding partners rather than seeking the capital which public limited status provides for expansion. To float your company on the stock market would mean giving up your rights to a high salary.

sufficient responsibility. Sportspeople and creative types largely seek fame and self-fulfilment in any case. Jobs of great value to society (e.g. politics, teaching, civil service) are likely to gain in status, become better-paid, and produce better applicants or candidates.

Possible motions:

This House would set a maximum limit for salaries.

This House would put the fat cats on a diet.

Related topics:

Capitalism v. Socialism

Legislation v. Individual Freedom

Marxism

Privatisation

Taxation (Direct, Abolition of)

[3]   Enjoyment and medium salaries could not satisfy those with short-term, ephemeral careers – sportspeople, actors and actresses, or singers, who create vast amounts of money for their 'employers' in a short space of time and deserve to profit from it before the bubble bursts. Politicians, teachers and civil servants *should* be utterly dedicated to their careers and not merely attracted by a generous salary.

Sunday Entertainment and Shopping, Restricting

Pros

[1]   Britain has a Christian heritage, traditionally recognised by making one day special – 'the Lord's Day'. Sunday entertainment and shopping erode any spiritual value for the whole of British society, whether church-going or not, by removing an opportunity for reflection. Although the government should not promote a specific religion, it should ensure that there are opportunities for worship and ponder non-materialist values – as it does with religious education and assemblies in schools and prayers in parliament. Religions other than Christianity may not share a commitment to Sunday worship but they do respect

Cons

[1]   Britain is no longer a Christian country. Church attendees are far fewer even than those who would profess a faith in God. There is neither a duty nor a democratic mandate for a government effectively to endorse a particular faith. Why should Sunday be kept special and not Friday (for Muslims) or Saturday (for Jews)? Allowing people to negotiate days off with their employers is more likely to satisfy everyone's wish to honour particular holy days.

[2]   The majority of the population in non-retail business have to work Monday to Friday. Pressures of work with long

spiritual beliefs, and they may value the Sunday restriction for this reason.

[2]   Even for the non-religious, it is advantageous to have a day when most of the population is at home, allowing families to spend time together or visit relatives. If Sundays are treated like any working day, family life will fragment and communal gatherings or days out are much harder to organise. For these reasons many other countries, notably the economic giant Germany, heavily restrict economic activity on Sundays.

[3]   Only a few people work in essential services which must be maintained on a Sunday. Without restrictions on Sunday trading, shop workers may be forced to work six- or seven-day weeks without sufficient rest. Most workers greatly value a two-day break at weekends. For this reason trade unions broadly support keeping Sunday special.

hours and short lunch breaks greatly restrict opportunities to shop, go to the bank, sports clubs, garden centres, theatres, and so on. Even those with families need somewhere to go, and one day at the weekend is not enough. For this reason liberalisation of the Sunday trading laws in the late 1980s was, unsurprisingly, very popular.

[3]   Many people like the flexibility of the work patterns offered, and the chance of extra pay when working on Sundays. Given the number of part-time employees in the retail/service work-force, it is easy to find extra cover if usual staff prefer a two-day weekend.

Possible motions:
This House would keep Sunday special.
This House says 'Never on a Sunday'.

Related topics:
Churches in Politics
Disestablishment of the Church of England
God (Existence of)
Licensing Laws (Relaxation of)

Taxation, Direct, Abolition of

Direct taxation covers any government revenue raised from income or wealth, for example Income Tax, National Insurance, Corporation Tax and death duties. *Indirect taxation* is levied on transactions between one individual and another, for instance, customs charges on imports, excise duty on certain products (mostly 'harmful' ones such as tobacco, alcohol or petrol) and Value Added Tax. Thus indirect tax is paid only on goods or services you purchase or consume, whereas direct tax is paid irrespective of your own expenditure.

Pros

[1]   Direct taxation is also a direct intrusion into the lives of citizens by the

Cons

[1]   Any form of taxation is a direct intervention into the affairs of citizens;

state, and it affects personal behaviour. A significant part of the wealth of each citizen is effectively confiscated; this removes the incentive of the right to find better jobs or work harder, and people may move abroad in search of lower taxes. The elderly dispose of much of their property in trusts and tied gifts to avoid death duties for their heirs. Companies distort their own behaviour by minimising direct tax payments through complex investment and shareholding. This power of intervention and distortion by the government is undesirable.

[2]   Although the level of direct taxation is lower than in many countries, the British public would not accept a rate much higher. The lowest earners find the level particularly high, thinking (justifiably or not) that the burden of direct taxation weighs more heavily on them than on higher income groups. Many feel that a widely generalised system of indirect taxation, replacing direct taxes, would be more equitable.

[3]   Since indirect taxes are paid only on goods or services used by the taxpayer, the poorest members of society can ensure that they pay tax only in strict proportion to their spending, whereas currently they may have to meet a disproportionate share of the tax burden. Indirect taxation rates could also be varied for different things, to take account of the probable income levels of people using them; for instance, Bollinger champagne would be taxed more heavily than Carlsberg Special Brew, or a Rolls Royce more than a Ford Escort. These distinctions are perfectly consonant with variable rates of VAT and sales tax in other countries.

and such intervention is a right of the government given that citizens receive a great deal in return. This is the give and take nature of the 'social contract' between individual and state, as outlined by Hobbes, Locke and many socialist writers.

[2]   Indirect taxes violate the first principle of taxation, in that they cause more to be taken from the taxpayer than they bring to the state – there must always be a cut for the middlemen. Direct taxation is actually fairer since those on higher income pay a higher proportion of their earnings to the state. With indirect taxation, the poor end up paying a higher proportion; although an individual earning £100,000 a year may spend more on food, clothing, and holidays than someone on £10,000, he or she is very unlikely to spend anything like ten times as much.

[3]   Tax revenue pays for much more than goods and services – it is impossible to measure how much an individual 'consumes' in the way of education or national defence. Variation of VAT is impossible within the European Union and has failed in Britain when tried in the past – when, for example, electrical appliances such as refrigerators ended up being classed as 'luxury goods'. Any system which could accurately tax in proportion to consumption would be too complex to administer.

[4]   Fraud is a problem with any tax system, and in fact in advanced economies it is probably easier to avoid indirect taxes through car boot sales, black market goods, unlicensed trading and so on than it is to avoid direct taxes levied

[4]   Evasion of income tax is common – so common that in some continental European countries governments already have to rely on indirect taxation for the bulk of their income. Indirect tax is much harder to avoid, as the strict application of VAT in Britain has shown.

[5]   Indirect taxation can be imposed on articles for moral reasons, when their excessive consumption should be restricted – as it is on alcohol, tobacco and petrol.

[6]   If Britain were to abolish direct taxation while others retained it, we would create an attractive tax haven for foreign high-spenders. Industry would become more competitive as tax is shifted away from business towards consumption, and the transparency of indirect taxation reduces costs in tax management.

through computerised company and bank accounting systems.

[5]   The higher the 'moral' tax on these goods, the greater a drop in revenue from them is suffered by the government. This is also the sort of intervention by the state that the Proposition claims to abhor.

[6]   In fact the high cost of living created by indirect taxation would drive our citizens to purchase much cheaper goods in Ireland, France and the Low Countries. This can be compared with sales distortions near state borders in the US, when one state has a lower sales tax than a neighbouring state.

Possible motions:
This House would abolish direct taxation.
This House believes taxation is theft.

Related topics:
Anarchism
Legislation v. Individual Freedom
Welfare State
National Health Service (Privatisation of)
National Lottery (Abolition of)
Pensions (Ending State Provision of)
Graduate Tax
Tuition Fees for University Students

Trade Unions, Modernisation of

In the Thatcher era in Britain, after the bitter disputes with the National Union of Mineworkers in the 1980s, the powers of trade unions were severely restricted; and with the advent of 'New Labour' and Tony Blair in the 1990s their traditional influence over Labour policy was called into question for the first time. Is there more to be done?

Pros

[1] The trade union movement in Britain anachronistically pits the 'workers' in a class war against the 'capitalists', or employers. The old view of the Conservative Party representing company owners and the Labour Party the workers has long been outdated. New Labour has deleted Clause IV of its constitution, which committed it to the socialist principle of state ownership of the means of production, and has struck up a positive relationship with organisations such as the Confederation of British Industry (CBI) which represents interests of employers generally. The Trades Union Congress (TUC) must be reformed urgently to have any relevance to a modern world where productivity and co-operation rather than strikes and disruption are the order of the day.

[2] The trade union movement still functions in a confrontational way. Today, however, society depends on partnership, between state and private businesses in health, education and transport, and between employers and employees (e.g. the John Lewis Partnership which is owned by its staff). All parties now have common aims – working conditions *and* high productivity – and the obsession of the unions with the former obscures progress.

[3] It is in the trade unions' own interests to modernise. Their traditional affiliation with the Labour Party has tended to mean that unionists are socialist and political activists more interested in campaigning than in providing services. Trade unions should return to their

Cons

[1] The rhetoric of New Labour and of modernisation is simply another method to oppress workers and deny them proper employment rights. The rejection of Clause IV was an outrageous betrayal of the roots of the Labour Party and the interests of its supporters, and it was no surprise when, in 1998, the Labour government sided with the CBI rather than the TUC in its dispute over the level of the minimum wage and union representation in the workplace. To 'modernise' is to give up the fight for fair pay, good working conditions and a voice for workers, and an irreplaceable mechanism to check exploitation by greedy directors.

[2] Trade unions have never *sought* confrontation, nor are they in the least opposed to high productivity. It is the unreasonable intransigence of government (in the case of the miners' strikes), employers (over union representation) or both (minimum wage) that has led to confrontation. The first priority of the unions must be to protect the fundamental right to work in good conditions and be paid above the level of poverty wages; productivity is criticised only when it conflicts with these rights.

[3] Trade unions were independent organisations in the nineteenth century only because the Labour Party did not exist. It came about from developments in the trade union movement, and it should remain the party with the political goal of protecting the rights of workers. There could be no such thing as an apolitical trade union movement.

nineteenth-century roots as independent organisations existing to represent 'the common man'.

Possible motion:

This House believes that trade unions must modernise or die.

Related topics:
Capitalism v. Socialism
Civil Disobedience
Marxism

Workfare

The debate over how to reduce the burden of the welfare state upon taxpayers, and how to avoid a 'dependency culture' where individuals learn to rely on the state for income, housing, healthcare, and so on, has raged for many years. Since the early 1990s interest has centred upon 'workfare' – the concept of withholding unemployment benefits unless the recipient is working in a community project. Various workfare schemes have been piloted, notably in Wisconsin, USA.

Pros

[1]   The cost of the welfare state has become a major financial burden on the government and its taxpayers. Resultant high taxes leave us struggling economically behind the US, various Asian tigers, and potentially Eastern Europe. Simultaneously a 'dependency culture' has developed whereby 'work-shy' individuals rely on income benefits, not seeking proper jobs and 'sponging off the state'. A new approach to unemployment benefit is needed.

[2]   The economic and social cost to society of dependency is enormous. Workfare would lower the cost of the unemployed, by extracting at least a minimal return from their labour (perhaps in the form of street cleaning, unskilled

Cons

[1]   Currently, to claim unemployment benefit you must declare yourself ready for work at short notice. 'Work-shy' people are therefore lying to the state and this is an argument for better safeguards against benefit fraud, not for workfare. Unemployment benefit is also a tiny part of the welfare state; there are many other 'middle-class' targets for cost-cutting such as free health care, pensions and university education. Economically, workfare could hurt society by taking jobs that 'real workers' would otherwise be paid to do, creating even more unemployment – not to mention reducing the number of people available to work in the voluntary sector.

farm labour, environmental projects, etc.). Those who might otherwise seek to avoid work will therefore be encouraged to find better jobs, in order to avoid the workfare tasks.

[3]   Victims of dependency are encouraged to learn habits of regular labour, time-keeping, teamwork, and so on, which are crucial to holding down proper jobs. Many will welcome the chance to do something constructive, out of the house and around new people.

Possible motions:
This House would introduce workfare.
This House would get those on welfare to work.

Related topics:
Capitalism v. Socialism
Welfare State
School-leaving Age

[2]   The idea that people enjoy living off the meagre unemployment benefit is insulting – few would choose it over a real job. But to be forced onto workfare is truly humiliating, and will do nothing to improve confidence or motivation. The work is unlikely to be well done; pointless tasks provoke resentment and more meaningful work cannot be trusted to short-term workers.

[3]   At the same time, those on workfare are prevented from actively seeking proper jobs, with all the research, form-filling, cold-calling and attending interviews required.

SECTION D

Politics and Economics: International

Armaments, Limitation of Conventional

Conventional armaments include guns, mines, missiles, tanks, ships, warplanes – effectively everything except nuclear, biological and chemical weapons. The Proposition should avoid general platitudes ('Let's all be nice to each other – give peace a chance!') and instead suggest a plausible mechanism; the arguments below focus on a unilateral end to arms sales and limitation of defence spending rather than abolition, retaining the capacity for Britain to defend itself.

Pros

[1] Horrific though the effects of nuclear, biological and chemical weapons are, the vast majority of deaths and injuries are caused by conventional arms. Action must be taken to engineer peace where possible and stop the proliferation of weapons; a unilateral end to the sale of such weapons by Britain would be the logical first step.

[2] Even if a unilateral end to arms sales would not stop others selling them, we should end our complicity in wars and violence. British-made weapons are among the 'best' and most destructive in the world and our boycott would have a greater global impact than might be expected. Such moral leadership would shame others into following suit.

[3] Arms may be supplied to oppressive, non-democratic regimes which use them for internal repression (e.g. Indonesia, some Gulf states). It is hypocritical to argue for the respect of human rights while supplying the means to suppress them.

[4] The threat to defence industry jobs cannot justify our involvement in bloodshed, and the government could

Cons

[1] Weapons are a feature of society and have always been so, as have wars. It is naive to suppose that everlasting peace can ever be obtained. Given that war is inevitable, there will always be a large international economy based on weaponry in which we may justifiably be involved.

[2] Britain's refusal to sell arms would have little impact on a world awash with them. Others will simply take our place.

[3] Foreign policy is about promoting our national interests, a process which is not always compatible with whiter-than-white ethical considerations. At least if we are on friendly terms with such regimes they are more likely to listen to our human rights message; if we ignore them, they will side with other countries with no such considerations.

[4] The arms industry is a large and successful one providing many jobs and economic benefits. It would be wrong to throw this away for a gesture of pointless symbolism.

[5] Arms sales to states such as Iraq, Libya, Serbia or Cuba are already

support the redeployment of industries and workers. The need to defend Britain would continue to support most of the arms industry.

[5]   Not only does our sale of weapons involve us in conflict abroad, but British weapons may often be used against us in the future (as happened with Iraq). It is almost impossible to control the re-export of arms to potentially hostile end-users.

prohibited by international agreement. Applications of such sanctions could be more widely made and enforced, but this is not tantamount to a worldwide ban. Why should we deny weapons to friendly, democratic governments, who may be our allies in times of conflict?

Possible motions:
This House would end the arms trade.
This House would keep morality out of the market.

Related topics:
Ideology v. Pragmatism
Pacifism
Nuclear Weapons (Banning of)
United Nations (Standing Army for)
United States (Fear of)
Handguns (Ownership of)
Science: a Menace to Civilisation?

China, Fear of

This debate is not about 'disliking' a nation, although we may reject its values, leaders or national behaviour. The Proposition must show that there is a perceived threat to international peace or prosperity.

Pros

[1]   We should fear China because, as one of the very few communist states remaining, it refuses to adhere to international norms of human rights and democracy. Tibetans, Muslims and Christians within its borders are under particular threat, and yet China's huge population and growing economy make it an example to others and hinder the spread of the values of liberal democracy.

Cons

[1]   Many states have poor domestic human rights records and yet are not an international threat — Saudi Arabia, for example, is a key ally of Britain. Given the perceived failure of communism in the 1990s it is unlikely that other states will copy China's pattern of behaviour, and at any rate its record on these issues is improving, with increasing political openness and personal freedoms.

[2]   China has clear territorial claims which may lead it into conflict with neighbours, and through alliances with the US and other Western powers. There are minor border disputes with almost all its neighbours, but major arguments with Taiwan (which it regards as a rebel province) and the South China Sea (where seven countries are claiming mining and fishing rights).

[3]   In both the Taiwan Strait and the South China Sea, China has made a show of armed force in the past few years. It is a nuclear power and has the largest armed forces in the world. Although its military strength is not particularly impressive, this may hasten the use of nuclear weapons in crisis situations.

[4]   There is little internal stability in China, with a central government struggling to control the regions and the Red Army. Growing crime, corruption and ethnic unrest suggest the leadership in Beijing is losing control. This may lead either to aggressive, populist action such as seizing Taiwan, or to a situation where the peaceful intentions of the leaders are rejected by a more assertive military.

[5]   China poses a threat in terms of economic dominance; its ability to flood with cheap exports is increasingly hurting our own industries. Its rapid development also poses problems to the global environment, since the Chinese demand for cars, energy, CFCs, timber, and so on undermines international attempts to deal with pollution and resource depletion.

[2]   Every country wishes to pursue its own national interest – and the peaceful transition of Hong Kong and Macau to Chinese rule shows that China does not necessarily seek to achieve its ends with violence. Its other priority is a more open foreign policy and improved trade relations (e.g. joining the World Trade Organisation) which will restrain it from upsetting the international community.

[3]   The Chinese military is largely untested and almost certainly overestimated; few of its forces have roles in combat, and its equipment is poor. Most analysts believe that even tiny Taiwan, with its hi-tech, Western technology and weaponry, could counter a Chinese invasion without assistance. The use of nuclear weapons is wild conjecture, equally true of Russia, Pakistan or India.

[4]   There is no evidence that the military is not under governmental control, as key generals and commanders are appointed by the leadership. Nor is there a logical link between internal strife in China, should it happen, and a threat to the rest of the world.

[5]   A trading China is even less of a threat to world peace. Its economic development is slow enough to allow our businesses to adapt to its presence in the market. The opening of the Chinese population also presents an enormous opportunity for our investors, as Rupert Murdoch has identified with his efforts to service them with satellite television.

Commonwealth, Abolition of

The Commonwealth (or 'The British Commonwealth' until 1949) is a voluntary association of fifty-four nations (as of 1997) – each (excepting Mozambique) having once been a colony, protectorate or dependency of Britain, or of another Commonwealth country. In 1991 the Commonwealth Heads of Government issued the Harare Commonwealth Declaration stating the principles and purpose of the Commonwealth – co-operation in pursuit of world peace, commitment to the United Nations' Universal Declaration of Human Rights, opposition to all forms of racial oppression, commitment to the removal of disparities in living standards among member nations, equal rights for women, the rule of law and democratic government.

Pros

[1] The Commonwealth is founded upon an outdated and oppressive colonial system. Now that the European empires have been dismantled, we should base international co-operation on truly international foundations, not on the imperial maps of the past. The Commonwealth fosters neo-colonialism and blinds its members to non-English-speaking culture. If there is a need for an international talking shop and network of trade and technical support for developing nations, it should be truly global, not based on the British empire, with the British monarch as its head.

Cons

[1] The British Commonwealth is a marvellous testimony to how injustice and oppression can be transformed into co-operation and harmony, using the linguistic and historical links of post-colonial nations in a positive way. The nations of the Commonwealth share, for example, English as a first or major language and are almost all governed by parliamentary systems modelled on the British one.

[2] There is no reason why the voluntary association of nations of the Commonwealth should be forced to disband and lose all their mutual support

[2]   International organisations (notably the UN and Amnesty International) already exist to promote education, human rights and equality worldwide. The Harare Declaration is simply an empty repetition of these organisations' principles. Trading blocs such as NAFTA, the EU, and ASEAN based on real economic and political interest foster international trade. In all its supposed roles the Commonwealth is merely duplicating functions performed better by other international organisations.

[3]   The Commonwealth is a sham. Its members, especially powerful ones such as Britain, will always act in accordance with self-interest rather than in alliance with their Commonwealth colleagues. In 1986 Britain refused to place sanctions upon South Africa even though the Commonwealth voted in favour of sanctions, and in 1991 Britain refused to join in protesting against France's nuclear tests in the South Pacific.

[4]   The Commonwealth is indecisive and impotent. Despite declarations in Singapore in 1971 and Harare in 1991, vacuously asserting obvious moral truths about the iniquities of oppression, racism, sexism and so on, the Commonwealth has no means of enforcing its principles or curtailing human rights abuses. The 1995 Millbrook Commonwealth Action programme provides only for 'collective disapproval' and suspension from ministerial meetings if a member nation violates human rights. Technical aid will continue to be provided for two years after a military coup before its provision is even *reviewed*. In 1995, the Nigerian government executed the writer Ken

and co-operation simply because other organisations exist with similar aims. There is room in the world for many such organisations with particular emphases and interests. Membership of the UN and membership of the Commonwealth are not mutually exclusive.

[3]   Powerful countries such as Britain can afford to ignore the policies and interests of the rest of the Commonwealth, and they sometimes do, unfortunately. But the real beneficiaries are the less developed and less powerful countries (e.g. St Kitts and Nevis, Sierra Leone, Tonga, The Gambia), whose heads of state can negotiate with the big world players at Commonwealth Heads of Government meetings, and who can foster bilateral trade agreements and programmes of technical co-operation and education through the NGOs of the Commonwealth network. The fact that Britain does not need the Commonwealth is no reason to deny its benefits to those smaller countries that do.

[4]   It is acknowledged that the Commonwealth is not an agency for the enforcement of international law − it is a low-budget network of mutual co-operation. The principles of democracy, equality, rule of law and individual freedom are not at all obvious in many developing countries − e.g. in the cases of women's rights or child labour, which the Commonwealth combats through educational programmes.

Possible motions:

This House believes that the Commonwealth has had its day.

Saro-Wiwa and eight other opposition activists. Two years later the Commonwealth had still failed to impose sanctions upon or expel Nigeria, but limited itself to official letters of disapproval.

This House believes that if the Commonwealth didn't exist no-one would think of inventing it.

Related topics:
Devolution of Scotland and Wales
Immigration (Relaxation of Laws against)
Democracy (Imposition of)
European Union (Expansion of)
United Nations (Failure of)

Democracy, Imposition of

Pros

[1]   Democracy is desirable in itself as the best system of government. Despite its obvious flaws, any other system is bound to be worse. It ensures that governments are accountable to their people, guards against corruption, protects individual liberty, and allows flawed policies to be corrected. Economies are more likely to be open, competitive and prosperous. If we believe in these benefits, we should promote them vigorously to others.

[2]   Democracy is not a purely domestic issue, as it tends to produce governments that co-operate internationally. There has never been a war between two democracies.

[3]   Democracy carries with it a self-correcting mechanism; if Western pressure leads to the replacement of a dictatorship with democracy, then the electorate can always choose to return to dictatorship – an unlikely prospect. So-called Western cultural imperialism actually consists of trusting the people to choose for themselves.

Cons

[1]   It is one thing to believe our system to be the best, and quite another to impose it on other countries. This is a blatant breach of the UN policy of non-intervention in the domestic affairs of independent nations. Just as Western citizens fought for their political institutions, we should trust the citizens of other nations to do likewise if they wish to. Democracy is also not an absolute term – Napoleon used elections and referenda to legitimise his hold on power, as do leaders today in West Africa, Serbia and Indonesia.

[2]   It is true only in the strictest sense that democracies have not gone to war; the collapse of Yugoslavia and continuing tensions between Greece, Turkey and Cyprus or between Pakistan and India witness this. States with partial democracy are often more aggressive (e.g. Napoleon) than totally unelected dictatorships which are too concerned with maintaining order at home (e.g. Myanmar).

[4]   The Proposition is not advocating invasion *in order to* impose democracy; even if this were justifiable, the lives of our own citizens should not be put at risk. However, when a war is won, it is then reasonable to impose democracy as a condition of peace as done after 1945 in Germany and Japan. Not to do so was a great missed opportunity at the end of the Gulf War.

[5]   As well as imposing democracy through force, it should be promoted peacefully through diplomacy, trade and aid. In such cases countries can choose whether to listen to us, but we can make their people well aware of our commitment to democracy and the reasons for it, for instance through the BBC World Service. Choosing only to trade with or give aid to other democracies is sensible as their economies are more stable and any use of aid can be openly monitored.

Possible motions:

This House would take action to promote democracy.

This House believes that democracy is so good, everyone should be made to have it.

Related topics:

Democracy
Ends v. Means
Voting (Compulsory)
Commonwealth (Abolition of)
Dictators (Assassination of)
Sanctions (Use of)

[3]   The differing types of democracy make it impossible to choose which standards to impose. Britain, the US and European countries all differ in terms of restraints on government and the balance between consensus and confrontation. In Africa, tribal allegiance may make party politics inappropriate – Uganda holds elections but bans parties, forcing all candidates to stand independently. Given that few states today do not at least go through the pretence of holding elections, what standards should we apply?

[4]   Imposition of democracy can backfire, especially after postwar partition, as minority groups become victimised by the majority – as with ethnic Russians in some Baltic states, Arabs in Israel, gypsies in Romania and so on.

[5]   Of course we should be prepared to engage constructively with countries and pressurise them to hold elections, or in some cases boycott them, but this is not the same as imposing democracy. The use of force against other countries, other than in self-defence, is fundamentally incompatible with the qualities inherent in democracy.

Dictators, Assassination of

This can be defined in two ways: whether subjects of a dictatorship should assassinate their leader, or as a policy debate about international relations. Try to avoid using Hitler as an example!

Pros

[1]   Murder is rightly seen as wrong in all societies; but the specific circumstance of a dictatorship, where one unelected individual rules a state through force and fear, means that there are no other ways of removing the dictator from power. If the harm dictators cause is great enough, and their death would remove clear and present dangers, then assassination may be justifiable as a last resort – the end justifying the means.

[2]   Dictators pose a danger to international peace. Their unpopularity at home frequently causes them to launch foreign wars as a distraction (e.g. the Argentine military junta invaded the Falkland Islands in 1982, and Saddam Hussein invaded Kuwait). The removal of one individual through assassination may prevent thousands from dying and millions from suffering.

[3]   Dictators often promote terrorist activity against other states, as in Iraq, Iran, Syria or Libya, to strike at former domestic enemies now in exile or as revenge against governments which have supported their opponents.

[4]   Most dictators care little for ethics and ignore international conventions, law, or standards of behaviour. Examples include Myanmar's collusion in drug

Cons

[1]   Assassination is simply unjustifiable as murder is always wrong. A soldier killing in war is a special case, but the cold-blooded killing of a political leader is not. The ends may not always justify the means; dictators are usually replaced by other members of their military regime, and should the attack fail it would only make them more bloodthirsty and paranoid than before.

[2]   Dictators may threaten their neighbours but so do leaders in democracies such as India and Pakistan, Egypt and Israel, and even the US in Vietnam. Even under a dictatorship such conflicts may be very popular with the people for patriotic, territorial or ideological reasons. Assassinating dictators will not, therefore, prevent international conflict.

[3]   Even the world's greatest democracy, the US, has employed terrorist activity, notoriously against Nicaragua in the early 1980s. Assassination itself is a form of terrorism in any case and to use it is to descend to the level of dictators.

[4]   Many unpleasant regimes have actually been supported by Western powers, such as Marcos in the Philippines as a counterweight to communism. This is not justifiable, but certainly gives us no right to preach to others about

trafficking or Iraq's refusal to restrict its nuclear, biological and chemical weapon development.

[5]   In their own countries, dictators are dangerous in several ways: the use of violence to maintain power (e.g. Tiananmen Square when Chinese tanks crushed student protesters); deliberate policies of attack on their own citizens (e.g. Stalin and the kulaks, or Pol Pot against the Cambodian middle class); and the lack of consultation about their policies which may have disastrous consequences (the failure of China's Great Leap Forward or the famine in Ethiopia). Even relatively 'moral' dictators may be surrounded by corrupt advisers using power to serve their own interests, as happened in Indonesia under Suharto.

[6]   The security with which dictators surround themselves and the climate of fear which they create make it virtually impossible for either popular or elite (i.e. army) opposition to remove them from power, as the career of Saddam Hussein has shown. If widespread suffering and death of their citizens is commonplace, this justifies removing them from power in the only way left.

international responsibilities. Assassination would become a tool of our national interest rather than a moral requirement.

[5]   Such dictators should be removed, but in different ways – preferably by being put on trial (as Ceausescu was in Romania) and allowing justice to be seen to be done. The entire military regime behind a dictator must also be removed or one dictator will simply be replaced by another, as happened with the natural deaths of Kim Il Sung of North Korea and General Sani Abacha of Nigeria.

[6]   The internal security of a dictator can be destabilised by isolating the regime diplomatically and economically, while keeping the people informed through global communication. Constructive engagement remains the best solution; history has shown that authoritarian regimes do not survive when a wealthy middle class is opposed to them. Creating the middle class through economics is our best attack on dictators.

Possible motions:
This House would assassinate a dictator.
This House believes it is never right to take a life.

Related topics:
Civil Disobedience
Ends v. Means
Democracy (Imposition of)
Sanctions (Use of)
Terrorism (Justifiable)

Environment: Links to International Trade and Relations

Pros

[1]   With the threat to the future of the planet posed by global warming, ocean and air pollution, depletion of natural resources and threats to biodiversity, the environment must be a top priority for all nations. International aid, trade and diplomacy should be used to promote environmental protection and conservation.

[2]   Environmental protection could be made a condition of receiving international aid. This can be done either by directly offering aid to finance programmes of environmental protection, or by refusing to give aid of any kind unless environmentally sensitive policies are put in place. It is in the interest of the country receiving aid in the long term and the planet as a whole that aid should be linked to environmental protection in one of these ways. Therefore the World Bank should consider the environmental implications of any lending decisions it makes.

[3]   Environmental aid given now will save money in the long run by averting long-term environmental crises. To take one example, investment in safe and non-polluting forms of energy production will reduce the health bill of future generations who might otherwise suffer from the effects of disasters such as Chernobyl, from the unsafe handling and storage of nuclear waste, and from respiratory diseases resulting from the burning of fossil fuels.

Cons

[1]   Environmentalism is a luxury of rich nations. The evidence for the real causes of global warming is inconclusive. Environmentalism is a Western bourgeois fad that should not be imposed on developing countries. Linking environmental protection to trade, aid and diplomacy is an unacceptably coercive form of neo-colonialism (i.e. the West imposing its policies and values on the developing world).

[2]   Aid should not be tied to any particular policies. Aid should be used to relieve poverty and disease and to finance the education of the underprivileged, not as a political tool by the West. Such a linking of aid to environmental protection is also deeply hypocritical. The rich and powerful countries of the world (and the World Bank itself, which administers many loans and aid grants to developing countries) have been responsible, in their accumulation of wealth, for massive environmental destruction (e.g. emission of greenhouse gases, destruction of rainforests).

[3]   In the past, foreign aid has very rarely been effective in achieving its aims. Foreign aid to Somalia, for example, did not prevent famine and civil strife overwhelming that country. The reason for this is often that conditions attached to aid are ignored by unscrupulous or undemocratic regimes which use the money to invest in their own military and industrial programmes. It is, in any case,

[4]   The principle that 'the polluter must pay' is already put into practice by some countries in their domestic policies – fining companies that pollute the atmosphere, rivers or oceans. The same principle should be applied internationally by rich countries and multinational corporations refusing to trade with countries and companies with records as polluters.

[5]   Countries which show disdain for human rights are subjected to diplomatic exclusion and economic sanctions by the international community. By the same token, we should extend this practice to countries which show disdain for their fellow humans, their children and their own ecosystem by polluting and depleting the environment.

Possible motions:
This House would put the environment first.
This House would cease trading with polluters.
This House would not give aid to the polluter.

Related topics:
Ends v. Means
Legislation v. Individual Freedom
Population Control
Global Warming (More Action on)
Nuclear Energy
Smoking (Banning of)

unreasonable to expect poorer developing nations to plough money into unprofitable environmental and safety measures rather than into measures to increase economic growth.

[4]   First, it is naive to believe that any corporation will genuinely put the environment before economics in its choice of trading partners. Second, as long as there are *some* countries (as there inevitably will be) which will trade with companies and countries no matter what their environmental record, trade embargoes of the kind proposed will fail. Those countries that refuse to trade with polluting companies and countries will lose out to the less scrupulous, and so ultimately no country will be able to afford to disadvantage itself economically for the sake of environmental principles.

[5]   The abuse of human rights is in an altogether different league from the neglect of environmental protection, which may be undesirable but cannot reasonably be judged to be malicious and immoral. The use of diplomatic and economic sanctions against polluters is unreasonable and extreme.

European Union, Expansion of

Pros

[1]   The European Union has had great success in reuniting a continent shattered

Cons

[1]   The EU in the past may have achieved these benefits, but its members

by the Second World War. Members get clear benefits from co-operation and avoiding confrontation. Trade and prosperity are promoted, and citizens have increased opportunities to travel and work abroad. Through demonstrating liberal democracy to Eastern Europe, it may also have helped win the Cold War. All of these benefits should be extended to others.

[2] The world is dividing into major trading blocs and the time is right for the EU to expand. NAFTA and Mercosur are growing and a Free Trade Area of the Americas is proposed, as are deeper links with ASEAN. Europe needs to strengthen itself for future competition with these other blocs. A Union with twenty or twenty-four members would carry more international clout than with the current fifteen.

[3] Historically, the addition of new countries – whatever their circumstances – has worked because each country has contributed from its strengths (as the economist Adam Smith suggested, free trade works because it encourages everyone to specialise in what he or she is good at, rather than waste time and money competing in other areas). Britain's specialities lie in international finance, high-technology and creative industries, and the service sector. Greece, Spain and Portugal were all integrated without undue difficulty.

[4] Generosity must be shown in welcoming former Warsaw Pact states into the European mainstream, reuniting Europe after its wars. Our future security depends on avoiding the resentment that might be caused if we do not.

are merely nation states acting in their own interests. If further expansion were to sacrifice these interests, then it should not be attempted. Given that all likely new entrants to the EU are relatively poor, formerly communist states, the advantages to current members of including them are doubtful. Cheap farm produce from Eastern Europe would hurt our agricultural sector, and cheap wages there undermine our industries.

[2] The time is not right, even if the idea were good in theory. Huge changes are being undertaken by the current members (Single Market, Single Currency, Social Chapter, Schengen Agreement, etc.) and they need time to consolidate. Attempting to expand simultaneously could be disastrous.

[3] The last expansion of the EU was uncontentious because it involved richer, north European countries such as Sweden and Austria. With the exception of Norway and Switzerland there are no such countries left; instead we would only be welcoming states that would take more from the EU than they could give, as Greece and Portugal currently do. The Union can bear a few poorer countries without problem, but not many.

[4] The greater geopolitical danger in expanding the EU would be the alienation of Russia, which (largely correctly) identifies it with NATO as an alliance designed to strengthen Western Europe against Soviet expansion. With no clear physical limits to the European Union, Russia will naturally be suspicious of where natural expansion may end. Antagonising Russia is in no-one's interest.

Possible motions:

This House believes a wider Europe is not in Britain's interest.

This House would let them in.

Related topics:

Immigration (Relaxation of Laws against)

Commonwealth (Abolition of)

Single European Currency

United Nations (Failure of)

United States of Europe

Islam, Fear of

See the notes on a similar debate under 'China, Fear of'.

Pros

[1] Islam in this context really means Islamic fundamentalism, which places religious ideology over considerations of democracy, human rights, and so on. Such a creed is a threat to regimes in a number of Muslim countries (e.g. Egypt, Algeria). Its adherents in countries such as Iran, Afghanistan, Sudan and Pakistan have introduced laws based on their interpretation of Islamic law, such as restricting the role of women in society. We should fear this form of Islam as it conflicts with our conception of human rights.

[2] Fundamentalist Islamic movements derive their authority from religious belief rather than from popular mandate (although they sometimes claim this too). This means that they are not bound by normal conventions of political behaviour and are more likely to use violence to achieve their aims, as with terrorist groups such as Islamic Jihad, Hezbollah, the GIA in Algeria or the Taliban in Afghanistan.

[3] The opposition of Islamic groups to Israel will perpetually destabilise the Middle East, and will inevitably bring

Cons

[1] A different religious or political belief does not mean that we should be afraid; Christianity, Hinduism and communism all have belief systems which could be taken to challenge concepts of human rights and democratic government. Islamic fundamentalism is also a dubious concept, imposed as an umbrella term on a number of diverse movements – we might as well speak of 'Christian countries of the West'.

[2] Islamic groups are no more likely to resort to violence than those of any other religious affiliation (IRA, Tamil Tigers, Basque ETA, etc.). Their use of international terrorism stems from the particular political circumstances of the Middle East; religion is not the motivator. Internal violence such as exists in Egypt and Algeria is a response to authoritarian governments denying Islamic groups a voice.

[3] The Israel–Palestine dispute is more about territory than about religion; in fact many Palestinians are Christian. The opposition of Islamic states to Israel long pre-dates Islamic fundamentalism. In

Islam into confrontation with Israel's friends in the West. This has led Iran in particular to sponsor international terrorism.

recent times, anyway, it could be argued that Israel bears more of the blame for the failing peace process than do any of the Arab states.

Possible motion:

This House fears Islam.

Related topics:

Churches in Politics
China (Fear of)
Democracy (Imposition of)
Terrorism (Justifiable)
United States (Fear of)

Nuclear Weapons, Banning of

Pros

[1]   Despite the end of the Cold War, the danger of a nuclear exchange remains. Previously, it was held in check by the doctrine of MAD (Mutually Assured Destruction) by which a super-power launching a nuclear strike upon its opponent would itself be destroyed. With the end of MAD, the risk of use by a rogue state or a limited exchange in a regional conflict becomes more likely. Recent events in the Middle East and in the Indian sub-continent highlight these concerns.

[2]   As the Russian military dis-integrates, mistakes become more likely. In 1995 a Norwegian scientific rocket was mis-identified by under-trained radar operators, placing the Russian missile systems only a few minutes away from a full strike; power-cuts to missile silos and

Cons

[1]   The end of the Cold War has seen a diversification in the nature of a possible nuclear threat, to include use by a number of rogue states and by terrorists. The size of the nuclear arsenal may therefore be reduced, but in today's complicated political climate, a flexible nuclear deterrent is as vital as ever.

[2]   There is no 'quick fix'; the process of disarmament is long and complex. The nuclear material in the warhead cannot be destroyed, and must therefore be stored in a secure facility. The demoralisation and disorganisation of the Russian military, protecting some thousand such facilities, often leaves them unguarded; moreover, the Russian government has no accurate records to track nuclear materials, making it impossible to tell when a quantity is missing.

thefts of vital control equipment for sale on the black market have likewise caused near-accidents. The only way to ensure that these do not happen is to eliminate the weapons.

[3] Nuclear weapons are a deterrent, guarding against a perceived threat. To avoid an imbalance of power, disarmament must therefore be universal. Moreover, it is vital that the superpowers disarm. As India and Pakistan have shown, the so-called 'nuclear club' is still prestigious; treaties such as the Comprehensive Test Ban Treaty cannot succeed while the perception remains that the superpowers are simply making permanent their nuclear advantage.

[4] The trend in modern warfare is towards 'surgical strikes', with the minimum of civilian casualties. Nuclear weapons are designed to result in the maximum loss of life. Were a modern rogue state to employ nuclear weapons, the justification for a retaliatory strike would be unclear; the citizens of a modern democracy would not accept the resultant deaths of civilians not responsible for their government's actions. Hence, the deterrent role of such weapons has ceased to be effective.

Disarmament therefore increases the risk of theft and proliferation.

[3] Universal disarmament is impossible. It requires only one state to maintain a secret nuclear capability for the system to fail – without any deterrent, it would be free to strike at its enemies. Moreover, the large nuclear arsenals of Russia and the US help to reduce the danger of arms proliferation; in extending a 'nuclear umbrella' over friendly countries, they remove their need to form an individual deterrent.

[4] The danger of escalation of regional conflicts, and the knowledge on both sides of their mutual ability for destruction, are powerful incentives for governments to seek peaceful solutions to their problems. Whatever our feelings on the Cold War, it may well have prevented a devastating third – conventional – world war from breaking out between East and West. Although the use of nuclear weapons would be horrifying, the fear of their use may have saved countless lives in the past fifty years, and will continue to do so in the future.

Possible motion:
This House would ban nuclear missiles.

Related topics:
Ideology v. Pragmatism
Armaments (Limitation of Conventional)
China (Fear of)
United States (Fear of)
Nuclear Energy
Science: a Menace to Civilisation?

Population Control

Unlimited population growth cannot be a good thing; Thomas Malthus pointed out 200 years ago that the human capacity for reproduction could disastrously overtake the resources available to mankind. The debate now is whether we are heading for a 'Malthusian' disaster, and whether measures to avoid it should be 'soft' (education of women, economic growth) or 'hard' (promotion of free contraceptives, abortion, penalties for large families, etc.). A Proposition which ducks the second type and sticks only to soft measures does not deserve to win this debate.

Pros

[1]   Malthus argued that human reproductive potential was geometric (1–2–4–8–16 etc.) while growth in resources was only arithmetic (1–2–3–4–5). Eventually a disparity between the two will end in crisis, such as war over resources, famine, malnutrition, epidemic disease and environmental devastation. Such tragedies are clearly identifiable today and are sure to become worse unless steps are taken to limit the population growth. We owe it to future generations to give them a chance of existence free from malnutrition, poverty and so on.

[2]   There are, of course, other global problems, but population control still needs addressing; problems of inequality are often exacerbated by those of overpopulation. Human prosperity and happiness and the environment are all affected.

[3]   Many different means exist to restrict population but it is not necessary to compel individuals to undergo vasectomies, abortions, contraceptive injections, and so on. Instead, governments can apply economic pressure on those with large families, as in China where second

Cons

[1]   Malthus predicted a major population crisis in the mid-nineteenth century, but none came. In the 1970s the neo-Malthusian *Limit to Growth* predicted another catastrophe, also erroneously. Most disasters are caused by ideological or ethnic rivalry, poor government management of resources (famine) or greed (which causes much environmental devastation, such as the Bangladeshi floods). It is difficult to prove any link between natural disasters and overpopulation.

[2]   The real problem is not rapid population growth but inequitable distribution of resources between a rich Northern hemisphere and a much poorer South. More urgent priorities to address are different and fairer trade and development policies. An end to EU agricultural protectionism would greatly aid Africa, for example, while the large quantities of meat eaten in richer countries currently require a much less productive use of agricultural land than if our diets were more vegetarian.

[3]   Attempts to limit population growth have traditionally been very

and subsequent children disqualify families from a range of state benefits. Contraception can be distributed widely and cheaply (often a big issue in Africa), and educational programmes can enthusiastically promote the advantages of small families – as can better provision for parents in old age.

[4] Restricting population growth has other spin-offs, particularly the empowerment of women who can be given control of reproduction. This allows them to pursue education and job opportunities, as well as better health and longer life expectancy. The spread of sexually transmitted diseases is contained when condoms are more widely used.

unpleasant, ignoring basic human rights with state intervention (e.g. China with its one-child policy) or attacking deeply held religious beliefs (Catholicism and Islam) through promoting contraception and therefore, by implication, relaxed sexual morality. Such measures are often deeply unpopular within societies on which they are imposed, and only totalitarian governments (such as China) are able to implement them.

[4] If our aim is the empowerment of women then legislating against families of more than one child, for example, seems entirely counterproductive. Such a measure radically reduces the control of women over their reproductive life. It is certainly a good idea to increase the availability of condoms and provide education on safe sex and STDs, but that does not mean that we should make contraception (or sterilisation or one-child families) compulsory. This would be an unacceptable constraint on personal freedom.

Possible motions:
This House calls for further population control.
This House would go forth and stop multiplying.

Related topics:
Legislation v. Individual Freedom
China (Fear of)
Abortion on Demand
Euthanasia
Feminism (Devaluation of Parenthood by)
Marriage
Co-education
Sex Education
Prostitution (Legalisation of)
Contraception for Under-age Girls
Eugenics: IVF and Genetic Screening
Genetic Engineering

Sanctions, Use of

By 'sanctions' we mean here economic sanctions, including cultural boycotts (such as the ban on sporting ties with South Africa in the 1980s), the denial of expected aid packages, and restrictions on trade. The debate must address the principle of sanctions, but should also include salient examples (at the time of writing, Iraq, Nigeria, Cuba and North Korea, for example).

Pros

[1]   Economic sanctions are the best method available to the international community for altering the behaviour of unpleasant regimes. Bloodshed is avoided and direct intervention into another country's affairs is eschewed. By linking sanctions to specific behaviour we wish to change, we can send a clear message to regimes which abuse human rights, defy democratic election results, proliferate nuclear weapons and so on.

[2]   There are limited examples where economic sanctions have been conclusively effective, but that is because sanctions have seldom been applied effectively by the whole international community. Following the end of the Cold War, new opportunities exist to gain fuller co-operation and enforcement (e.g. against Iraq) and thus to succeed. In recent years Western pressure on President Moi of Kenya and other African leaders to hold elections has been notably successful.

[3]   Sanctions can be designed in such a way that the suffering of the people is minimised and pressure on the leadership maximised. Medical supplies continue to be sent to Iraq, and food exports to North Korea are carefully monitored to

Cons

[1]   Sanctions are fine in theory, but they have little effect – and can even do more harm than good. The standard example of success against South Africa is questionable; many factors were at work there and change was a long time in coming. Cuba, Iran, Iraq and Nigeria have all been under sanctions for long periods without any sign of crumbling to Western pressure.

[2]   Elections in Africa have been largely cosmetic; none of the leaders involved has lost power through elections, which are conducted amid menacing military presence at the polling stations. It will always be difficult to obtain full international consensus on sanctions; and the targets are usually more insular states which depend less on wide trade links in any case. Even when potentially effective, they may be circumvented by smuggling, corruption and other forms of sanction breaking.

[3]   Too often the sanctions hurt the people they are meant to help; the poor will always be a last priority in times of economic crisis, while the ruling elite will take first pick of available resources. Sanctions can also be exploited by leaders – fostering a sense of national resentment

ensure that they go directly to the starving people, not into military storehouses.

[4]   Even if sanctions are often ineffective, to continue to trade with nasty regimes is complicity in their actions. Too often in the past we have sold them arms, trained their soldiers or bought their oil, diamonds, gold or crops.

[5]   Sanctions can be effective not only by changing the domestic behaviour of regimes but also by limiting the resources available to them for future external aggression. Without arms, fuel, communications technology and so on, capacity for mischief making is severely curtailed.

against the 'foreign oppressors' who deny them food, and using the suffering of the people as a stick to beat Western consciences.

[4]   To claim the moral high ground in this way is pure hypocrisy. Sanctions have invariably been used selectively, putting national interests first – despite their questionable behaviour, China, India and Nigeria have not been the targets for heavy sanctions because they are seen as valuable strategic and economic partners. Serbia, Kenya and Cuba – which are targeted more seriously – are seen as of little value to the West.

[5]   Again, there will always be someone else willing to trade – and dictators are much more likely to find arms and technology on the black market than grain and medical supplies! The determination fostered by refusal to give in to sanctions can also outweigh the loss of resources suffered.

Possible motions:
This House believes that sanctions do more harm than good.
This House believes that sanctions are always preferable to war.

Related topics:
Ends v. Means
Armaments (Limitation of Conventional)
China (Fear of)
Environment (Links to International Trade and Relations)
Islam (Fear of)
United Nations (Failure of)

Single European Currency

Pros

[1]   Britain should join the European single currency in its own self-interest. All European countries except Britain and

Cons

[1]   Monetary policy decisions (e.g. interest rates) must be linked to fiscal policy decisions (regarding taxation and

Denmark are fully committed to a single currency, which will be the currency for every consumer in the European Union by 2002. If Britain does not fully opt in, we will be left out of the most important and powerful political and economic bloc to emerge since the end of the Cold War. The single currency is a crucial part of a really free market within Europe and a stable European Union. Economic and political self-interest should over-ride rhetorical jingoism. Real patriotism is doing what is best for Britain in the long term.

[2]   A single currency brings many tangible benefits. For example, there are no longer bank commission charges taken out of your money when you have to change it from one currency to another. So travellers in the EU will save money by having a single currency. In 1998, if you started off with £100 and travelled through every EU country simply changing it into the local currency without spending anything, by the time you got back to Britain you would have had only £50.50 left.

[3]   With a single currency there will no longer be the problem of varying exchange rates that make business unstable and insecure. For example, in 1997–98, the British manufacturing industry went into recession because the strength of the pound on the currency market meant that British goods were prohibitively expensive compared with those made in countries with weaker currencies. With a single currency these dangers would be eliminated and the purchasing power of your money in one EU country would be the same as in any other, and your produce

expenditure) in order to have a balanced, healthy economy. If we surrender monetary policy to a European Central Bank (which is the institution through which the single currency will be administered), then we will also have to surrender fiscal policy to the EU – i.e. Europe will have to set levels of taxation and public spending for all its member countries. In other words, all important policy decisions will be taken out of the hands of the British parliament and given to European bankers. That is why a single European currency will mean a loss of sovereignty and a loss of democratic accountability. Real patriotism is safeguarding the power of the British people and their parliament.

[2]   There are ways other than having a single currency to seek to reduce commission charges for travellers. 'Eurocheques', for example, can be used in all European countries, and will minimise bank charges. Credit cards can also be used throughout Europe. No travellers (except perhaps the very stupid) actually travel through several counties simply changing cash into the local currency at each new border. The loss of political sovereignty and democratic answerability that the single currency would bring is much too high a price to pay for small savings over existing payment methods for travellers that minimise bank charges.

[3]   Each nation state has its own currency as a sign of the economic strength of the nation. Currencies *could* be merged indefinitely until there was only one global currency, but that would be to ignore facts of national differences in productivity and wealth. Variations in exchange rates are not arbitrary

could be expected to earn a stable and predictable price. A single currency will bring stability and security for business and thereby job security for employees. Jobs will no longer be at risk from the vagaries of currency markets.

[4] A single currency for the whole of the EU is more likely to enjoy a strong position on the financial markets, in competition with the US dollar and the Japanese yen than individual currencies are.

[5] For all the alarmist rhetoric of the anti-Europeans, a single currency will have little effect on individuals' everyday lives. The coins of the 'Euro' will have one side the same throughout the EU but the other side left to each individual country so that in Britain they can still bear the monarch's image on one side. The fact that it is no longer called the 'Pound' is of no material consequence, any more than decimalisation and replacing imperial (inches, pounds) with metric (centimetres, kilogrammes) measurements had any profound political or cultural effects.

[6] There are stringent 'convergence criteria' for inclusion in European Economic and Monetary Union (EMU) and so strong members of the single currency will not have to 'carry' weaker ones. Only countries that have reduced their national debt to acceptable levels and reduced unemployment sufficiently will be allowed to join. Economic convergence has been facilitated in the run up to EMU by fixing exchange rates through the European Exchange Rate Mechanism (ERM). In any case, every currency and

inconveniences but an inevitable aspect of an international market. To have a single currency for the EU would not eliminate this fact but would simply put British businesses at the mercy of the entire European economy. So a strong Euro or a weak Euro, resulting from economic changes in other nations, would have repercussions for British businesses. Having a single currency is to put all your eggs in one basket. The whole of the European Union will go into recession together if a few national economies fail. Currently fluctuations reflect real national changes. We do not want Britain's economic prospects to be determined by developments in Italy, Portugal, Spain and Greece.

[4] The Euro will not be guaranteed, simply by the fact of its existence, to be strong against the dollar or the yen, especially if the convergence criteria for EMU are fudged, as they increasingly seem to be. Such a fudged currency would be in danger of losing international confidence – a crucial factor in financial markets. The whole of the EU would then suffer.

[5] The pound is a central part of British heritage. Decimalisation of our currency (until 1971 there were 240 pence to the pound, threepenny and six-penny coins, and one and two shilling coins) was a major concession to European integration; to give up the pound altogether would be many times more significant. The notes of the Euro will have no national symbols on them, but the EU flag and examples of European culture. These changes are not superficial but part of an insidious erosion

its associated monetary policy, from the yen to the dollar to the pound, is inevitably used over a wide range of different economic circumstances (e.g. the south-east of England is currently much richer than the north-east). A single currency builds stability on a widely diverse economic base. If the United States can function with a single currency then so too can the countries of the EU.

Possible motions:

This House welcomes the single European currency.

This House believes in the Euro.

This House believes that the pro-European is the true patriot.

Related topics:

European Union (Expansion of)

United States of Europe

from the everyday level upwards of Britain's heritage and historic culture.

[6]   The effect of a single currency in the EU will be that the economic strength of the richer countries (Germany, Britain, France) will prop up the poorer countries (Greece, Portugal). The poorer countries will benefit at the expense of the taxpayers in richer countries. The economies of the countries of the EU are too diverse to be unified by a single currency. The analogy with the United States is, indeed, telling. The only way in which a single currency can be administered effectively is in a *politically* unified country with central direct tax-raising powers. The inevitable implication of EMU is *political* unification and the creation of a United States of Europe. The desire to retain national political sovereignty and identity thus demands opposition to a single currency.

Terrorism, Justifiable

Be careful not to let this descend into a definitional debate about the exact meaning of 'terrorism'. The Proposition *is* expected to defend violent behaviour towards civilians, at least in some cases; however, the Opposition cannot necessarily expect blowing up kindergartens to be defended.

Pros

[1] Sometimes minorities under oppressive regimes have no other means of expression, as they are denied access to media, the political system or the outside world, as were the ANC in South Africa under apartheid. As a last resort it may be defensible to resort to violence.

[2]   The end justifies the means; it may

Cons

[1]   Having no other means of expression is no justification for harm done to innocent civilians. Gandhi and others showed the potential success of peaceful protest. A noble cause is devalued if it is fought through violence.

[2]   There are very few cases of terrorism actually working. In some cases

be that the eventual outcome of a terrorist campaign is beneficial and this outweighs the harm done in achieving it. History will be the judge, as when terrorism in East Pakistan helped to bring about the creation of Bangladesh, or the Jews forced the British out of Palestine and led to the creation of Israel.

[3] Terrorism draws international attention to your cause in a way in which nothing else can.

[4] 'One man's terrorist is another man's freedom fighter.' The terrorists may see themselves as fighting a genuine war, directed against military targets; we condone killing soldiers and even an inevitable number of civilian casualties in wartime.

[5] Terrorism is about causing fear. Although some civilians will usually have to die, much of the campaign may not involve actually violence but merely the exploitation of existent fear. In 1997 the IRA threatened to blow up several railway stations in south-eastern England without doing so; and they have used phony warnings to evacuate buildings, exploiting the fear caused by previous explosions. The level of violence can be − and often is − kept to the bare minimum necessary to be taken seriously.

the satisfactory outcome is only achieved once the terrorists are forced to renounce violence, but in most cases the fighting continues and nothing is achieved. The IRA won no concessions from the British government in seventy years of violent campaigning, and the PLO was forced to renounce terrorism before negotiations began.

[3] In fact, terrorism tends to draw international condemnation; the countries that support terrorist groups tend to be Islamic fundamentalist states and the US with its notoriously immoral foreign policy.

[4] War is a two-way process, and if the military targets are not attacking you then it is not war. There must also be sensible criteria for defining war, or any lunatic could declare himself a soldier and kill with impunity. Civilian casualties in wartime are usually accidental; any attack deliberately targeting civilians therefore devalues the claim to be 'freedom fighters'.

[5] The bare minimum is still unacceptable − no amount of phony warnings from the IRA will erase the stark reality of their surprise bombing at Omagh. The more often a terrorist exploits the fear from a previous attack, the more the public will begin to see through it and the terrorist must attack again.

Possible motions:
This House believes that terrorism can be justifiable.
This House believes that one man's terrorist is another man's freedom fighter.

Related topics:
Civil Disobedience
Ends v. Means
Pacifism
Dictators (Assassination of)
Terrorists (Negotiation with)

Terrorists, Negotiation with

As with the previous topic, much depends on the definition – both of 'terrorists' and of 'negotiation'. A brave Proposition will define it as 'listening, and being prepared to make concessions, to those who use violence against civilians to achieve their political aims'. The debate is really only relevant to democracies, as dictators would have no interest in negotiation.

Pros

[1]   Negotiation may lead to lives being saved, and this must be any government's first priority. Hostages tend to be civilians who are not the property of the government to be sacrificed for other matters. If the price to pay for their safety is the release of 'political' prisoners, it is cheap.

[2]   Negotiation in its simplest form means 'talking to'. We must keep an open dialogue with terrorist groups, to understand them and encourage them to take part in the political process without arms.

[3]   History shows us that negotiations have led to ceasefires. The British government under John Major held secret talks with the IRA in the early 1990s, which led to the first, breakthrough ceasefires; Bill Clinton negotiated with the PLO in making advances towards peace in the Middle East.

[4]   Non-negotiation – the refusal to make any concessions to terrorists unless they give up their weapons – has no effect on terrorists, who are unlikely to be brought to their knees by their enemies not talking to them. Margaret Thatcher's firm stance of non-negotiation, for

Cons

[1]   'Political prisoners' tend to be imprisoned terrorists who will kill again on their release, so any hostages saved in the present must be weighed against probable future casualties. Second, there is no guarantee that hostages will not be killed anyway once their demands are met.

[2]   Keeping an open dialogue with terrorist groups gives them political legitimacy which they do not deserve. It is better to have no relationship whatsoever with them until they renounce violence, to show that they are voluntarily excluding themselves from democracy.

[3]   Terrorists want all or nothing, and in many cases negotiations have failed. Several IRA ceasefires were abandoned due to impatience on behalf of the Provos, and meaningful peace has not been established in the Middle East.

[4]   Once any concessions are made to terrorists, a dangerous precedent is set; other terrorist groups will be encouraged to believe that they can achieve their aims with violence. The only possible prevention of this encouragement – which could lead to a disastrous escalation of terrorist violence and government

example, merely let violence continue in Northern Ireland for her decade in power.

capitulation – is consistent non-negotiation, even if it is not always successful.

Possible motion:
This House would talk to terrorists.

Related topics:
Ends v. Means
Ideology v. Pragmatism
Terrorism (Justifiable)
War Crimes (Prosecution of)

United Nations, Failure of

This debate can often descend into example-swapping. A better tactic is to use examples, but to focus on the nature of the organisation and whether or not it has fulfilled its own aims.

Pros

[1]   The United Nations was founded in the aftermath of the Second World War, in an attempt to preserve peace and to build a better world founded upon respect for human rights. There have been so many conflicts, with so much loss of life, in the past fifty years that it is clear that the UN has not satisfied the hopes of its founders. Not only do many regimes still abuse basic human rights, but the UN has been powerless to prevent ethnic cleansing and genocide in Central Africa and the Balkans.

[2]   The UN cannot be credited with preventing another world war; this is entirely due to the US/USSR arms race and nuclear technology, which has made it too dangerous to escalate local conflict. Similarly, human rights and democracy have been promoted through the determination of the West (what used to

Cons

[1]   To a large extent the UN has fulfilled its remit, helping to prevent a global war, standing up to aggression (especially in Korea and Kuwait) and making human rights a powerful worldwide concept which states can flout but not ignore – or else why would China have tried to justify its record as better than that of the US? Some UN failures are tragic, but it cannot be expected to succeed in every case; it should be judged against the outcome if it had never existed.

[2]   Mutually assured destruction may have prevented nuclear warfare, but the UN has been the global focus for negotiation and co-operation in the way its predecessor, the League of Nations, never was. Both formal and informal compromises can be reached in tense situations. The end of the Cold War has made co-operation via the UN even

be called 'the free world') to stand up to communism, and by the obvious link between democracy and material prosperity – not by the UN.

[3]   Many of the UN's failures stem from its intrinsic bureaucratic short-comings, such as the ability of any permanent member of the Security Council to veto decisions. The selection of these members is looking increasingly arbitrary and is not dependent on com-mitment to the UN ideals (China, for example, sells arms and nuclear tech-nology to dangerous regimes, while the US refuses to pay its contributions to the UN). Some resolutions passed by large majorities in the General Assembly (e.g. against Israel) have not been imple-mented, in large part due to obstruction by the US and other Security Council members.

[4]   International development has been promoted more through the loans of the World Bank and through the benefits of free trade (under GATT and the WTO), which are independent of the UN. Nor is the UN involved in the majority of development aid from national governments.

easier, as shown by prompt action against Iraqi aggression and attempts to make peace in Central Africa, Angola, the Balkans and Cambodia. Where it has failed recently, it tends to be in conflicts *within* sovereign states, where the UN has little mandate to act.

[3]   The Security Council could cer-tainly be changed to reflect the evolving nature of world powers. Rotating seats, allocated on a continental basis, would be a possibility. This is not a reason to condemn the whole work of the UN.

[4]   The UN's greatest successes, which have changed the face of the world, have not been in the area of peacekeeping and diplomacy. Through its agencies (e.g. the World Health Organisation, the FAO, and Unicef) it has co-ordinated and promoted efforts to improve the lives of billions. Smallpox has been eradicated, and the basic calorific intake significantly raised on the Indian sub-continent, for example. It is hard to believe that volun-tary agencies or national governments would or could have had these effects.

Possible motions:
This House believes that the United Nations has failed.
This House believes that the UN is a tooth-less watchdog.

Related topics:
Ideology v. Pragmatism
Democracy (Imposition of)
Sanctions (Use of)
United Nations (Standing Army for)
United States (Fear of)

United Nations, Standing Army for

A 'standing army' is one that is always ready for action, rather than one assembled only on an ad hoc basis in times of crisis. The Proposition should have a broadly plausible plan for such an army, but need not go into very specific detail – an Opposition that argues the scheme would fail because soldiers would disagree whether to drive on the right or left is missing the point!

Pros

[1]   At present the ability of the United Nations to enforce its decisions, even if reached through broad international consensus, is very limited. Too often, by the time it has persuaded member states to contribute a meagre number of troops for peacekeeping or aid protection, the crisis has peaked and many lives have been lost unnecessarily, as happened in war in Croatia, Rwanda or Albania. Knowledge of such limitations may even prevent the attempt being made at all.

[2]   To solve the problem, the UN should be given its own standing army: recruited, equipped, financed and commanded independently of any national army. Like the Roman army, or the French Foreign Legion, these soldiers would be a multinational force, loyal to their own flag and the principles for which it stands. Funding could be contributed by member countries, in the knowledge that they would not have to contribute arms and troops to UN ventures as they previously did.

[3]   With committed, independent soldiers, the UN might be more prepared to commit such troops to dangerous situations in which Western powers have no direct economic or strategic interest (e.g. Rwanda) than is the case at present.

Cons

[1]   The extent to which this problem is one of rapid reaction is questionable. Ultimately, the UN is called upon to act in a wide variety of complex situations, none of which offers a simple solution. Reaction could easily be speeded up since many crises can be predicted and troops committed in advance by national governments.

[2]   The United Nations is not a government in its own right and should not be given the trappings of one. Its effectiveness is due to its being a trusted intermediary, not a policeman; and its unelected leaders (the Security Council) would fail to give its army any democratic legitimacy. Funding is already a major problem for the UN and a hugely expensive army would not be funded by national governments which it could one day oppose. Countries currently commit troops to the UN for valuable training opportunities; this incentive would be lost. The secrets of advanced weapon technology would never be released by the countries which had developed them.

[3]   There are countless conflicts around the world where UN troops could usefully be deployed, and no possibility of it affording all of them. The only

[4]   Policy co-ordination would be easier if only one organisation was involved. At the moment, a number of countries contribute small forces which have to be co-ordinated despite having a wide variety of strategic traditions, languages, communication standards, weapon systems, and so on.

[5]   The nationality of current forces 'lent' to the UN can make a great difference to their effectiveness. Traditional friendships and foreign policy interests of their home countries will affect their reading of the situation and behaviour on the ground, and may result in certain forces being pulled out to avoid a conflict of interests. The UN can be subject to accusations of favouritism. A professional standing army would avoid this.

Possible motions:

This House would create a United Nations standing army.

This House would use force to defend human rights.

Related topics:

National Service ((Re-)Introduction of)

Armaments (Limitation of Conventional)

Sanctions (Use of)

way of distinguishing is, unfortunately, to prioritise major conflicts and the interests of the countries contributing most of the funding to the UN.

[4]   At the moment, the UN can ask for a wide variety of equipment and types of troops (e.g. tanks, paratroopers, marines, engineers, bombers, surveillance aircraft) to meet the needs of a specific situation. Either a standing army would have to be well enough equipped to deal with any conceivable situation in any terrain in the world – at unthinkable expense – or it would lack essential equipment.

[5]   Some soldiers even within a standing army will face divided loyalties in any conceivable conflict situation – would their allegiance to the UN flag outweigh loyalty to their own religion, country or even family? In the present situation, individual nations volunteer troops and an attempt can be made to match neutral donors to specific problems.

United States, Fear of

See the notes on a similar debate under 'China, Fear of'.

Pros

[1]   The USA poses a significant threat to world peace through its tendency to

Cons

[1]   Every country's foreign policy is influenced by domestic considerations

let its short-term domestic agenda drive its foreign policy, as has happened towards Cuba, Colombia, Libya, Israel and Iran. It ignores the realities of international affairs and may prevent realistic and effective settlements being reached.

[2]   The USA also threatens with its combination of vast military and economic power with isolationism. The difficulties successive presidents have had in securing the passage of international treaties – most recently, the ban on chemical weapons and the authority to negotiate free trade agreements – and in obtaining funding for international programmes through Congress demonstrate that American politicians are not prepared to face up to the responsibilities of power. Given the country's influence, this behaviour sets a bad example to the rest of the world – and so does its abysmal record in paying dues to the United Nations.

[3]   The US is clearly guilty of cultural imperialism, dominating the world with its tastes in films, TV, popular music, clothes and food and drink which are eradicating other traditions of great antiquity and value – as with McDonald's in Asia, Disney in Europe, Coca-Cola worldwide, the influence of American tastes on French wine-making and basketball in the Caribbean. Not only is the erosion of local cultures regrettable, but American culture tends to be shallower, cuter and less earthy than more sober traditions.

and America is not unusual here. More important is its long-term commitment to the causes of democracy, human rights and free trade, which it does seek justifiably to export to the world.

[2]   The US provides leadership within the UN, NATO and even in Asia, and frequently acts to protect the weak and uphold international norms of behaviour, as in Kuwait (1991), Taiwan (1996), Bosnia (1996–8) and Kosovo (1998). US presidents have brokered many peace treaties, using the implied threat of US displeasure and the incentive of US investment and subsidy to cajole the people of former Yugoslavia, Koreans, and Israelis and Palestinians into compromise. Precisely because the US could retreat into self-sufficient isolation if it wished, when it does intervene it is respected and listened to.

[3]   No-one forces people to like Walt Disney, Big Macs or soft drinks; American products are popular because they are appealing to anyone's tastes and represent a culture which values freedom and opportunity. Nor is the US universally successful; EuroDisney was forced to stress European influences on its food and management style, while the local ThumpsUp! cola is still the biggest seller in India. When the US does succeed, this is a natural by-product of the global communication network which the whole world welcomes.

Possible motions:
This House fears the US.

This House would support its friendly neighbourhood superpower.

This House wishes that the Plymouth Rock
had landed on the Pilgrim Fathers.

Related topics:

China (Fear of)

Democracy (Imposition of)

Environment (Links to International Trade
and Relations)

Islam (Fear of)

Sanctions (Use of)

United Nations (Failure of)

Nuclear Energy

United States of Europe

With the rapid advance of economic and monetary union in Europe in the 1990s the
question still remains open as to what *political* shape the European Union should take.
Opinion spreads between two opposing poles – the pro-Europeans (in this case the
Proposition side) who value European integration above all, and the anti-Europeans,
or 'Eurosceptics' (in this case the Opposition side) who argue for the maintenance of
national autonomy and political sovereignty of member states above all else. More particularly, this debate is about the merits of a 'United States of Europe' – a federal
European Union modelled on the US with a central federal government which passes
legislation, raises taxes and determines levels of public spending, a federal judiciary
and a central bank. The alternative is power remaining principally in the hands of the
governments of individual member states.

Pros

[1]   It is in the individual self-interest of
all the member countries of Europe to
continue the process of integration so
successfully initiated by the Single Market
and the implementation of European
economic and monetary union (EMU)
subsequent to the Maastricht treaty. This
process constitutes the European Union
as a political and economic unit that has
greater power and stability than the sum
of its parts. For this unit to be strength-
ened and stabilised still further, full federalisation is required. This will provide
a central government to set levels of

Cons

[1]   Economic matters need to be
separated from political matters. The
EU as a trading bloc is indeed beneficial
to its member states. But trading blocs do
not need to turn into politically centralised federations. NAFTA and ASEAN
are successful trading blocs, but they
do not feel the need to have a common
currency or one single federal government in order to maintain that success.
The benefits of an economic alliance or a
relatively loose 'confederation' between
countries need not become a *federation* for
the economic benefits to be maintained.

taxation and spending throughout Europe, set down a common foreign and security policy, a common legal system and so on. This will result in a United States of Europe that can compete as a true 'superpower' with other major world powers such as the US and China.

[2] Economic and monetary union cannot succeed without a central government making crucial decisions on taxation and spending – political decisions that need to be taken out of the hands of national governments, and put into the hands of a central European legislature. This will not be 'undemocratic', since such a legislature will be elected by the population of the entire EU, just as in the US members of the Senate and of the House of Representatives are elected by all States. The central legislature will be an extension of the existing European parliament. The relationship between this parliament and national governments will be analogous to the current relationship between national and local governments.

[3] A federal Europe, as envisioned by the Maastricht treaty of 1991, will be governed on the principle of 'subsidiarity'. In other words, federalism is not just about centralisation but about devolving power to the appropriate level. Regional decisions will be made regionally while other decisions will appropriately be made centrally – e.g. decisions on immigration controls, trade policy, and security policy.

[4] Even in the US there is no longer one shared language – some US schools now teach in Spanish as a first language,

[2] EMU has already gone too far. A single currency should itself be opposed since it does indeed inevitably lead to political decisions being taken out of the hands of national governments. This is undemocratic. European bankers and legislators will take control of our lives, leaving our own elected representatives impotent. As for the European parliament – low turn-outs in elections have repeatedly shown apathy and a lack of confidence in that institution from the people of Europe. They have also shown that people vote on national issues rather than Europe-wide issues. The correct level of representative democracy is the level of the nation state.

[3] 'Subsidiarity' is just a piece of 'Euro-speak' to disguise the fact the federalism is about taking power away from national governments. If federalism meant devolving power to the appropriate level, then decisions about national security, levels of taxation and spending on schools, hospitals and social security would be made by the government of the nation state.

[4] The EU is not a logical political or cultural unit. Unlike the US it does not even have a shared language. Each of the nation states of Europe has its own particular culture, language, legal precedents, constitution, customs and traditions. It is not an appropriate candidate for federalisation. Entry into a United States of Europe would mean the 'normalisation' of each country so that it lost its historic traditions and institutions. The British monarchy, and the judicial system would go the way of Imperial measurements and the pound – sacrificed in the name of

for example. The United States of Europe would similarly have several languages. Switzerland and Canada are other examples of countries with successful federal governments but no single shared language. There is no need for alarmism. As the example of the US in particular shows, federalism is quite compatible with cultural pluralism and the retention of different national and ethnic traditions.

European unity. The fact that we can retain 'national traditions' such as morris dancing, Yorkshire puddings or football hooliganism is no consolation for the fact that the historic way the British people govern themselves has been lost.

Possible motions:

This House believes that Europe should be the next United States.

This House welcomes European federalism.

Related topics:

Legislation v. Individual Freedom

Devolution of Scotland and Wales

Regional Government

Immigration (Relaxation of Laws against)

Commonwealth (Abolition of)

European Union (Expansion of)

Single European Currency

War Crimes, Prosecution of

Traditionally, this has been a debate about the prosecution of suspected Nazi war criminals, often camp guards and civilian officials responsible for many deaths. Often they were not German and were able to evade prosecution after 1945 by settling around the world, while evidence was lost in the chaotic postwar period or was hidden behind the Iron Curtain. Since the fall of communism in the 1980s it is now possible to identify many more suspects, often in their eighties, and considerable debate has raged about whether it is desirable to prosecute such old men. Atrocities in Rwanda and Bosnia have led to prosecutions of 'current' criminals.

Pros

[1] No matter how long ago war crimes – such as participation in genocide, torture and murderous reprisals against civilians – took place we must never forget them. If evidence had come to light immediately after the Second

Cons

[1] There comes a point where a line has to be drawn under the past; prosecution of very old men and women serves no purpose. The atrocities are remembered anyway, and the civil and military leaders most responsible are already dead.

World War, the suspects would have been prosecuted; they should not escape trial simply because it did not. Age is no defence.

[2] We owe justice to the victims of war crimes, especially those who died in Hitler's 'Final Solution'. Crimes without motive apart from bigotry are so abhorrent that they must be punished. We cannot claim to have learned the lessons of the past without settling its unfinished business.

[3] Victims are among those most in favour of prosecution, and we should not assume for them whether they can cope with the pain of testifying. Many have had to live with horrifying memories for years, and to see justice done may achieve a cathartic closure.

[4] With the terrible genocide in recent years, it is especially important to prosecute past war criminals to show that such atrocities will never go unpunished.

[5] Airing of the issues will remind the world of the history of the crimes, and promote tolerance so that they never happen again.

Possible motions:

This House would continue to prosecute Nazi war crimes.

This House would hunt them down to the ends of the earth.

Related topic:

Ideology v. Pragmatism

Those who may be prosecuted now were generally very young, very junior and frequently non-Germans who were in fear of the consequences of non-co-operation. This does not excuse their actions, but it suggests that there is no overwhelming case for prosecution at this stage.

[2] Such trials are very likely to fail, as the experience of many countries in the past decade has shown – conclusive identification is very difficult after fifty years have elapsed, and there is a real danger that innocent men and women will be convicted, not least because of the great pressure on courts, witnesses and juries to satisfy the demands of victims.

[3] It is questionable whether such trials are in the best interests of surviving victims; many may be subpoenaed to testify against their will, while even volunteers may find the process hideously traumatising. Given that many such trials will collapse for lack of evidence, even the most committed witnesses may find their testimony discounted for errors of memory, and suffer the anguish of watching their former tormentors go free.

[4] Those who commit such atrocities do not care for legal niceties like this. War crimes are committed from fanatic hatred and bigotry, while rational evaluation of the future plays little part.

[5] In fact, prosecution of elderly suspects, even if guilty, may generate sympathy for them and spark a rise in far-right movements and ethnic tensions across Europe.

SECTION E

Moral and Religious

Abortion on Demand

Abortion was always considered sinful, and was criminalised in Britain and most states of the US in the nineteenth century. Back-street abortions became the most popular way to limit the size of families. In Britain, the 1967 Abortion Act legalised abortion when advised by a doctor on medical grounds. In the US, the Roe *v.* Wade case of 1973 in the Supreme Court set down the principle that in the first three months abortion is to be allowed, and in the second trimester it is to be allowed if it is required in the interests of maternal health. In neither country is 'abortion on demand' – abortions undertaken principally as a form of birth-control at the wish of the pregnant woman – officially allowed, but doctors (especially those in private clinics) will happily certify that carrying the pregnancy to term would cause severe mental distress to the woman.

Pros

[1] It is a woman's right to decide, in conjunction with the father when appropriate, whether she wishes to have a baby. It is her body and she ultimately should control what happens to it. It is people, not fertilised eggs or foetuses, that have 'rights'.

[2] If abortion is not allowed on demand, women will go to 'back-street abortionists' where lack of expertise and of sterile conditions can be a serious risk to health. Such back-street abortions result in an estimated 500 deaths per day world-wide.

[3] There is no definitive answer to when a foetus becomes a person in its own right, but up to around 24–28 weeks the foetus is so undeveloped that it is not reasonable to consider it a person and to accord it rights.

[4] In many areas of the world where overpopulation and chronic food shortage are perennial problems, abortion

Cons

[1] The right to do as we wish to our bodies must be curtailed by the rights of others to be free from harm. In many instances the right to do as we wish to our body is overruled, e.g. drug laws exist to guard against my making myself a danger to others by altering my mind with drugs. In this case the mother's rights are overruled by the right to life of the unborn child.

[2] We could argue against banning *anything* on the grounds that people will carry on doing it on the black market. The fact is that abortion is morally wrong and banning it will reduce the number of abortions that occur.

[3] A foetus can survive if born prematurely from as early as 20 weeks, and this boundary is being made earlier all the time by improved incubator technology. Given that we cannot be sure at what point a foetus is a person or can feel pain, we should err on the side of caution and consider the foetus a person from

helps prevent bringing children into the world who would probably know only deprivation, illness, starvation and early death.

[5]   In an increasingly secular and scientific world, the religious views of some about the infusion of a foetus with a soul by God at conception, for example, should not be imposed upon the rest of society.

[6]   Many young girls who become pregnant would have their future, their education, their family relationships and their career ruined by the birth of a child. Others are pregnant as the result of rape or incest and would have their suffering multiplied indefinitely by carrying the child to term. We cannot put the alleged 'rights' of a dividing cluster of cells ahead of such concrete harm to a person.

[7]   We allow contraception. Abortion is, in effect, no different – the prevention of the development of a potential human being. In the case of the 'morning after pill' the analogy is even closer. If we allow these measures then we should also allow abortion.

Possible motions:

This House would put the mother first.

This House believes that the unborn child has no rights.

This House believes that a woman's body is her temple.

Related topics:

Ends v. Means

Population Control

Euthanasia

conception or shortly afterwards. Abortion, therefore, is murder.

[4]   We can address overpopulation in the developing world with other measures such as increased availability of contraception as well as economic and technical aid programmes.

[5]   Human life is sacred, as is recognised by the billions of adherents of the main world religions. God creates each individual at conception and so abortion is murder, and an act against the will of God that destroys God's work.

[6]   Young people should be encouraged to have a more responsible attitude to sex and pregnancy, and should deal with the consequences of their actions whatever they may be. There are even schools now specifically for teenage mothers and their babies to attend. In cases of rape or incest, either the child can be immediately put up for adoption, or possibly exceptions could be made just in these distressing instances.

[7]   Barrier methods of contraception (condom, cap) are qualitatively different from abortion in that no fertilised egg ever exists to be destroyed. Other methods (coil, morning after pill) that are logically equivalent to abortion should not be allowed.

Surrogate Mothers

Sex Education

Contraception for Under-age Girls

Eugenics: IVF and Genetic Screening

Science: a Menace to Civilisation?

Animal Experimentation and Vivisection, Banning of

Human treatment of animals can be a highly emotive subject. A dolphin trapped and killed in a trawler net, a rat deliberately mutated by genetic engineering, a red deer hunted to the point of terrified exhaustion and shot, a rabbit with eyes and skin blistered from chemical and cosmetic tests, a captive lion robotically pacing its tiny cage at the circus or zoo – all of these are distressing images that arise in the context of debates about the human treatment of animals. But what are the arguments behind these emotional appeals? The Australian philosopher Peter Singer was one of the first, in the 1970s, to argue that animals have rights. This is still a contentious claim, but one that more and more people seem to accept. The arguments in the next topic consider whether animals have rights, and whether, if they do, we should be doing more to recognise and respect those rights. We currently use animals from bacteria to primates in many different ways – for food, clothing, entertainment in circuses and zoos, medical experiments, biotechnology (e.g. using bacteria to synthesise human hormones) and cosmetic testing, and in sports such as greyhound racing and horse racing, and even as objects of 'field sports' such as fishing, shooting, fox-hunting and hare-coursing. Some would argue that all of these uses of animals are wrong and that they should never be used as a means to a human end. Others would take the opposite view that it is right and natural for us to use other species for our own benefit and that this is indeed the key to our continuing evolutionary success. This debate, and the four other debates on animals in this section, weigh up the pros and cons of our treatment of animals in various contexts.

Pros

[1] Vivisection involves the exploitation and torturing of innocent animals to benefit humans, and this is wrong on principle. Mice are bred to be susceptible to skin cancer, exposed to high levels of radiation and allowed to die. Rats are genetically engineered to grow full size human ears on their backs, and baboons are deliberately infected with the AIDS virus. No economic or medical gain can justify such cruel and cynical exploitation of our animal cousins. More advanced mammals – especially primates (monkeys and apes) – have complex nervous systems like ours and are similarly susceptible to pain and fear.

Cons

[1] On principle it is right and natural that we humans study, use and exploit the natural environment for our own benefit. That is the way that our species has come to thrive and prosper and it is right that we should continue to do so through experimentation on and exploitation of both vegetable and animal resources. Animals are not people and do not have 'rights', and anthropomorphic sentimentalism should not get in the way of scientific and medical progress.

[2] Experimentation on animals saves lives. Animal experimentation and research has historically produced innumerable

[2]   The successes, necessity and efficiency of animal research have been greatly exaggerated. In fact vivisection is wasteful, inefficient and often unsuccessful, as well as being cruel. In the US alone an estimated 50–60 million animals are killed annually in the name of scientific research, but with highly unreliable results. Half of the drugs given approval in the US by the FDA (Food and Drugs Administration) between 1976 and 1985, all of which had been tested on animals, produced side effects serious enough that they had to be taken off the market or re-labelled with warnings; the Thalidomide disaster is another awful case. This is because vivisection is flawed as a scientific method. One species (e.g. rats, rabbits or dogs) cannot serve as a reliable experimental model for another (humans) – penicillin is fatal to guinea pigs, for example.

[3]   There are more humane and more efficient alternatives to vivisection. For example, in the 'Eytex test', vegetable proteins extracted from the jack bean mimic the cornea's reaction to foreign matter and so can be used in the place of live rabbits, to test for eye irritancy of products. Tissue and cell cultures can be grown in the laboratory from single cells from humans or animals – these can be used for tests in the place of live animals. Computer simulations of diseases and drug treatments can also be used in the place of vivisection.

Possible motions:

This House would ban all experimentation on animals.

This House believes that we have no more right to risk the health of animals than we do to risk the health of humans.

medical and scientific breakthroughs that could not have been made in any other ways: experiments on cows were instrumental in developing the vaccine that eliminated smallpox world-wide; experiments on dogs in the 1920s led to the discovery of insulin for the treatment of diabetics; genetic experimentation on mice and primates is currently helping to develop gene therapy for cystic fibrosis; and so on. Animals from mice to primates to humans share the same essential biology and physiology (with analogous organs, nervous systems, immune systems and hormones).

[3]   There are no alternatives to animals for research into complex immunological, neurological and genetic diseases. Computer simulations are only applicable to simple conditions of which we have full understanding. In more complex cases, our lack of understanding of the diseases (e.g. AIDS, cancer, muscular dystrophy) means we must experiment on animals or on humans. Human subjects cannot in general be expected to be guinea pigs for untested drugs at all stages of their development.

Related topics:

Animal Rights

See the introduction to the debate on 'Animal Experimentation and Vivisection, Banning of'.

Pros

[1]   Particularly since the revolution in biology associated with Charles Darwin in the nineteenth century, science has forced us to acknowledge the continuity between humanity and all other animals. If we, ourselves animals, have rights, then it is logical to extend rights to all animals. Animals, like us, have feelings, even if they do not have reason and language.

[2]   Animals, according to the theory of evolution, have common ancestors with us – they are our blood relations. As such we should respect their rights. Having risen to a position of dominance in the natural world, we only have a right to make use of its resources in so far as it is balanced by our duty of stewardship over the natural world and our duty of care to our animal cousins.

[3]   It is not, as some might say, necessary for a being to be conscious and aware in order to be given rights. Unborn children and those in comas are accorded rights, especially the right to life. Rights are something that we decide to confer. And, especially in cases where it can be seen that animals can suffer physical pain and emotional distress (as in the cases of bull-fighting, battery hen farming, cramped and unnatural confinement in zoos and circuses, grotesque examples of vivisection), we should confer on them

Cons

[1]   It has always been acknowledged by philosophers and scientists that man is almost infinitely removed from the other animals, particularly by the powers of speech, rational thought and moral conscience. The Bible teaches Christians the same moral – that humans are put above the animals to use them as well as to look after them. It is only humans who have rights; animals are qualitatively different from us and it is nonsensical to speak of them having rights. According animals rights can lead to absurd conclusions – such as that we should respect the right to life of bacteria or mosquitoes.

[2]   The theory of evolution tells us that nature is 'red in tooth and claw' and that only the strongest and most ruthless survive in the struggle for life. It is most *unnatural* to refuse to fulfil our role in nature, at the top of the food chain, using animals to ensure our own survival.

[3]   Animals do not have the kind of consciousness that we do. They are more like automata than like people, they work on instinct and reflex, not by rational thought. Therefore they are not capable of understanding the ideas of what is just or fair for them. They have no expectations about how they will be treated and no emotions in anything like the human sense. The argument for animal rights is based on a philosophically

the rights that we do on humans to pro- tect them from suffering and death.

[4] It is not true that we need to exploit animals to the extent that we do. There are synthetic alternatives to almost all animal products such as leather, ivory, animal fat, fur, and even meat. Our lifestyles should be changed to acknowl- edge the rights of animals to be free from cruelty and exploitation.

and scientifically false anthropomorph- ism. We should, perhaps, seek to eliminate obvious cases of gratuitous cruelty such as bear baiting or cock fighting, but in general animals do not have rights.

[4] Perhaps we do not need to use animal products to the extent that we do, but synthetic alternatives are often many times more expensive, and inaccessible to the vast majority. Also, there is nothing wrong with using animals for our own benefit – it is only natural.

Possible motions:
This House believes that animals have rights too.
This House calls for an end to all exploitation of animals.
This House would put ecology before economics.

Related topics:
Pacifism
Bill of Rights
Abortion on Demand
Animal Experimentation and Vivisection (Banning of)
Blood Sports (Banning of)
Vegetarianism
Zoos (Abolition of)

Beggars, Giving Money to

Pros

[1] 'Beggar' in itself is a pejorative word that is inappropriately applied to many unfortunate people in our society who find themselves homeless and desti- tute through unemployment, repossession of their house or, frequently, an abusive family background. These people should not be treated as human vermin – they simply need our help. It is all too easy to end up as a beggar on the streets with no family or community support in our increasingly selfish society. Individually

Cons

[1] While we cannot doubt that there are some beggars who are the victims of circumstance, all too often people choose to live on the streets and beg for money rather than facing up to difficult family or financial problems. We should not be expected to support these people on a random individual basis. The welfare state, which is financed by working peo- ple, exists as the safety net that can help those in dire circumstances. In the UK, the Housing Act of 1985 makes it the

and as a society we have a duty to help 'beggars' through individual giving on the streets as well as through charities and through government action. A society only succeeds through co-operation.

[2]   If we can afford to give to someone on the street then we should. Sometimes we may indeed be giving money to a fraud who is not genuinely in need – but our moral imperative to help those in real need outweighs this.

[3]   If we do not give to those who beg on the street they will get their money in other ways, for example through theft or prostitution. By denying them money we are driving them towards these alternatives.

[4]   If you are concerned about what someone may spend the money you give them on, you can always buy them food or clothing and give it to them.

[5]   Society works on the principle of 'reciprocal altruism'. Helping behaviour is observed in many animal species, other than humans. It is by such behaviour that a community survives and flourishes. That is the basis of our obligation to less fortunate members of our community.

responsibility of Local Authorities to find housing for the unintentionally homeless. Those who are intentionally homeless cannot expect to live on other people's charity.

[2]   There are many 'professional beggars' who are not even in dire need but play on people's sentiments as an easy source of money. How are we to know who is in genuine need and who is a fraud? We should give money to established hostels and charities instead.

[3]   Giving money to beggars guarantees that they will remain beggars, rather than going to seek a job or the help from the state to which they are entitled – we should not reinforce their dependency on the charity of others.

[4]   Most beggars only want money from people to pay for alcohol and cigarettes or to feed a more serious drug habit. We do not help people by financing their health-destroying addictions.

[5]   There is no such thing as society, just a collection of individuals. Biologists such as Richard Dawkins have shown that we are ruled by our 'selfish' genes. Our concern must be with our immediate family, especially our offspring, who carry our genes. It is their survival that is our first priority, not the survival of unfortunate strangers. Charity must begin at home.

Possible motions:
This House believes that charity begins with the homeless.
This House would help beggars become choosers.

Related topics:
Capitalism v. Socialism
Welfare State
Workfare
Zero Tolerance

Blood Sports, Abolition of

See the introduction to the debate on 'Animal Experimentation and Vivisection, Banning of'.

Pros

[1]   There is a continuum between humans and the rest of the animal kingdom. Animals such as birds, hares, foxes and deer can, like us, experience stress, fear, exhaustion and pain. As conscious beings we should accord these animals rights and not inflict suffering and death on them for the sake of our entertainment. The infliction of unnecessary suffering on domestic and captive animals is already a criminal offence – this offence should be extended to cover all animals.

[2]   Hunting with hounds – killing the quarry only after hours of terror and exhaustion – is not an effective way to kill hares, foxes and deer. Shooting is more humane and efficient, if they really need to be killed to protect livestock or reduce populations.

[3]   Hunting is defended on the grounds that it is legitimate pest-control or legitimate hunting for food. Claims that hunting is a form of 'pest control' are usually bogus. Foxes, for example, are particularly inefficient predators, accounting for only a tiny percentage of livestock lost each year. Foxes were imported into Britain specifically to be hunted, when deer populations waned early in the twentieth century, and fox hunts still deliberately nurture fox populations. Game birds are bred specifically to be shot. These practices are a particularly

Cons

[1]   Humans are at the top of the food chain and of the evolutionary tree and as such may use other animals to their own ends, while preferably minimising the suffering of other species. Blood sports exist as a way to derive community enjoyment from the hunting of animals that would be killed anyway. The opposition to blood sports is largely based on anthropomorphic sentimentality and squeamishness. People have always had to kill animals to feed and protect themselves. In the modern metropolitan supermarket age, people have the luxury of distancing themselves from the actual business of doing so.

[2]   Shooting, poisoning and trapping – the alternatives to hunting with hounds – are not more humane. All these methods potentially leave animals to die a slow and painful death (most farmers are not trained marksmen – a shot is more likely to wound a fox than kill it, leaving it to starve through its inability to hunt). The death of an animal caught by hunting hounds is over in a second or two.

[3]   Blood sports only kill animals that are pests or food. The huge majority of farmers agree that foxes are pests. In any one year 30 per cent of farmers in Britain suffer damage or lose livestock because of foxes. And it is hardly logical to complain about the shooting of birds that

stark example of the abuse of humanity's position as 'stewards' of the natural world.

[4]   In the case of fox-hunting, not only is the quarry not a genuine pest, it is also not of use as food. Oscar Wilde famously described the sport as 'the unspeakable in pursuit of the inedible'. In the case of animals that *are* edible, such as deer, hares etc. there are more humane ways of killing them that do not involve terrorising the animal first.

[5]   Public opinion in Britain is clearly opposed to hunting wild animals with hounds.

[6]   There are alternatives to blood sports that could maintain employment for those involved in the industry and maintain the pursuit as a hobby but without the cruelty to animals. An example of this is 'drag-hunting' where an artificial trail is laid and followed by hounds.

Possible motions:
This House would ban hunting with hounds.
This House believes that the unspeakable should leave the inedible alone.
This House believes that blood sports are legalised barbarism.

Related topics:
Legislation v. Individual Freedom
Pacifism
Animal Experimentation and Vivisection (Banning of)
Animal Rights
Vegetarianism
Zoos (Abolition of)

were bred to be shot. As it is, they have a perfectly comfortable life ended instantaneously when they are shot. If it were not for blood sports these birds would never have had a life at all – they would not have been born.

[4]   It is true that foxes are not eaten by humans, but they are pests (see above). Other blood sports kill animals that can be eaten – pheasants, grouse, deer, hares, and fish – some of which are also a pest to agriculture and forestry (e.g. hares, deer).

[5]   Most of those who oppose hunting have never been on a hunt and are city-dwellers. They live a life detached from the realities of rural life and farming, and hence can afford to take an idealistic stance on 'animal rights'. This is totally inconsistent if these same people rely on the efficiency of agriculture for the affordable produce they expect to find in their supermarkets. In rural communities there is very little support for a ban. The banning of blood sports would undermine the rural economy, since hunting provides jobs for many and protects agricultural land.

[6]   As explained above, there is no need for such an alternative, since blood sports are not gratuitous entertainment but the carrying out of legitimate and necessary killing of pests or game in an enjoyable fashion.

Divorce, Easier

Pros

[1]   The idea of life-long marriage and the promises to stay together 'till death do us part' arose in the early Christian church, when life expectancy was much shorter. Nowadays we live around forty years longer and many people question whether humans are naturally monogamous creatures. At any rate, when there is no love left in a marriage it is foolish to continue it for the sake of some high-minded principle. The practical thing to do is to admit that in some cases marriages fail, and to provide for easy divorce in such cases. Parties should not have to prove adultery, neglect or unreasonableness by their spouse. A simple declaration of the desire to divorce should suffice.

[2]   It is bad for children to grow up with parents who are in conflict. Such parents will provide role models only of bitterness and resentment rather than of the mutual love and support that they should teach their children. In such cases the best solution is a quick divorce for the sake of the children.

[3]   We wish to maximise sexual fidelity. If divorces are hard to obtain and a long time in coming through, there will be an increase in adultery involving married people seeking divorce unsuccessfully. Easy divorce means less adultery.

[4]   We should be realistic about the nature of promises that we make to each other. A promise represents a commitment

Cons

[1]   Marriage is never going to be a bed of roses, and couples should be encouraged to persevere through inevitable difficult patches. It should not be assumed that marriage is all about romantic love – that is only the first stage of a marriage. Beyond that stage it is a partnership that needs to be worked at and maintained. Those divorcing should have to prove a concrete reason such as adultery or neglect by their spouse before they are allowed to divorce.

[2]   It is bad for children to live through the break-up of their home. Children whose parents have divorced are at a higher risk of underachievement at school and of anti-social or criminal behaviour. The first duty of parents is to struggle through difficult times in their marriage with as little strife as possible for the sake of the future of their children, at least until they have left home.

[3]   What we wish to maximise in society is life-long commitment, especially to the raising of families, not serial monogamy. The view that sexual fidelity is the ultimate goal takes an individualistic and selfish view of parents as sexual operators in their own right rather than as parents *per se* first and foremost. Harder divorce means fewer broken homes and broken commitments in the long run.

[4]   Easy divorces devalue the meaning of the vows solemnly made at the wedding ceremony. A society that allows easy

to a certain goal. But we all know that the best intentioned efforts to attain a goal can fail. It is cruel to punish people for a promise they made which they have sincerely tried but failed to keep. To avoid the complaints of people who take the wedding vows at a very literal level, they could be reworded in terms of a commitment to stay together as long as the relationship flourishes rather than as long as both parties shall live.

[5]   However easy divorces are to come by, they are still personally and financially undesirable. Those who divorce will be less well off separately (they will lose the economies of shared living expenses as well as possible tax breaks for married couples) than together, and will endure personal emotional trauma. No-one enters upon a marriage thinking divorce desirable, however easy it is.

divorce implicitly acknowledges that even people's most important vows need not be wholly reliable. Such an attitude will erode trustworthiness and commitment throughout society.

[5]   If divorce is made easy too many couples will enter into marriage lightly and unthinkingly with the knowledge that if it does not work they can always get out. Such a situation devalues marriage as a stable relationship and makes it just like any other. It also, in itself, makes failed marriages more likely by reducing the amount of thought and mental preparation put into a marriage, and increasing the social acceptability of divorcing rather than persevering.

Possible motions:
This House believes marriage is not necessarily a life sentence.
This House would make divorce easier.
This House celebrates the advent of the easy divorce.

Related topics:
Feminism (Devaluation of Parenthood by)
Marriage

Euthanasia

The term 'euthanasia', coming from the ancient Greek words meaning 'good death', is used to refer to voluntary rather than compulsory euthanasia. Voluntary euthanasia is when an individual asks to be given a lethal injection to put them out of pain and end his or her life. Compulsory euthanasia – killing those who are terminally ill or who are above a certain age regardless of their wishes – is everywhere regarded as murder. In the Netherlands voluntary euthanasia has been legal since 1983; around 3,000 people formally request it there each year. The Northern Territory in Australia, where three-quarters of the population support voluntary euthanasia under due safeguards, legalised it only for the bill to be overthrown by the federal Senate.

Pros

[1] People should be allowed to request 'mercy killing' to end their suffering. Victims of cancer, AIDS or motor-neurone disease may know, in the later stages of their illness, that the only prospect for the short remainder of their life is more physical degeneration and acute suffering. They should be allowed to die with dignity with the help of, for example, a lethal injection or an overdose of morphine from a doctor.

[2] Someone may wish to write a 'living will' stating that if they ever become a 'vegetable' or are in a persistent vegetative state (PVS) as the result of an accident that they do not wish life support to be continued. We should respect the wishes of such people rather than preserve them against their wishes with virtually no quality of life.

[3] At present doctors are sometimes allowed, in effect, to carry out euthanasia on the grounds that the amount of painkillers they had to use to alleviate the patient's suffering in fact turned out to be fatal. Instances of this 'double effect' of a drug are not currently considered wrong, and allowing euthanasia is only an extension of this principle.

[4] Just as the right to vote includes the right to abstain and the right to free speech includes the right to be silent, the right to life should be seen to include the right to choose to die. It is 'my body, my life, my choice'.

[5] Not allowing those who are too physically ill to commit suicide to do

Cons

[1] However much a patient is suffering, it is the role of a physician, as expressed in the Hippocratic Oath that all doctors have to swear, to cure disease and restore patients to health, not to kill them. Doctors should not be forced to compromise their professional oath nor be put under the great moral pressure of deciding when to advise a patient that euthanasia might be the best option. With the highly effective painkillers now available there is never any need even for the terminally ill to suffer great pain. Use of painkillers, not euthanasia, is the answer to painful terminal illness.

[2] People have been known to recover from comas and PVS after considerable periods, and some 'terminally ill' patients make miraculous recoveries. Allowing euthanasia would risk killing people who could otherwise have had years more life. With euthanasia, as with capital punishment, the price of a mistake is too high.

[3] There is a qualitative difference between seeking to reduce someone's pain and their dying as a secondary effect, and deliberately killing them. Doctors should not be allowed or required to kill their patients.

[4] There is no such thing as a 'right to die'. Suicide is always wrong, and is only legal because of the absurdity that can exist of sentencing people to death for unsuccessfully attempting suicide.

[5] While it is true that suicide is not illegal, *assisting* suicide is. Allowing such a

so amounts to discrimination against the physically handicapped, since it is not illegal for others to commit suicide. Euthanasia, or 'doctor assisted suicide', should therefore also be allowed.

[6]   Euthanasia also spares the loved ones of a patient the needless agony of watching them slowly degenerate and die in great pain, and gives them the comfort of knowing that they carried out the patient's last wishes.

[7]   A person who dies 'naturally' by having life support removed, when in a coma or persistent vegetative state, de-hydrates over a period of five days before death and their organs are then unusable. Euthanasia would increase the number of organs available for transplant in those cases where the patient's and family's consent had been obtained.

practice will immediately open up grave dangers of abuse by unscrupulous doctors and relatives who would like to see a certain patient 'out of the way' for the purposes of inheritance or freeing up scarce medical resources.

[6]   A patient in a coma or PVS may have changed their mind subsequent to writing their 'living will' but not altered the document. In such cases the loved ones would be authorising the killing of someone against their wishes and ruling out the possibility of their recovery or cure.

[7]   Carrying out euthanasia in order to use somebody's body parts for transplants is morally repugnant in that it reduces them to just one more medical resource to be exploited.

Possible motions:
This House would legalise voluntary euthanasia.
This House believes in the right to die.
This House would assist suicide.

Related topics:
Ends v. Means
Legislation v. Individual Freedom
Abortion on Demand

Feminism, Devaluation of Parenthood by

There are now fewer people than ever who would claim that feminism was a 'bad thing', or would wish to disassociate themselves from the core principle of feminism that women should have equality of opportunity and status in society and the work-place. However, like any powerful cultural movement, feminism is open to criticisms, one of the most persistent of which in recent years has been that feminism has devalued motherhood and child-rearing, and more generally has portrayed parenting as a chore rather than a joy. Is parenting undervalued in today's society? Is feminism to blame?

Pros

[1]   Feminism has been responsible for many successes such as the legal recognition of women's rights to vote, and to have equal access to education and equal pay. However, it has systematically devalued the role of the parent and home-maker. Women have been driven by feminism to want to 'have it all', which too often means they feel pressure to spend as little time as possible away from their careers with their children. They have become 'surrogate men' driven by ambition at the expense of time and closeness with their family.

[2]   Women who wish to work at home caring for their children and making a stable home are made to feel that they lack ambition, are inferior beings, are giving in to patriarchy and injustice, are mere drudges, and are letting down their fellow women.

[3]   Women driven by feminist beliefs to be 'high achievers' are coming to realise that they have been sold down the river through implicitly accepting the anti-family rhetoric of well-meaning feminist campaigners. Feminists may claim that they never *forced* anybody into any particular decision, but the coercive power of social movements and popular political rhetoric cannot be denied. The result is that millions of women have realised too late what they missed out on by working through the early years of their children's lives.

[4]   Recently, feminism has complained that, despite equal opportunities legislation, women make up a disproportionately

Cons

[1]   Feminism has attained a measure of equality for women but there is still much more to be done. There are 'glass ceilings' in many professions – i.e. despite equal opportunities legislation, women in fact fail to be promoted to the top jobs. In the United Kingdom fewer than 10 per cent of judges, 20 per cent of MPs and around 10 per cent of Oxbridge professors are women. Women in identical management jobs to men still receive a 10–20 per cent lower salary, on average. Feminism *rightly* directs its resources at socio-economic injustice rather than the celebration of the family since the role of mother and home-maker is not one that women need to struggle for.

[2]   It is extremely naive to imagine that across the world there are billions of women celebrating the role of home-making, positively deciding that they do not want any sort of career. Of those women who devote their time entirely to child-raising and home-making, it is unlikely that a majority are doing so out of positive choice. It is still a task for feminism in many parts of the world to break down the *assumption* that the role of the woman is in the home. No feminist denies the right of a woman (or a man) to *choose* to devote time to the family, but in most cases the woman does not have that choice.

[3]   Feminism has never forced anybody to do anything. It has merely made it possible.

large number of part-time workers (who have no employment rights) and lower-paid workers. This is to attack exactly those sorts of work that mothers who wish to split their time between family and work seek to find. Feminists implicitly tell mothers that they are collaborating with sexism and injustice if they do not seek high-paid, full-time employment.

[5] Government policy increasingly emphasises the duty of single mothers to go to work to support themselves rather than staying at home to work caring for their children. Such policies, undermining the value of family life, are the result of feminist campaigns for women and men not only to be given equal opportunities but to be treated identically. The resulting position is that all are expected to conform to the old male stereotype of the breadwinner.

[6] In reacting against an imbalanced male-dominated workplace, feminism has ended up arguing for a society in which women free themselves from family commitments and revel in sexual freedom and professional achievements. We must reclaim work in the home and within the family as something to be highly valued in society as a source of fulfilment and of well-balanced children, not as a chore. Feminism has consistently failed to appreciate the value of this.

[4] It is right that feminists should campaign against low pay and lack of employment rights for part-time workers. That is not to undermine the value of splitting one's time between work and family but to insist on fairer treatment for those – predominantly women – who do.

[5] Feminists do not want to see women forced into the old male stereotype of the breadwinner. Welfare policies encouraging people to come off welfare and get into work will serve to enrich the experiences of single mothers (and single fathers) while, crucially, ensuring that they are not financially worse off by going into paid employment – something that was too often the case in the past. These policies therefore bring greater freedom to women.

[6] Feminism has traditionally encouraged men to take a more active role and a fairer share in the work of child-raising and home-making. It is still only in a minority of families that such division of labour is found. While feminism does not wish to undermine the value of parenting, its priority must be basic equality and social justice, and that will not be achieved while the majority of men remain voluntarily blind to the duties (and joys) of parenthood.

Possible motions:

This House believes that feminism has undermined the family.

This House celebrates the value of motherhood.

Related topics:

Gambling, Immorality of

Pros

[1]   Gambling is immoral because it gives false hopes to those least able to afford the financial outlay involved. This is particularly true of state lotteries and football pools. The psychological lure of a huge prize is immorally used to lure the poor into parting with money they cannot afford for the sake of a near-zero chance of becoming a millionaire.

[2]   The more widely acceptable and available gambling becomes, the more people will become addicted to it. Gambling is as addictive as any drug and as ruinous. Those who become addicted invariably turn to crime to fund their habit. All gamblers lose in the end – that is why bookmakers, lottery companies, fruit machine companies and casinos continue to make huge profits year after year. We should regard gambling with the same moral disapproval that we regard other activities (e.g. taking hard drugs) that lead via addiction to anti-social behaviour, financial ruin and crime. The introduction of 'scratch cards' has seen a worrying increase in child gambling addicts.

[3]   The social toleration and state-sanctioning of gambling inculcate materialistic values in society. People are led to believe that their greatest aspiration should be to increase their wealth by whatever means possible – the advertising of state lotteries suggests that huge amounts of money would transform a person's life immeasurably for the good.

Cons

[1]   Gambling brings a bit of real excitement and hope to the lives of many, especially those whose daily realities bring them very little of either. *Someone* will win the jackpot in a lottery, and *some* people win each time there is a horse race, dog race etc. Those who say gambling is immoral are puritanical kill-joys who do not appreciate the value that simple fun and escapism can have in the dreariness of life.

[2]   Virtually anything can be the object of an addiction – sex, coffee, jogging, television, computer games – but that does not mean that it is of itself immoral. Gambling is, for the huge majority, an affordable luxury, an inexpensive distraction, not a problem on a par with heroin addiction. The gambling addict's problems do not derive from the existence of gambling but from her own psychological disorder.

[3]   People do not gamble expecting huge wealth – they gamble for fun, for the buzz, and they spend money on gambling as on any other form of entertainment. In any case, it is silly to assert that material wealth does not improve one's standard of living. It is all very well for someone who is financially secure to eschew the importance of material goods, but for the many who live in poverty the acquisition of wealth could buy them security, education, healthcare and many other opportunities that are central to human fulfilment.

This is not the case. Many who have become millionaires through luck in a lottery have found that their marriages, families or friendships have been destroyed through greed, envy and bitterness. The materialistic life idealised by the gambling ethos is shallow and unfulfilling.

[4]   It is fundamentally against the ideals of social justice that wealth should be acquired by chance and without skill, industry or merit. This applies to all forms of gambling, including city traders in futures, options and derivatives.

[5]   There comes a time when – as with the firearms or drugs industries – we must take a moral stand against certain ways of making money. It should be hoped that those employed in the gambling industries could be employed in alternative, more constructive industries.

[6]   The huge amounts of money wasted on gambling every year could be put to any number of more constructive – e.g. charitable – uses.

Possible motions:
This House would ban all gambling for under-21s.
This House condemns gambling.

Related topics:
Legislation v. Individual Freedom
National Lottery (Abolition of)

[4]   Our lot in life is inherently random. Good education and lucrative employment are almost always accidents of birth rather than the result of hard work or real ability. In any case, those who make money out of gambling (professional poker players, horse tipsters and financial speculators) do so through their mathematical prowess and extensive knowledge of horses, markets, etc.

[5]   The gambling industries and financial speculators provide services that bring people excitement, hope and, sometimes, wealth. The demand for gambling industries is there and its supply does not harm anybody other than those voluntarily taking risks for themselves. Gambling is not immoral, it is harmless fun.

[6]   Following that line of argument, all money 'wasted' on pastimes or luxuries – such as sports equipment, expensive food and wine, cosmetics – would compulsorily be redirected to charity. Gambling is not an immoral waste of money, it is a pastime or luxury that we are free to spend our money on if we choose to enjoy ourselves that way. Furthermore, taxes on gambling make it a valuable source of government revenue.

Gay Marriages

Great strides have been made towards equal rights for homosexuals in the century that has passed since Oscar Wilde was sentenced to hard labour for his homosexuality. However, in most countries homosexuals still do not have completely equal rights and status in the eyes of the law. In Britain and the US homosexuals are not officially allowed to serve in the military. In most countries homosexuals may not marry or adopt children, and most denominations of Christianity still publicly oppose homosexuality and the ordination of homosexuals, despite the fact that many Christian ministers are gay. The gay rights movement has much popular support, especially among the 'politically correct', but should there be limits? Is it true that homosexual couples are equally good as parents as are heterosexual couples? Is it right for a child to be brought up by homosexuals? Can a religion that speaks out against homosexuality really ordain homosexuals in good faith? In short, does equality of opportunity for homosexuals necessarily entail *identical* treatment for homosexuals? Many still think it does not. This and three other topics below explore some of the most contentious issues in the ongoing debate about gay rights. A fifth, on 'outing', is not about the rights accorded to gays by law but about their treatment of each other.

Pros

[1] To complete the world-wide movement towards equal rights for homosexuals in society, we should allow homosexual couples the right to a public legal and religious recognition of their life-long loving commitment to one another. Homosexuals, as equal members of society, should have equal access to both civil and religious forms of marriage.

[2] Whatever its historical roots, marriage is clearly not just for the purpose of reproduction. Infertile heterosexual couples are allowed to marry, therefore homosexual couples should be allowed to marry. Homosexual couples, like heterosexual couples, may wish to marry as a prelude to adopting or fostering children, and this should be encouraged as part of a modern reconception of the idea of the family and family values.

Cons

[1] The equality of homosexuals with other members of society is achieved by decriminalising homosexual activity and allowing equal opportunities to homosexuals in terms of broad education and employment rights. Gay rights does *not* mean ignoring the obvious differences between homosexuals and heterosexuals. Marriage is historically and logically a heterosexual institution, the extension of which to homosexual couples would be meaningless and even repressive of their distinct identity.

[2] Marriage is primarily an institution to allow for the creation of children in a stable family environment. Homosexual couples can never produce a family and to allow them to marry is to overlook the history and meaning of marriage. We can endorse their love for one another

[3]   Society has always been able to adapt religious teachings and develop interpretations of religious principles proper to each new era. Religions should respond positively to the role that homosexual couples can play in communities. Those sectors of religious communities that condemn homosexuality outright will simply find themselves increasingly marginalised as society progresses. Those homosexuals who wish to marry may choose, in any case, to reject the homophobic religious traditions and marry in a civil ceremony.

[4]   Many societies give certain financial advantages to married couples – e.g. tax allowances. To deny these advantages to committed homosexual couples is an unjustifiable case of discrimination on the grounds of sexual orientation.

[5]   It is circular to argue that homosexuals are not parents and so are not candidates for financial rewards open to parents. If homosexuals were routinely allowed to adopt and foster children then it would be appropriate to reward and encourage stable homosexual family homes with financial incentives. What we want to see is a reinvention of 'family values' in which homosexuals can marry, be parents, and receive the same rights and benefits as their heterosexual counterparts.

without pretending that they are just like a heterosexual couple. Furthermore, their relationships, not being child-producing, do not *need* the same permanence for the sake of children that a marriage provides. Homosexual relationships can last as long as the love lasts but need not be constrained to last longer.

[3]   Marriage is primarily a religious service and all the main religions condemn homosexuality. The Jewish and Christian communities would be being hypocritical to endorse homosexual marriage when their sacred Scriptures condemn homosexuality.

[4]   The financial advantages offered to married couples are not to encourage marriage for its own sake but to encourage the creation of traditional family units. Child support payments and tax relief on mortgages serve the same purpose – to encourage the creation of stable family homes. It is this that society seeks to encourage, not sexual unions *per se*.

[5]   Homosexuals, by definition, will not produce children, and so are not appropriate candidates for financial incentives to home-making and the maintenance of family values.

Related topics:

Possible motions:

This House would allow homosexuals to marry.

This House celebrates homosexual homemakers.

This House demands new family values.

Gays, Adoption of Children by

See the introduction to the debate on 'Gay Marriages', above.

Pros

[1]   There are many accepted forms of departure from the supposed 'ideal' family of a married heterosexual couple with their own biological offspring, which is increasingly rare. If we allow single parents to care for children then why not homosexual couples? In fact the sexual orientation of their care-givers is irrelevant to the psychological and physical well-being of children. The only difference displayed by children raised by a homosexual couple is that they are more tolerant of homosexuality.

[2]   There are many ways of rearing children in nature. If one parent dies then often an uncle or aunt without their own offspring can help to take the place of the lost parent. It has been suggested that during evolution this role has been taken by homosexual relatives.

[3]   Above all, children need love and nurture. Some parents may be victimised in society for their race, colour, beliefs, physical appearance, handicap or social status, but that does not mean that they should be banned from adopting or fostering children. In the same way, homosexuals should not be barred from adopting or fostering children. Such banning merely fosters prejudices. It may be that in some extremely violent and homophobic localities adoption by homosexuals would not be recommended, but this would be a question for individual cases, not a guiding principle.

Cons

[1]   A child should be brought up by its own parents, and if that is not possible, by parents who can as closely as possible fulfil the role of the absent parents in a traditional family environment. Children should be raised by a mother and a father who are in a loving relationship. Therefore homosexual couples are not suitable adoptive or foster-parents.

[2]   The way that has evolved in nature for caring for children is by a mother and a father. We should not positively encourage ways of rearing children that are unnatural. The natural way evolved because that is what is best for the children.

[3]   Our first concern must be the welfare of the children being adopted or fostered. In society at large homosexuality is not yet fully accepted as a way of life and children of homosexual couples would be subjected to teasing, abuse and social exclusion. It is not right to subject children to this pain and misery for the sake of our high-minded liberal adult ideals. The children do not have a voice of their own so it is up to us to protect them and oppose their being unnecessarily put in a situation of victimisation and exclusion.

[4]   A child should not be brought up with minority sexual role models as his or her only view of sexual relationships. Parents have a huge effect on the

[4]   It is increasingly accepted by scientists that there is a 'gay gene'. A significant minority of children are born with a homosexual orientation. Banning adoption by homosexuals means that none of this large population of children will grow up with the role model that they need but will all be subjected to a struggle against the dominant heterosexual norms. Homosexual and heterosexual parents alike need to be sensitive to the messages they give their children and be open to the child's autonomous sexual development – be it gay or straight.

[5]   Masculine and feminine roles are principally socially constructed – they are not tightly linked to male and female biology. A homosexual couple are just as likely to provide a variety of masculine and feminine traits.

sexuality of their children, and allowing homosexuals to adopt would unacceptably skew and narrow the growing child's view of sex. Heterosexual children might often find hostility from their parents to their emerging sexuality.

[5]   A child not only needs a biological mother and father, he or she also needs masculine and feminine role models. Homosexual couples do not give this variety but tend to fall at one end of the masculine-feminine spectrum for their sex.

Possible motions:
This House would let homosexual couples
    adopt.
This House believes in happy families.

Related topics:
Gay Marriages
Gays in the Military
Homosexuals (Ordination of)
Homosexuals (Outing of)
Surrogate Mothers

Gays in the Military

See the introduction to the debate on 'Gay Marriages', above.

Pros

[1]   Britain and the United States are alone in NATO in maintaining a policy barring homosexuals from serving in the armed forces. In Australia, Canada and New Zealand it is an offence to discriminate against gay and lesbian servicemen and women. It is time that the UK and

Cons

[1]   While we should not sanction discrimination against gay men and lesbians in general, the armed forces present a special case. In military life, the closeness in which colleagues must live, sharing bedrooms and showers in single sex accommodation, day and night

the US came up to date and allowed homosexuals to serve in the armed forces. There is no empirical research or scientific opinion to support the view that homosexuals are less physically capable, less mentally determined, less in control of their sexual impulses or in any other way less able to serve in the military than their heterosexual counterparts.

[2]   There are many jobs that involve close comradeship, stress and danger, such as the civilian emergency services (police, paramedics, fire-fighters). Homosexuals are not barred from serving in these capacities in the UK or in many parts of the US. It is, therefore, inconsistent to ban them from military service

[3]   Many people do not come to realise that they are homosexual until their early twenties, which is often many years after they have already committed themselves to a career in military service. It is not right that they should at that stage have their career destroyed. Those who do know they are homosexual should in any case be allowed to serve their country in the way they wish, and this may currently involve concealing their sexuality.

[4]   Even in the US, where investigations are not undertaken or admissions sought, the armed services lose hundreds of personnel each year who are dismissed when it emerges that they are homosexual. An anti-homosexual policy carries a huge cost in terms of lost expertise and lost investment in personnel through training.

[5]   Now that homosexual activity has

for extended periods, is such that homosexuality, if allowed, could intolerably undermine group unity, discipline, trust, stability and morale. This is not true of any other career. It is not claimed that homosexuals cannot fulfil other requirements of military service.

[2]   The armed services are also special in the intensity of emotional stress and the levels of danger involved in performing one's job. In life-or-death situations the serviceman or woman must keep his or her head. Homosexual feelings, though unavoidable, could be fatal in obscuring professional judgement in such situations. The risk is too high.

[3]   Since people in the US and the UK know, when applying for military service, that a ban exists on homosexuals, it is surely their own fault if homosexuals join up regardless and are later found out and sacked.

[4]   It is, of course, the case that anybody who is found to be unsuitable for a job (on grounds of deceit, sexuality or both) and dismissed will represent a loss to the employer in terms of training and investment. That does not mean that we should do away with all constraints on what is and is not acceptable in certain careers. It remains the case that homosexuality is not appropriate in the unique career of military service.

[5]   Homosexuals in the military present a security risk. If their sexuality became known to enemy agents or, for example, terrorist organisations, it could become the basis of blackmail threats being used to extract security information.

been decriminalised and is increasingly socially accepted, the threat of blackmail is unrealistic. Furthermore, the force of any blackmail would be significantly reduced if the exposure of a serviceman or woman as homosexual did not result in dismissal. A 1988 US Department of Defense report found no statistical link between homosexuality and security risk violations.

[6]   The way to reform society and the military is to make it clear, from the top down, that homosexuals are equally capable, have equal rights and should equally be free from unjust discrimination and abuse. The way to do this is to allow them to serve in the military. Maintaining the ban will simply maintain the invidious homophobic prejudices in the military.

[6]   Society in general, and the military in particular, are not yet ready for the full incorporation of open homosexuality. Open homosexuals in the military would be in danger of abuse or attack from their colleagues. The time is not yet right.

Possible motions:

This House would lift the ban on homosexuals in the military.

This House would let queens fight for Queen and country.

This House believes that you do not have to be straight to serve.

Related topics:

Ideology v. Pragmatism

Affirmative Action

National Service ((Re-)Introduction of)

Gay Marriages

Gays in the Military

Homosexuals (Ordination of)

Homosexuals (Outing of)

God, Existence of

It is commonly held in educated culture that religious belief is irrational and unsubstantiated. But can all the great geniuses of Christianity and other religions throughout the ages have been simply mistaken, not to mention the billions of religious believers world-wide today? Some twentieth-century theologians, such as Paul Tillich, have redefined God as 'the ground of being', in an attempt to get away from simplistic and anthropomorphic conceptions of God as a very powerful person, or even as an old man with a long beard. Does this idea of God make any sense? Can traditional conceptions of a personal, intelligent, benevolent Creator God be rejuvenated? Or is all talk of God rendered meaningless in a modern scientific world?

Pros

[1]   The universe is governed by natural laws and forces that seem to be the product

Cons

[1]   We do not need God to explain natural laws and forces – they would simply

of an intelligent mind. That mind is God, who created the universe. This fact of the universe's dependence on God is expressed in the Genesis myth of the Jewish and Christian traditions, and in other myths around the world.

[2]   Unlike other animals, we are moral beings with consciences. This is because we were created by God, who is a moral being who set down the moral as well as the natural law.

[3]   Around 40 per cent of people in Britain report having had a 'religious experience' of some kind in which they were aware of a power greater than themselves or of a supernatural personal being. People have had such experiences of the 'numinous', the 'sublime' and the divine throughout history. It is arrogant to think that we can write off all these experiences as being entirely mistaken.

[4]   The fact that there are saints in the world capable of supreme charity, devotion and healing (such as the late Mother Teresa of Calcutta) reveals that there is a source of ultimate love to which humans have access (God) and which can triumph over human evil and selfishness. Evil in the world is a result of human disobedience to God, as symbolised in the story of the Fall of Adam and Eve from their original state of paradise. Natural suffering, such as famine, is a sign that the world is not only disobedient but also free. God's love and forgiveness could make no sense in a world without freedom for humanity and for nature.

[5]   The universe, like everything else, must have a meaning, purpose and destiny.

have to exist for us to be here at all and for there to be a universe. The fact that we find laws and forces should not therefore be a source of surprise. In any case, the universe being a 'brute fact' that we cannot explain is a more intellectually honest answer than inventing a supernatural Creator.

[2]   Moral rules are created by human communities so that people can live harmoniously with one another. They vary from culture to culture and are merely human constructions. It is a mistake to take moral feelings – the result of the moral rules set down by a group of people – to be the result of the existence of something supernatural.

[3]   Such feelings and experiences can be explained in terms of natural psychological needs and of brain processes. It is no coincidence that Christians but not Buddhists have religious visions of Christ or of the Virgin Mary. These experiences are the product of religious teaching and often also of sensory deprivation, drugs, sleep deprivation, fasting, meditation or other deliberately mind–altering practices.

[4]   Human beings are so selfish and, often, evil in their dealings with nature and each other, that it is impossible to believe that a loving God exists. Why would a loving God allow the sexual abuse of children, the starvation of innocents in Africa or the Nazi holocaust? On top of evil perpetrated by humans there is the suffering of animals in nature and of people in natural disasters such as famines, earthquakes and floods (e.g. Bangladesh). The natural world as much as the human world reveals indifference and evil as much as goodness or divinity.

It is God who provides and guarantees that meaning and purpose to the universe and to individual people. The universe and humanity can be redeemed in the end by the love of God. There is objective meaning and redemption above individual human lives – there is a greater cosmic process of which we can have intimations through belief in God.

[5]   The universe is ultimately meaningless. We have limited mental powers and there is no rational way for us to find meaning in the 'brute fact' of the universe's existence. On top of this, the strong link made by modern brain science between what used to be called the 'soul', and the brain, makes it impossible that we could exist in any form after our death. Subjective meaning is confined to individual, mortal human lives.

Possible motions:
This House believes that God is not dead.
This House believes that God created the world.
This House believes in God.

Related topics:
Churches in Politics
Disestablishment of the Church of England
Homosexuals (Ordination of)
Religious Teaching in Schools

Homosexuals, Ordination of

See the introduction to the debate on 'Gay Marriages', above.

Pros

[1]   One of the merits of the Christian religion has always been its ability to adapt its principles of love and inclusion to societal values as they evolve. It is now clear, scientifically (the discovery of the 'gay gene') and sociologically, that homosexuals are not deviant or diseased but equal, normal members of human society. There is no reason why they, any more than, for example, women, should be excluded from serving God and society as Christian ministers. Homosexuals and heterosexuals alike are sometimes guilty of the misuse of their God-given sexuality in abusive and unloving ways. However, it is not right to bar all homosexuals from ordination any more than it

Cons

[1]   The strength of the Christian religion rests on its ability to stand up for unchanging moral standards in a changing and morally degenerating world. Homosexuality is a misuse of natural gifts from God, a rejection of His design, and even if it is socially tolerated it cannot be an acceptable way of life for a Christian minister who must stand as a moral example to the members of the church and provide a role model of Christian living. The existence of a 'gay gene' does not make homosexuality morally right any more than other biological predispositions (e.g. to aggression, alcoholism or promiscuity) make their outcomes morally right. The analogy with the

would be right to bar all heterosexuals from ordination on the grounds of the misconduct of which some are guilty.

[2] The Bible (especially the Old Testament) contains many regulations (e.g. regarding diet, cleanliness, clothing, circumcision, etc.) that Christians do not feel obliged to follow. The biblical opposition to homosexuality should be treated by Christians like these other forgotten 'purity rules'. In biblical times homosexuality was not socially integrated and probably generally took place in unstable situations detached from love and open to abuse. That is no longer the case, so the view should be rethought. Jesus himself, the central figure of authority in the Bible for Christians, never made any statement against homosexuality.

[3] Many parts of the Christian community are happy for their ministers to have sex purely for recreation – i.e. married ministers using contraception. It is therefore illogical to deny homosexuals the right to ordination on the grounds that they have non-reproductive sex.

[4] The argument that homosexual sex is wrong because it is outside the sacrament of marriage is circular. It should only remain outside the sacrament of marriage if it can be established on *other* grounds that homosexuality is wrong.

[5] Since heterosexual ministers who condone homosexual love within their congregation are not (generally) sacked, it is illogical to sack celibate homosexuals for holding the same view.

[6] A large minority of the Christian

ordination of women does not hold either: people have no control over their sex, but they do have control over their sexual behaviour.

[2] The Bible, on the authority of which Christianity is based, condemns homosexuality. If Jesus had wished to see the age-old Jewish condemnation of homosexuality overturned he could have taught his disciples accordingly. In other cases (e.g. rules about the Sabbath) Jesus was prepared to challenge the orthodox view. However, he did not do so in this case. Therefore we must assume that he was happy with the Old Testament view. The unequivocal condemnation of homosexuality is repeated in the New Testament in St Paul's letter to the Romans.

[3] It is also clear from the Bible that sex is intended to produce children. The Bible condemns 'fornication', which is the use of sex for pleasure rather than procreation. All homosexual sex falls into this category and those who practise it cannot be role models for the Christian community.

[4] Sex is also something that should take place only within marriage. Marriage is a sacrament of union between a man and a woman for procreation. So, again, homosexual sex is necessarily outside the proper Christian life.

[5] Even non-practising homosexuals are unacceptable as Christian ministers since they condone a form of sex rejected by the Bible and Christianity as against the natural purpose given to sex by God.

[6] Homosexuals should indeed be

community is homosexual. Those gay men and lesbians need spiritual direction as much as heterosexual Christians do. It is right that there should be a significant minority of homosexual Christian ministers who can truly empathise with the needs of this portion of the church.

given spiritual guidance by Christian ministers, but simple affirmation of homosexuality is not the Christian answer. Lesbians and gay men need to be encouraged by ministers to overcome their urges and to live in a truly Christian way. The simple existence of homosexuality is not an argument for ordaining homosexuals. The clergy are there to lead and guide, not as a representative microcosm of society.

Possible motions:
This House would ordain homosexuals.
This House believes that the road to God isn't necessarily straight.
This House calls for a representative clergy.

Related topics:
Legislation v. Individual Freedom
Tradition v. Innovation
Gay Marriages
Gays (Adoption of Children by)
Gays in the Military
God (Existence of)
Homosexuals (Outing of)
Privacy of Public Figures

Homosexuals, Outing of

See the introduction to the debate on 'Gay Marriages', above.

Pros

[1] Prejudice against homosexuality is linked to the fact that gays are seen as a tiny minority in society. In fact, it is estimated, as many as one in ten people are gay. If this were known by the general public it would greatly reduce the existing prejudice and discriminatory behaviour. Therefore, 'outing', or the naming of gay individuals who are currently 'in the closet', is in the long run a valuable weapon against bias. This is particularly true in the case of gay celebrities who can serve as role models.

Cons

[1] There are quite enough gay celebrities to fight the cause already – most of whom have come out voluntarily – and society is changing to embrace homosexuality even without widespread outing. Declaration of sexuality is one of the most important decisions in life and must be made by the individual concerned. Even if outing were to help the fight against discrimination, each individual case must be the choice of the person concerned, not anyone else's.

[2]   Many closet homosexuals are in fact hypocrites, maintaining heterosexual lifestyles and even campaigning against gay rights (two members of John Major's Cabinet, widely believed to be gay on Fleet Street but never exposed, voted against an equal age of consent). It is doubly important that they be outed.

[3]   It is an unpalatable truth that many people do not know what is good for them. Because of the traditional prejudice against homosexuality, 'coming out' can be a terrifying experience that gays resist through fear of rejection, condemning themselves to a lifetime of secrecy, un-happiness and unfulfilment. In fact society is more embracing than ever and coming out will usually drastically improve one's quality of life, with very little backlash – as the comedian Michael Barrymore found in the mid–1990s when he was exposed. Outing can there-fore be beneficial for individuals, even if they would not choose it at first.

[2]   It is society's fault, not that of politicians or bishops, that people are forced to cloak themselves in hetero-sexuality for the sake of their careers. The British election of 1997 made great progress in bringing several openly gay MPs to Parliament, but there are many constituencies where they would have stood no chance of success. Until society accepts gay men and women in all walks of life, those with ambition are faced with a stark choice: admit their homosexuality and give up their chance of being a politician, a vicar, or so on; or pretend otherwise. This is hypocrisy, yes, but we can understand why it is done.

[3]   The consequence of outing can be terrible. Coming out frequently entails rejection by family and friends and the destruction of careers. It can lead to a complete change of lifestyle and requires careful and meditative preparation. To out someone who is not prepared can lead to nervous breakdowns or even suicide. Many public figures have indeed given up their careers or killed themselves to avoid being outed.

Possible motions:

This House would name them but not shame them.

This House believes that staying in is the new coming out.

Related topics:

Marriage

Frank Sinatra once sang that 'love and marriage go together like a horse and carriage'. Did this view die with Sinatra in 1998 or is it still a defensible one? Is there something special about marriage that differentiates it from the ever more popular arrangement of cohabitation? Does marriage provide children with a more stable family home, or is the marital status of their parents (or parent) immaterial?

Pros

[1]   Marriage is the foundation of the stable family unit within which children can have the best possible start to life. Studies repeatedly show that children who grow up with married parents are the best-adjusted and most successful. Therefore, for the sake of their children, prospective parents have a duty to marry in order to provide the real security and trust that children need. A couple who are not married will never be able to offer the same psychologically crucial promise of security to each other or to their children.

[2]   It is important that marriage is valued in order to uphold a healthy and rational view of what loving relationships are about. Loving relationships are about working together for mutual respect and support over a long period – not just about 'falling in love', sex and romance, which are relatively superficial ends. It is interesting to note that arranged marriages have a high success rate – perhaps because they do not give couples false and superficial expectations of total sexual and romantic compatibility.

[3]   The fact that marriages fail does not mean that we should give up trying. Social and legal institutions such as

Cons

[1]   Parents do not need to be married in order to provide a stable home life for their children. In the place of an old-fashioned marriage, couples can sign 'child care orders' committing themselves to care for their children, while not un-realistically committing themselves to a lifelong partnership with the other parent.

[2]   Marriage is an unnecessary curb on freedom and happiness. True love in all its intensity does not actually last a lifetime and it is unreasonable to sentence oneself to a lifetime of enforced fidelity to some-one with whom the spark has gone. Especially now that we are living longer and longer, lifetime commitment is un-realistic and unnecessary. Therefore we should not make unkeepable promises but instead acknowledge that even long-term relationships can end when the love is lost or one partner falls in love with somebody else.

[3]   In the face of the huge divorce rate (up to 50 per cent in some places) in today's world we should re-think our approach to relationships and parenting. It is time to admit that marriage does not work in today's society and to look at alternatives. It is often the rigid and

marriage, the church, the criminal justice system, and so on exist to provide ideal models to which to aspire, often with success. We should not abandon the ideal of truly loving couples providing stable homes for their children.

unrealistic constraints of traditional marriage itself that make a relationship stifling and unbearable.

Possible motions:

This House would get married for the sake of the children.

This House believes that marriage is an out-dated institution.

Related topics:

Disestablishment of the Church of England

Divorce (Easier)

Feminism

Gay Marriages

Surrogate Mothers

Political Correctness

Political correctness is a movement that originated in the US in the 1980s. Its aim is to promote liberal and egalitarian attitudes especially through modifications to language and behaviour. In Britain the main initial reaction to political correctness was one of derision, especially based on extreme examples of 'PC' talk. However, some examples of political correctness, such as the use of 'she' and 'her' rather than 'he' and 'his' as the default personal pronoun (e.g. 'the reader is asked to use her imagination'), have become widespread and accepted. The central question in this debate is whether modifying language and behaviour at the everyday level can really have a large-scale impact on equality and social justice. As always, address the principles and beware of playing 'example tennis'.

Pros

[1]   Political correctness is concerned with social justice. It is paying attention in detail to language and behaviour in order to rid it of ingrained prejudice, discrimination or oppression. It aims in particular to combat racism, sexism, heterosexism (homophobia) and discrimination on the grounds of physical

Cons

[1]   Political correctness may be well intentioned, but it has no really important consequences. The real battle ground for social justice should not be incidental uses of language but real attitudes in the workplace and in society at large. It is implausible and patronising to suggest that people cannot understand that 'man'

appearance or handicap. The great value of political correctness is that it recognises the need to challenge attitudes and behaviours from the bottom up – starting with the very language that has embodied prejudice and discrimination over the years. Political correctness has successfully argued for using something other than just 'he' as the default personal pronoun, for the use of 'Chair' or 'Chairperson' instead of 'Chairman', and for 'Ms' instead of 'Miss' and 'Mrs' (to abolish the discrimination between men and women, the latter unlike the former being defined – by their marital status).

[2]   Political correctness recognises the important role of language in shaping attitudes and behaviours. If it is socially acceptable to call people 'fat', 'ugly', 'stupid', 'short', 'spastic', 'bent', 'bitch', 'Paki' and so on in derogatory ways then attitudes will not change. It is right to challenge such name-calling and discrimination wherever it is found. And we have political correctness to thank for alerting us to this and making us watch the way we think, speak and act.

[3]   It is easy for opponents to pick out silly examples where political correctness has been taken to extremes. The existence of such examples does not mean that the whole movement should be abolished.

[4]   It is up to the groups in question to find their own names. However, it is still right to challenge the use of names that have been part, in the past, of discriminatory ways of thinking and talking – that was the original reason for challenging the uses of 'black' and 'white'. It may be that terms such as 'black', 'queer' or even

just means 'all people' or that they really use it in a way that implies men are superior to women. Political correctness is a distraction from real issues of discrimination.

[2]   It is absurd to believe that political correctness is to be thanked for drawing our attention to discrimination and abuse. The movements campaigning for women's rights, black rights and gay rights all pre-date political correctness. Political correctness reveals an unhealthy and patronising obsession with so-called 'rights' and discrimination. Adults can cope with being teased about their height, weight, age or IQ without the need for the verbal witch-hunt of political correctness. More serious issues of discrimination are dealt with by the law.

[3]   Political correctness is too often taken to extremes. A London teacher forbade her class to see the film of *Romeo and Juliet* because it was heterosexist and did not provide gay role models. A teacher in America suspended a six-year-old boy from school for kissing a girl – this, it was claimed, was sexual harassment. Political correctness fosters paranoia, prudery, and smug judgmentalism.

[4]   Political correctness is often self-defeating in that it creates exclusive, patronising or just silly names for groups that it believes are being discriminated against. Using the term 'African American' , it could be argued, implies that black Africans in America are not 'real' Americans. Calling someone 'differently abled' rather than 'disabled' is patronising. Calling a bald person 'follically challenged' is just silly.

'bitch' can be 'reclaimed' by a group and used positively in future. Political correctness is not committed to any particular names but seeks to challenge the unthinking use of old discriminatory ones.

Possible motions:

This House would be politically correct.

This House believes political correctness has reduced discrimination.

This House believes that political correctness will bring social justice.

Related topics:

Censorship by the State

Legislation v. Individual Freedom

Pornography

Pornography

Pros

[1]   We aspire to live in states free of censorship. Censorship is only to be used as a last resort to protect groups who might be put in danger by certain material. So, for example we have legislation against incitement to racial hatred. This is a form of censorship. But in the case of pornography this does not apply, since no-one is harmed by the photographing or filming of consenting adults for publication to other adults for their sexual pleasure.

[2]   Pornography legitimately explores the realms of sexual fantasy, which is a rich aspect of human experience that it is merely prudish, oppressive and ignorant to deny. Admittedly it is desirable that the availability of pornography be restricted to adults, but for them there should be no restrictions. Pornography is used by many couples as a way to spice up their sex life, and hence even acts as a way to strengthen and stabilise marriages and relationships.

Cons

[1]   Young men and women are lured into debasing and objectifying themselves by the economic power of pornographers. Banning pornography would protect against this exploitation and against the objectifying attitudes pornography engenders. It is naive to say pornography is harmless.

[2]   The availability of pornography, even if it is properly restricted to those over 18 or over 21, sends a message of social consent to the objectifying of women in particular. It encourages young men to see women as sex objects. From an early age young men, through access to pornography, see women in crude sexual and repressed poses rather than seeing them just as fellow humans. Such attitudes are insidious and lead to disrespect and discrimination in the workplace and elsewhere.

[3]   Elements of human sexuality can be explored in music, poetry, literature,

[3]   Pornography can be part of a wide spectrum of approaches to sex and entertainment that are available. There is no need to ban it. Some people may be turned on by less pornographic films and novels, but that does not mean there is no place at all for pornography for those who enjoy its direct approach.

[4]   A clear distinction needs to be made between pornography made and used by consenting adults and pornography involving children. The latter is always unacceptable and should be attacked with the full force of the law. However, the people involved in popular adult magazines such as *Playboy* and TV stations are not in any way connected with child pornography.

[5]   Sadly, sexual abuse and rape will exist with or without pornography. Pornography does not cause these crimes, even if some of the perpetrators may like pornography.

[6]   The use of potentially suggestive pictures of attractive men and women to sell newspapers, magazines and other products is not an instance of pornography, but a normal and acceptable part of our consumerist culture.

theatre and films in infinitely more subtle, interesting and erotic ways. Pornography is trash in comparison – simply bad photography and bad writing of the most superficial kind.

[4]   The more that pornography is tolerated, the more it will spread, and the more cases of abuse and exploitation will occur. There is already a disturbing increase in cases of child pornography, which are the result of a lax attitude to pornography in the past.

[5]   Many rapists and sexual abusers are pornography fanatics. It seems likely that pornography fosters obsessive, unbalanced and violent sexual attitudes. We should ban and seek to wipe out pornography with the same strength as is currently applied to the war on drugs.

[6]   Pornography is infiltrating every aspect of the media, from pop videos and underwear advertisements to 'lifestyle' magazines and tabloid newspapers. Some urgent action needs to be taken to counteract this cultural trend. It is disingenuous to suggest that pictures of 'men and women' are equally used to sell products. It is almost exclusively pictures of the half-naked bodies of *women* that are used, and these pornographic images continue progressively to undermine respect for women as individual human beings.

Possible motions:
This House would legalise all adult pornography.
This House believes pornography is harmless fun.
This House believes pornography saves marriages.

Related topics:
Legislation v. Individual Freedom
Political Correctness
Sex Education
Prostitution (Legalisation of)
Internet (Censorship of)

Privacy of Public Figures

The death in a car crash in Paris of Diana, Princess of Wales in 1997 refuelled calls for restrictions on the paparazzi (press photographers) from whom she and Dodi al Fayed had been fleeing. Subsequently the press in Britain voluntarily agreed not to intrude into the privacy of Diana's sons, William and Harry, but it is yet to be seen if voluntary self-regulation of this sort will be enough. More broadly, the private lives of politicians, actors, singers and sports personalities are constantly subjected to media scrutiny. The details of such figures' sex lives are particularly popular topics in the tabloid press. In 1989 a bill in the UK that would have prevented the press from printing private information about an individual without his or her consent failed to become law. Is it fair that every aspect of the lives of public figures and celebrities should become public property, or should something be done to protect these figures' privacy?

Pros

[1]   Public figures and their families deserve privacy and protection from media intrusion. What they do in their private lives, unless it has implications for e.g. national security (as in the 'Profumo affair' in the 1960s when a cabinet minister and a Russian spy shared a mistress), should not be investigated and reported by the media.

[2]   What a politician does in private has no bearing on his or her ability to do their job. The distress caused to politicians and their families by revelations about sexual indiscretions is unjustifiable.

[3]   Politicians are public servants, entrusted with running the economy and the public services in an efficient and responsible way. They should not be seen as moral paragons. Religions are there to provide moral leadership. We should follow the example of France where there are strict privacy laws and the people accept that their politicians are not saints.

Cons

[1]   Public exposure is one of the prices of fame and power. Politicians and celebrities realise this from the start, and if they do not like it, they should not enter the public sphere. These figures rely on the media for their fame and wealth – they cannot then complain if their lives become, to a large extent, public property.

[2]   It is in the public interest to know whether a politician is unfaithful to his or her spouse. If someone cannot be trusted to keep a promise in their personal life, then it is to be doubted if they can be trusted more generally with important matters of state. If a person goes into politics, has sexual affairs, and is caught, it is he or she who is to be blamed for the distress caused to his or her family, not the media.

[3]   In an increasingly secular world, we need politicians to be the moral leaders that they claim to be. Hence it is right that the media scrutinise their personal life

[4]   Giving public figures a right to privacy is not a form of censorship. Investigative journalism into immoral and criminal activities with a demonstrable element of public interest (rather than seedy gossip) will still be allowed.

[5]   We should condemn the media for printing intrusive photographs of celebrities and 'kiss and tell' stories from their alleged lovers. The bodies that regulate the media should take the lead in banning the printing of such material, and if that does not work, privacy laws will have to be introduced.

[6]   Libel and slander laws are not good enough. People will assume that there is no smoke without fire, and so a politician or celebrity's name can be permanently smeared even if they subsequently win a libel suit or a small apology is printed – by then the damage to their reputation has been done.

Possible motions:
This House believes that public figures have a
  right to private lives.
This House condemns the paparazzi.
This House believes in the right to privacy.

Related topics:
Censorship by the State
Party Funding by the State
Politicians' Outside Interests (Banning of)
Broadcasting (Ending Public Control of)
Homosexuals (Outing of)

to reveal the all-too-frequent cases of hypocrisy (such as secretly gay politicians speaking out against the gay community, or a politician cheating on his wife and preaching 'family values'). The media perform an invaluable task as moral and political watchdogs and investigators. In any case, privacy laws do not work. France, indeed, has stringent privacy laws, yet it was there that intrusive photographs of the Duchess of York and a 'friend' were taken and published, and that Diana, Princess of Wales was hounded, right up to her death, by paparazzi photographers.

[4]   Giving public figures a 'right to privacy' is in effect condoning media censorship and gagging the press.

[5]   Interest in the private lives of public figures is an inevitable part of the modern media world. And as long as we keep on buying, in our millions, the newspapers and magazines that dish out the salacious stories and pictures it is hypocritical to feign outrage at each new media intrusion. These stories sell because of our fascination with fame and celebrity.

[6]   Libel and slander laws already exist to protect public figures from unfair press coverage. There is no need to introduce any more legislation.

Surrogate Mothers

A surrogate mother is a woman who carries and gives birth to a baby for another couple, who are unable to have children in the normal way. A couple in which the woman is infertile might use the man's sperm and the surrogate mother's egg to produce the foetus – the surrogate would not need to have sex with the man, but could be inseminated in another way. Alternatively, if the woman and man are both fertile but the woman cannot, for some other reason, conceive and bear a child, one of the woman's eggs, fertilised by the man, can be implanted into the womb of the surrogate. When it is born the child is handed over by the surrogate to be adopted by the couple. In the US and some European countries 'commercial surrogacy' is allowed (where the surrogate mother is paid). In the UK in 1984 the Warnock Report condemned surrogacy. Under the Surrogacy Arrangements Act of 1985, it became illegal for third parties to arrange any surrogacy for payment. The practice of surrogate motherhood continues to raise vexed moral and practical questions.

Pros

[1]   Surrogate motherhood is to be encouraged as it is a way for people who could not otherwise do so (infertile couples, gay men, single parents) to start their own family. There are always more would-be parents than there are children available for adoption. Couples who have been through a process such as surrogacy will love and value their children all the more.

[2]   Surrogate motherhood need not be a commercial arrangement. If it is, it is, of course, carried out within strict medical and legal guidelines (as is currently done in the US and some European countries) by official surrogacy agencies.

[3]   It is possible, however, to have instead a non-commercial system whereby the surrogate mother is not paid (except expenses) but agrees to hand the child over at birth to the prospective parents who can adopt the child. Such

Cons

[1]   Being a parent is not a right that everybody is born with. If a couple are unable to have children themselves then they should adopt or foster a child rather than bringing yet another child into the world, particularly through surrogacy, which is a method beset by emotional, legal and financial wrangling.

[2]   It is wrong to make a trade in human lives. Surrogacy will inevitably become commercialised. The result of commercial surrogacy will be that only the rich can afford to buy babies in this way. That is not the way that parenthood should be decided.

[3]   It is naive to believe that there will not be disputes in these instances of unpaid surrogacy. Such agreements would be legally unenforceable (since the surrogate mother would be the mother in the eyes of the law) if the surrogate decided to change her mind and keep the child

arrangements would be made with friends or family (e.g. the sister of a sterile woman) and hence would be less open to legal or commercial disputes.

[4]   A ban on this kind of surrogacy would be entirely unenforceable. A woman can easily be impregnated in the privacy of her own home by the would-be father's sperm without professional medical intervention.

Possible motions:

This House would allow surrogate mother-hood.

This House would allow paid surrogate motherhood.

Related topics:

Abortion

Feminism

Gays (Adoption of Children by)

Marriage

Eugenics: IVF and Genetic Screening

Genetic Engineering

Science: a Menace to Civilisation?

– which has frequently happened. Important biological and emotional links are made between mother and baby when it is in the womb – these will add to the pain and confusion for both the surrogate mother and the baby.

[4]   There may be some cases that the law would not be able to reach, but the principle is still to be laid down that surrogacy is wrong. It is a recipe for dis-aster for the would-be parents and the surrogate, and for the child in later life, growing up with the emotionally confus-ing state of affairs that its natural mother is not one of its parents but a friend or relative of its parents.

Vegetarianism

See the introduction to the debate on 'Animal Experimentation and Vivisection, Banning of'.

Pros

[1]   We are animals ourselves, with shared ancestors with all other creatures. We should take responsibility for our ani-mal cousins rather than exploiting and eating them unnecessarily. Furthermore, we cannot know exactly what feelings

Cons

[1]   It is natural for people to farm and eat other creatures. Humans have come to flourish and dominate through their successful adaptation to and manipulation of other species. It is a strange and un-natural idea that we have 'duties' to other

and emotions other animals can have. There is good evidence that they feel fear and pain like us. Therefore, we must err on the side of caution and not farm and kill animals at all. As Jeremy Bentham said, the question about animals is not 'Can they think?' but 'Can they feel pain?'.

[2]   Most mass meat-farming techniques are barbaric, especially the battery-farming of chickens and the force-feeding of veal calves. Supposedly quick slaughter techniques are often botched – leaving animals half-alive and in pain for hours when they were supposed to be dead. Cows are pumped full of antibiotics and steroids to force them to grow to an unnatural size, and are forced to produce a massive and unnatural quantity of milk so that they become exhausted and die at half the age they would in nature. By buying and eating meat the non-vegetarian is indirectly torturing animals that have unnaturally short, miserable and confined lives.

[3]   There is no need for meat in a balanced diet. All sorts of fruits, vegetables and pulses provide the variety of carbohydrates, proteins, fibre, minerals and vitamins that we need. Our closest animal relatives – the apes – have all-vegetarian diets. It has been suggested that this is our natural diet too.

[4]   The taste of naturally grown food is far superior to that mass-produced on a farm. Compared with organic chicken, for example, factory farmed chicken is watery, rubbery and tasteless. Free range eggs are also healthier and tastier than those produced by battery hens.

animals – rights and duties are exclusively applicable to humans. It is true that we cannot know what feelings or emotions animals have, but we can assume that they are minimal. Vegetarianism rests on sentimentalism and anthropomorphism. It is natural for us, like many other animals, to kill and eat other species to survive. Human dominance over the other animals is expressed in the creation stories of the book of Genesis in the Bible.

[2]   Modern farming techniques may often be cramped, but we cannot assume that chickens or calves really have much of an awareness of their quality of life anyway. Their slaughter is generally swift and painless. If it is thought to be very important, free-range chickens, eggs and meat can be purchased to ensure that the animal one is eating had a natural and more varied life.

[3]   Humans have evolved as an omnivorous species. Therefore the omnivorous diet (meat and vegetable) is what we are adapted to flourish on. By cutting out half of this natural diet we are bound to lose the natural balance and variety we need.

[4]   The issue is one of choice. Those who prefer to buy 'organic' food and have the money to spare should be able to do so. The rest of us should be left to buy what we please, unhindered by others' phoney sentimental morality.

[5]   A vegetarian diet may be healthy (if unbalanced) but it is exceedingly expensive. Vegetarianism is a luxury for the middle classes – fresh vegetables are prohibitively expensive compared with

[5] A vegetarian diet is safer and healthier. Factory farming is increasingly dangerous, both for us and for the environment. Agricultural slurry is poisoning our rivers and nitrates entering our water supply have been linked to increased rates of cancer. Antibiotics fed to animals in vast quantities are causing the evolution of 'super-bugs' – bacteria that are resistant or immune to antibiotics. The inclusion of animal brains in their own feed has led to the disastrous spread of Bovine Spongiform Encephalitis ('mad cow disease'), and the human equivalent, Creutzfeldt Jakob Disease. Animal fats are more likely than vegetable fats to cause clogged arteries. People in parts of the world that do not eat meat have lower rates of cancer. Almost all potentially deadly forms of food-poisoning (E-coli, BSE, salmonella) are transmitted through meat and poultry. The more vegetarians there are, the more demand for vegetables there will be, the more farmers will switch from meat to vegetable growing and the cheaper the vegetarian diet will become.

processed meats, burgers and so on, which are affordable and filling even if not full of vitamins. Safer farming techniques and increased health awareness, not a wholesale switch to an unnatural vegetarian diet, are the solutions to the problems of unsafe meat farming.

Possible motions:

This House believes that meat is murder.

This House believes that eating meat is a form of cannibalism.

Related topics:

Legislation v. Individual Freedom

Pacifism

Animal Experimentation and Vivisection (Banning of)

Animal Rights

Blood Sports (Abolition of)

Zoos (Abolition of)

Zoos, Abolition of

See the introduction to the debate on 'Animal Experimentation and Vivisection, Banning of'.

Pros

[1] Animals have rights just as humans do. They have evolved from nature and each belongs undisturbed in its own natural habitat, left alone to live, breed and seek food. To remove them against their will from this habitat is immoral.

Cons

[1] Animals do not have rights (and it is debatable whether 'rights' exist). It is entirely at our discretion how we treat them, since we are a stronger, predatory species. The use of a weaker species for the needs of a stronger one is entirely natural.

[2]   Even if animals do not have rights, we as humans still have a duty to treat them humanely in our role as 'stewards of the Earth'. Although we may breed them for our purposes, to use for entertainment, for company, or to wear or eat, we must still avoid causing them to suffer. Zoos do this in two ways. First, the animals frequently suffer abuse, neglect and even death, through boredom, unfamiliarity with their new habitats and cruel treatment by zookeepers. A San Francisco zookeeper, explaining an incident in which an African elephant was beaten with axe handles for two days, described the treatment as 'the only way to motivate them'. Birds' wings may be clipped, aquatic animals have too little water, herd animals are kept alone or in pairs, and many animals contract 'zoochosis', abnormal and self-destructive behaviour caused by their confinement. Second, the exhibition of animals in captivity tells an impressionable public that cruelty to animals can be condoned.

[3]   Few zoos approach satisfactory standards of care for their animals. Many make no attempt to do so, such as 'roadside' zoos or menageries, where the primary purpose of the animals is to attract customers to another facility such as a restaurant, store or hotel. There is no educational benefit to these zoos.

[4]   Larger, municipal zoos that claim to be for educational benefit are kidding themselves; visitors usually spend no more than a few minutes at each exhibit, using the animals rather for entertainment. Their primary use for research is to devise ways to breed and maintain more animals in captivity. If zoos ceased to exist, so would the need for their research.

[2]   It is easy to pick shocking, isolated examples of animal cruelty. In fact the general treatment afforded to most animals in zoos is very good. They are given regular food and water, comfortable environments suited to their particular needs, and most importantly medical treatment – something they would not benefit from in the wild. In many cases their chance of survival is better than in their 'natural' habitat. In other cases, it is certainly a comfortable existence. Zoos do not condone cruelty to animals; the public is taught that all animals are interesting and precious.

[3]   By all means close down roadside zoos, or at least subject them to the same stringent safeguards as municipal zoos.

[4]   Zoos are useful both for educational purposes and for research. In particular they allow children an opportunity to observe closely animals from other countries that they might never have a chance to see, as well as learn about all the species of the animal kingdom and how they are related. Scientists are also afforded valuable opportunities to study animals in strange environments, and draw conclusions about how we can affect their natural habitats.

[5]   Endangered species may be protected from extinction in zoos, or in wildlife sanctuaries.

Possible motion:
This House would free the animals.

Related topics:
Animal Experimentation and Vivisection (Banning of)

[5]   Animals chosen for zoos are usually the popular breeds, which will attract crowds. Endangered species in need of protection may not necessarily attract audiences.

Animal Rights
Blood Sports (Abolition of)
Vegetarianism

SECTION F

Education, Culture and Sport

Arts Funding by the State, Abolition of

Pros

[1]   The role of the state in the modern world is not to prescribe the means of expression of its citizens. Funding of the arts by the state amounts to such pre-scription – money will always go to one favoured art-form (often traditional figu-rative painting and sculpture) rather than others (e.g. more conceptual art-forms). To avoid having a pernicious influence over artistic expression and development, state funding of the arts should be abolished. The ideal of art is individual expression – this is incompatible with state (or, arguably *any*) patronage.

[2]   We have learned from the past (especially in Communist regimes) that funding of artistic projects (including the composition of music) all too easily slides into the realms of propaganda. Art should be free to criticise the Government.

[3]   There are many more important things that public money is needed for – obvious examples include books and equipment for schools, new drugs and technologies for hospitals, social security payments for single parents and the unemployed. Every spare penny should be channelled into these areas. Public spending should be on necessities, not luxuries. Art is of no material use to the nation and so is not a proper object of public expenditure.

[4]   If there is no demand for works of art then why are they being produced? It is simply a form of pointless self-

Cons

[1]   If the state does not provide care-fully administered funding for the arts, then only the independently wealthy or those given patronage by the rich will be able to practise as artists – this is un-acceptably elitist and haphazard. Art has always been associated with patronage of various forms from classical times onwards. Just as religion has always found a compromise with secular authorities, so the 'pure' artist will always find a com-promise between the ideal of individual expression and the economic realities of life as an artist. Only the state can fund the arts in a responsible way, appointing committees of artistic experts to make responsible, relatively impartial and up-to-date decisions about which art-forms and artists are funded.

[2]   We can, indeed, learn from history. What we learn is that arts funding must be given without any strings attached – that artistic freedom must always be guaranteed rather than the state dictating to the artist. Mistakes of past regimes do not mean that state funding of arts must be scrapped, any more than the fact that democratic processes have been abused by autocratic regimes means that democracy should be scrapped.

[3]   It is very simplistic to see benefit only in material goods such as textbooks and medicines. Civilised societies need moral and mental education and healing as much as they require educational and medical equipment. Artists (poets,

indulgence by artists. The state has no business subsidising plays, paintings or concertos for which there is no demand. Artists should compete on the free market like everyone else trying to sell a product. If there are too many artists for the limited demand, then some artists (actors, painters, musicians) should simply re-train, as did, for example, coal-miners in the 1980s when their usefulness was exhausted.

[5]   Arts are indirectly funded by unemployment payments to young musicians and artists who claim dole payments while not seeking work but simply developing their artistic talents. But there is no reason why such people should not organise their time to include part-time work as well as time for their artistic development. It is illogical to assume that artistic talent must go hand in hand with a chaotic, self-indulgent and undisciplined lifestyle.

Possible motions:

This House would abolish state funding of the arts.

This House believes that the arts are of no material benefit to society.

Related topics:

Capitalism v. Socialism

Broadcasting (Ending Public Control of)

National Lottery (Abolition of)

High Art v. Low Art

Museums (Entrance Fees to)

painters, actors, comedians, sculptors, musicians, film-makers) provide unique moral insights and function as irreplaceable critics of society and politics (a cross between academics and jesters). A society without arts would be soulless and blind.

[4]   There are some areas where we should not let the market dictate policy and spending. Public transport and health services, for example, should be kept in state ownership to ensure that they are run not according to supply-and-demand alone but on a moral basis, so that non-profit-making activities – e.g. train services to remote areas, or expensive treatments for rare medical conditions – are not scrapped. Arts funding is a similar case. The state should fund the arts to ensure that they are not sacrificed on the altar of heartless free market capitalism. Capitalists may be philistines, but that does not mean that the whole of society should be made culturally illiterate by abolishing state funding of the arts.

[5]   Young artists such as the Beatles or Oasis would never have had the time to develop their talents if they had been constrained by a nine-to-five job. The artistic temperament is not compatible with such a routine. It is perfectly acceptable for such gifted young people to live on state benefits while developing their unique talents.

Classics (Latin and Greek) in Education

Pros

[1] Latin and Greek language and literature have traditionally been the basis of education for many of the great scholars, authors and leaders of history. Milton, Shakespeare, T.S. Eliot *et al* relied heavily on classical literature for inspiration. Their study today can both inspire modern thinkers in the same way and help us better to understand past works influenced by them.

[2] The whole nature of a 'canon' of literature that survives the ages is that it is considered to be qualitively better than many current, ephemeral works. The literature of Greece and Rome is simply better than many of the texts studied in English Literature or modern languages.

[3] The study of Classics teaches valuable linguistic skills that can be applied to many other areas. A knowledge of Latin and Greek helps us understand the etymology of English words, while the almost mathematical decoding of grammar in both languages teaches the mind to be analytical.

[4] Just as the measure of a civilisation is sometimes said to be how well it takes care of its retired citizen – i.e how far it goes beyond the bare necessities for survival – surely the measure of education should be how well it teaches the student areas of knowledge that are not immediate requisites. The inclusion of Classics is a fine example of this: dead languages,

Cons

[1] Many great authors have had no education in Classics, especially notable writers of the twentieth century. Milton and Shakespeare had to study Latin and Greek as the source of most great pre-Chaucerian literature; now we have the benefit of several hundred years of literature in English to study instead. If we wanted to understand ancient influences there are also many others from which to choose: Ancient Egyptian and Anglo-Saxon in terms of culture; prehistoric in terms of science.

[2] This is nonsense for two reasons. First, it is impossible to define one work of art as 'better' than another; the only yardstick by which it can be judged is its relevance to an individual reader or viewer. If I prefer novels from 1960s France, then they are 'better' to me. Second, even if the use of language in Greek and Latin texts was more impressive, that is outweighed by the increasing irrelevance of the events and ideas described.

[3] The skills learned from Classics can equally be gained from the study of e.g. German or Russian which have use in the modern world. Mental discipline is more easily taught through the study of pure mathematics or philosophy.

[4] Luxuries are only to be applauded when they can be afforded. Unfortunately, the increasing demands of more relevant subjects – especially science and

yes, but poetic ones with immense relevance to the understanding of our own history and the birth of Western culture. This is the sort of unnecessary extra we should embrace.

Possible motions:

This House would put Latin and Greek on the national curriculum.

This House believes that Latin is a dead language, as dead as dead can be.

Related topics:

Tradition v. Innovation

High Art v. Low Art

Religious Teaching in Schools

technology, vocational skills, modern languages and business training – leave less and less time for the large number of optional extras: Classics, music, drama, art, etc. The limited benefit of studying the few ancient authors worth reading is not enough to justify their inclusion in the curriculum.

Co-education

Pros

[1]   It is only natural to teach boys and girls together, for social and economic reasons. Most high schools in the United States are co-educational, as are state schools and an increasing number of private schools in the UK. Primary schools are nearly always co-educational.

[2]   The benefits given to students in a co-educational environment are enormous. Both boys and girls are given an easy confidence when dealing with the opposite sex; those at single-sex schools frequently find this more difficult. Students from mixed schools are more fully prepared for adult life. The presence of girls usually leads to better behaviour among boys who would otherwise enjoy an 'oppressively male' atmosphere with its

Cons

[1]   In fact it is more natural for sexes to be taught apart, in the formative years between 7 and 15 when children prefer the company of their own sex. In the Caribbean, many single-sex schools are based on the belief that gendered responses from children confirm the natural differences between the sexes. There are also a number of subjects that cannot be taught in the presence of both sexes, or should not be taught in the same way: sex education, women's issues, etc.

[2]   Confidence is a product of maturity and children can be just as shy in co-educational schools as they can in mixed schools. In fact, co-education can lead to behaviour that is extremely detrimental to

associated traits: arrogance, crudity, juvenility. Teenage girls mature faster than their male counterparts and so are a good influence on them. Also, competition between sexes is greater than between same-sex rivals, and this competition leads to higher standards of academic achievement.

[3]   Adult relationships between alumni of co-educational schools often have a better basis. Both partners will understand the characteristics of their opposite gender, having experienced them in daily life to a far larger degree – in the same way that boys with several sisters are frequently thought to be 'more understanding of women'. Thus their judgements of each other will be better informed.

[4]   The system of single-sex schools arose from the chauvinistic society of the past, where men held all major positions in society and were accordingly given a better education. It is now recognized that the sexes have equal rights: of employment, of social benefit, and of education. The fact that single-sex schools tend to have a majority of teachers of that sex – especially in the higher positions such as that of head teacher – means that women teachers are discriminated against in boys' schools and vice versa.

[5]   The lack of finance in the state sector means that we must urgently address ways of directing funding more effectively. Distributing staff and equipment separately to single-sex schools is less cost-effective than their distribution to mixed schools where facilities for boys and girls can be shared.

education: boys are led to show off and even sexually harass girls, while both are distracted by each other. Teenage pregnancies are soaring in co-educational schools. Competition should be discouraged and students should not be used as pawns to provoke each other into working harder; it is the teacher's job to inspire them, and they should not be motivated by rivalry. Academic achievement is in fact generally higher in single-sex schools; in the 1990s, league tables have been topped by the likes of Manchester Grammar School and St Paul's Girls' School.

[3]   Divorce rates in the United States do not suggest that co-education leads to stable relationships.

[4]   Children of a certain age shy away from the opposite gender and prefer many activities characteristic of their sex. It is only natural that they should be taught during this period by same-sex teachers. While men and women should have equal rights, that is not the same as saying they are identical.

[5]   In fact mixed-sex schools are more expensive to run, having to provide facilities for both boys and girls, and teachers and subjects to suit both.

Possible motion:
This House would educate boys and girls
  together.

Related topic:
Sex Education

Contact Sports, Abolition of

Pros

[1]   There are some sports, specifically rugby and boxing, that involve high levels of violent physical contact. These sports should be banned in order to protect individuals from serious physical injury and to protect society from their brutalising effects. Young people are introduced to these sports at an impressionable age when they may not be old enough to make decisions based on all the relevant facts – there is also great peer pressure to be 'hard' and take part in contact sports. Banning these sports is the only way to ensure that young people in particular are protected from the dangers involved.

[2]   Unlike football, cricket, skiing or swimming, in which there may be some *incidental* injuries from accidents or (in football) illegal tackles, in contact sports injuries result from the central activity of the sport. The 'scrum' and the 'ruck' in rugby are central features of the game that place immense and dangerous pressure on the spinal column, hence endangering the central nervous system. The whole point of boxing is to knock one's opponent unconscious by temporarily detaching his brain from the inside of his skull. Both the British and the American Medical Associations have repeatedly called for a ban on boxing. Such forms of 'sport' are uncivilised and unacceptably dangerous, resulting in paralysis, brain damage and death for many unfortunate players.

[3]   The idolisation of boxers and rugby

Cons

[1]   It should be up to individuals to decide whether or not to take part in contact sports. We let people decide for themselves whether to drive cars or smoke cigarettes – both, proportionately, far more dangerous. In general we should let people decide for themselves what risks to take unless there is a good reason not to – for example, with heroin-taking, which is excessively and universally harmful and destructive.

[2]   In fact, there are relatively few deaths from contact sports compared with deaths from e.g. incidents of drowning in long-distance swimming and in sailing. There are risks inherent not only in all sports but in virtually all forms of travel and many forms of work. Cricket balls in the head, sliding football tackles, skiing accidents, crashes in 'Formula One' racing, are inherent risks of the games, not in some way incidental in a way that accidents in rugby and boxing are not. The distinction between inherently and incidentally dangerous activities is a spurious one.

[3]   It is simplistic to believe that admiration for boxers or rugby players leads to violent behaviour. People find all sorts of scapegoats for the incidence of violent behaviour – television, films, video games, sports – but in fact violence endures no matter what forms of sport and entertainment prevail. In the nineteenth century bare-knuckle boxing, a more brutal sport than modern boxing, was immensely

players gives young people role models who are revered simply for their brute force and ability to injure other people. Such role models can only have a negative effect and perpetuate the trend towards increased violence among young people. Rather we should revere sportsmen who display skill as well as physical prowess.

popular, but it does not seem that teenagers were more violent then than now. Violent behaviour is an unfortunate fact of human nature that cannot be blamed on one or two particular sports.

Possible motions:
This House would abolish contact sports.
This House would ban boxing.

Related topics:
Legislation v. Individual Freedom
Pacifism
School Sport (Compulsory)
Sport (Commercialisation of)

Corporal Punishment

Pros

[1] 'Spare the rod and spoil the child': especially in their formative years, before they have developed faculties of reason and fair play to which parents can (try to) appeal, children need to be taught the difference between right and wrong. A short, sharp expression of force, such as a smack or a spanking – which inflict no serious or lasting damage – is an extremely effective method. It is espoused by many childcare experts.

[2] The law in Britain allows parents the right of 'reasonable chastisement'. Ultimately it is the parents' responsibility to rear their children as best they may and by whatever methods they choose. The number of parents who have used smacking or spanking to produce well-raised children testifies to the usefulness of corporal punishment.

Cons

[1] The use of force is barbaric and there are many other methods that should instead be used to teach good behaviour: verbal correction, grounding, withholding of pocket money and so on. It is not morally sanctionable to cause pain to others even in a parent-child relationship.

[2] Parental use of force teaches children that violence can be acceptable. Too many criminals, bullies and children with other behavioural disorders have been beaten as part of their upbringing for the link not to be accepted. Parents are not necessarily trustworthy and many abuse the right of chastisement.

[3] In 1998 corporal punishment was finally banned in all forms from the remaining independent schools where it

[3] Corporal punishment has been outlawed in British schools because of the risks attached to its misuse. In the past too many school-teachers have been over-ready to use the cane, even deriving sadistic pleasure from it; and with the current fear of child abuse it is not appropriate to grant this right to teachers. This, however, is an argument against extreme empowerment of teachers, not against corporal punishment *per se*, which may retain a role in the home.

[4] Spanking and smacking should be seen as part of a wider strategy of child-rearing. They should be used only selectively, for acts of wilful disobedience and misbehaviour, and only after milder forms of discipline (removal of privileges, addition of chores) have failed. Encouragement and praise should be given for good behaviour.

was still employed – twenty-one years after the Plowden Report which first recommended the ban. Just as other methods are available to parents, so there are myriad options for teachers to employ in maintaining school discipline, none of which involves violence.

[4] Clearly some techniques of discipline or motivation work in some cases, and fail in others. Of course a variety of methods should be used, and stronger penalties employed when weaker ones fail. But this need not be extended to physical force; the fact that there are so many other options shows this.

Possible motion:
This House believes that parents should have the right to smack their children.

Related topics:
Ends v. Means
Capital Punishment
Child Curfews
Mandatory Prison Sentences
Sex Offenders (Chemical Castration of)

Examinations, Abolition of

Pros

[1] Examinations test the ability to memorise large amounts of information for short periods of time. It is well known that some students are much better at 'cramming' and revising than others and so do better at exams, despite performing less consistently well during the course of a year's study. Exams do not necessarily

Cons

[1] More use of *viva voce* examinations (face-to-face interviews) should certainly be made, as these test that the student has a proper understanding of the principles of a subject. There is also far more use of coursework components as part of most courses. But any exam will evaluate their ability to apply the knowledge they have

test creativity, imagination, or even a flexible understanding of the principles involved in a subject; on the whole they test the rote-learning of facts. It is therefore possible for students to idle for a year and then learn the course in a few days, just as they might successfully 'question spot' and only revise a few topics that happen to come up in the exam. It is unfair that university entrance and employment prospects are based to such a large degree on examination results.

[2] The pressure attached to exams, both because of their significance for the future and of the stress involved in intense revision, is extremely detrimental to the student. Not only can this pressure cause a pupil to perform less well in the exam than he or she would in a stress-free environment, it can also lead to breakdowns or worse. School drop-outs, discipline problems and even suicides are increasingly common, often due to worry about poor grades and the effect that failure in one set of exams will have for the future. Schools and parents are frequently culpable in reminding the student of the consequences of failure and hence increasing the pressure.

[3] Public exams (e.g. GCSEs, A-levels) are set outside the school by examination boards, not by the teachers who are familiar with the students. This means one of two things. Either the pupils will find that the exams bear little relation to the course they have been studying, which can cause disillusionment and surprisingly poor results, or the teachers must anticipate the exams so carefully that they are enslaved to the curriculum, without the ability to adjust their syllabus

learned to an unfamiliar question, and to communicate their knowledge to the examiner. Exams should be retained – and perhaps improved – as part of a course involving other means of evaluation as well.

[2] Pressure is a fact of working life, as are deadlines, and both need to be prepared for and tested. The number of people who cannot handle the pressure is very small and there is no indication that they would manage the increased workload that curricula without exams would involve; in many cases they are unbalanced anyway. Parents and teachers should encourage students to relax for exams.

[3] Exams are intended to make pupils think and use what they have learned to answer a question they have not thought about before. They should not be spoonfed the answer by teachers and should expect the examinations to surprise them.

[4] The disparity in mental maturity is significant only at primary school level, where separate tests are set for late developers. It is also the school's responsibility, rather than the examining board's, to deal with pupils of different abilities, putting them into sets or forward for different examinations.

[5] At some point opinions must be given about students, and their own teachers are much more likely to be partial than independent examiners who know them only as candidate numbers. Examiners mark primarily for knowledge and clarity of argument rather than for

to the needs of their classes. Creativity and initiative from the teachers are lost.

[4]   For the most part examinations are set and taken as if students had reached the same level of understanding at the same age. This is not true; boys and girls mature mentally at different rates, as do many individuals within the same sex. Exams make no allowance for this.

[5]   Examination success frequently depends on the individual examiner who marks a certain paper. Since academics often disagree over interpretation of the same facts, a student's essay or opinion may be thought correct by one examiner and incorrect by another. Two examiners could indeed mark the same set of papers and grade them in completely different orders. This is why marks given for exams are frequently moderated and raised or lowered by a second examiner – clearly the process does not provide an accurate evaluation of the candidate.

[6]   Intelligence tests should be used instead as a more reliable indicator of a student's potential, both for education and for employers. They do not favour the student with a good short-term memory over another. They may also be used to pinpoint exact strengths and weaknesses, profiling a pupil to say, for example, that he or she is 'strong at logical inference while poor at lateral thinking'. These evaluations are much more useful to employers in selecting the right candidate for the right job. Meanwhile, coursework and regular evaluation should be used in school and university to make sure the students are working consistently and understanding their entire course.

conclusion. Extensive moderation and examiners' meetings guarantee that all papers are marked to the same standard.

[6]   Intelligence tests are highly controversial and can only differentiate between right and wrong answers. They cannot judge whether the pupil used the right thought process in reaching the answer, and cannot measure creativity, initiative, hard work, structure and the ability to communicate. All of these qualities are evaluated by examinations.

Possible motion:

This House would abolish the A-level.

Graduate Tax

Another debate about the responsibilities of the state. The Opposition does not need to present a counter-plan but it may make the debate more constructive if they outline how else higher education could be funded, for instance, funding it fully through general taxation (as in Britain until 1997) or through loans taken out by students (the US). The Opposition arguments here concentrate more on the idea of full state funding.

Pros

[1]   Higher education is expensive for the state to provide but highly profitable for those who enjoy its benefits – graduates, who tend to monopolise many of the highest-paid professions. Given that graduates are currently a minority in British society, and are likely to remain so, why should bus drivers and factory workers who never went to university pay, through taxes, for others to gain a salary advantage? Equally, why should the childless or parents whose children did not go to university pay for other people's children to attend? A majority of university students come from middle-class backgrounds while most taxpayers are poorer; clearly this is inequitable.

[2]   A graduate tax would be progressive, linked directly to earnings in a way that a loans system could never be. This means that graduates who choose to pursue a low-paid profession (e.g. teaching) would not be penalised. 'Fat cat' lawyers, accountants and management consultants would pay much more, and overall the receipts of all graduate taxes would be enough to fund the higher education system.

Cons

[1]   Education is so important that it should be a responsibility of the state to fund it. It is a key factor in economic growth, as more graduates boost prosperity for all by using their skills. It also promotes social mobility and equality by allowing anyone with academic potential to make the most of his or her abilities. Because of the diversity of backgrounds of modern students, universities also promote tolerant, socially cohesive societies. The very nature of taxation means that many people pay for things they do not need themselves; in return, they draw on state services towards which others are contributing.

[2]   Graduates do earn more, generally, but not always – Richard Branson and many self-made businessmen disprove this. In addition, many graduates and non-graduates hold similar jobs in the same firms, for example in retailing and some financial sectors – it would not be fair for some of them to pay more tax than others. Graduates contribute more already through income tax and National Insurance, assuming they do have higher earnings – so a graduate tax would penalise them twice.

[3]   A graduate tax does not act as a deterrent to entering higher education in the way in which other systems do – private universities in the US which charge fees favour the rich or those with the confidence to take out loans, and the current requirement in the UK is for students to borrow from the government. In both cases the fear of large debts on leaving university may dissuade potential students from applying in the first place. This is especially true of working-class students; those from the middle classes are more accustomed to borrowing to finance investments (as in mortgages). The deterrent effect becomes strongest in times of recession.

[4]   Many of today's most productive careers require technical training which can be provided by companies rather than universities. University students are acquiring a surplus of unnecessary knowledge through their own choice. It should be their responsibility, not the state's, to fund this luxury.

[3]   Any extra charge on graduates is still a disincentive – France and Germany show that full state funding can create a society where university entrance is a common aspiration. But the US shows that fees and loans do not preclude a higher percentage of university attendance than Britain currently has. Tuition fees introduced in the UK in 1997 led to an immediate drop in applications but they soon returned to approximately their former level. Would-be students recognise that they will benefit from higher education and are prepared to invest in that. Unlike a graduate tax, loan repayments are fixed and can be fully repaid over time. In times of recession, those susceptible to a high graduate tax are more likely than anyone to move abroad – and these are the people society most needs to keep.

[4]   University education is of enormous benefit to society as whole (see [1]) and technical training is widely available at all universities. Industry, commerce and the culture of a country all need the benefit of graduates, and society should be prepared to invest in them.

Possible motions:

This House would introduce a graduate tax.

This House believes that higher education should be free.

This House would pay back its debt to society.

This House would make the student pay.

Related topics:

Ideology v. Pragmatism

Welfare State

Taxation (Direct, Abolition of)

Oxbridge (Abolition of)

Tuition Fees for University Students

High Art v. Low Art

Pros

[1]   There is such a thing as a 'canon' of art, including examples of music, literature, painting, sculpture, architecture and so on that are simply superior to others. Consensus and any sensible criteria of judgement tell us that Shakespeare, Beethoven and Van Gogh were among the best of their discipline. Modern culture is producing fewer and fewer works to add to the canon.

[2]   It is no longer possible, for the most part, for artists to devote themselves entirely to the production of high-class work, because their first priority must be to earn money. Whereas the system of patronage in the past, where artists were funded by wealthy benefactors, allowed them to work purely to their own tastes, now they depend on sales and must cater to the tastes of the public. Hence films feature more special effects than quality acting, conceptual artists must create unnecessary controversies to sell work, and teenage violinists must pose half-naked to sell classical concertos.

[3]   Art as it is traditionally thought of is becoming less important in our society. The advance of modern technology and media means that reading is in decline as computer games are rampant. Music has become increasingly dance- and rhythm-based (as it has evolved from rock 'n' roll to disco to hip hop to techno) and the traditional qualities of melody and harmony are lost. Museums and art galleries attract fewer visitors than ever before.

Cons

[1]   There is no such thing as a canon, nor a consensus on art. We all have different tastes and if something pleases one individual then it is good art to that person. Even if Shakespeare *et al.* are generally regarded as very good, the best exponents of dance music, of blockbuster films and so on can be equally good. The canon is foisted by older generations on the younger, but they have no superiority in evaluating art.

[2]   Artists have always had to cater to the public or to the benefactors who support them; Virgil wrote *The Aeneid* to please Augustus, and Dickens published his work in popular magazines. And if a work of art is popular, then surely it is doing its job.

[3]   The advance of technology has brought innumerable benefits and the decline of traditional recreation is inevitable – tastes change and we do not have enough time to enjoy everything available to us.

Possible motion:
This House prefers Sega to Shakespeare.

Related topics:
Arts Funding by State (Abolition of)
Classics (Latin and Greek) in Education
Museums (Entrance Fees to)

Mandatory Retirement Age

Currently there is a mandatory retirement age of 60 or 65 for most people employed by private businesses and corporations, and also for public sector employees (e.g. civil servants, teachers, doctors, the policeforce). Traditionally women have retired at 60 and men at 65, although this distinction is rarely made today. Private practitioners such as doctors and surgeons in private practice, barristers, artists and writers as well as people who run their own businesses and politicians are not subject to a mandatory retirement age. Judges in Britain have a mandatory retirement age of 75, except Law Lords, who sit as the highest court of appeal, for whom there is no rule.

Pros

[1]   Although many judges, surgeons or entrepreneurs will be able to work effectively after the age of 65, many will become less and less competent, lucid and reliable as the effects of old age (and possibly senility) set in. The impairment of judgement or skill may be slow and gradual, or dramatic. But without a mandatory retirement age there is no easy way to oblige someone whose faculties are impaired to stop working – even when it might be endangering life or causing miscarriages of justice. A mandatory retirement age of 65 for all will guarantee that this does not happen, and will put an end to the spectacle of senile, out-of-touch judges and politicians making crucial constitutional and judicial decisions.

[2]   At the moment, in the world of the arts, musicians, writers, actors and composers continue to work way past the normal retirement age. This prevents young talented performers and writers from breaking into the field. A mandatory retirement age would prevent those over 65 from taking paid jobs (book deals, film roles, positions in orchestras) and hence

Cons

[1]   This is a repressive and draconian measure and a complete over-reaction, especially in a world with an ever-increasing proportion of over-65s. There may be some who become incompetent as they get older but they must be dealt with on an individual basis – using existing mechanisms to prevent them from practising medicine, law or commerce on the grounds of their incompetence. The huge majority whose faculties are not impaired should be allowed to continue working as long as they are able to. Mandatory retirement would unnecessarily and unjustly curtail many careers and pointlessly deprive the community of the wealth of experience and ability that older lawyers, doctors and businessmen have accumulated. Most judges, for example, are over 60, because they require a huge amount of experience to be able to do the job.

[2]   Many composers (e.g. Michael Tippett who continued to work past his ninetieth birthday), actors (e.g. Sir John Gielgud who won an Oscar at the age of 77, and Jessica Tandy who won her Oscar for her role in *Driving Miss Daisy* at the

open up the field for young talent to come through. Mandatory retirement would thus encourage meritocracy in the arts as well as in business. Older artists could continue to do creative work on an unpaid basis, and should be encouraged to work for charities and teach younger artists, perhaps from underprivileged backgrounds, on a voluntary basis in their retirement.

[3] It is unfair that some people are allowed to continue doing their job past the age of 65 while others are not. In the interests of equality there should be a universal mandatory retirement age.

[4] Mandatory retirement should not be seen negatively. Too many people these days are dominated by their careers and the world of work. As more and more people live beyond retirement age by two decades, this period of life should be free from the stress and strain of work. It provides a time for people to pursue creative and educational interests, and also to give something back to the community with charitable work. Those who are 'workaholics' need a mandatory retirement age to give them the spur to develop other sides of themselves and broaden their lives.

[5] Looking at employment as a whole, we still suffer a problem of unacceptable unemployment levels. A mandatory retirement age will free up more working opportunities which can be offered to the young jobless – those who are more likely to be supporting families, buying houses, and so on.

age of 82), poets (e.g. Sir John Betjeman who became Poet Laureate at the age of 66) and writers (e.g. the phenomenally successful popular novelist Catherine Cookson who only started writing in her forties and produced huge amounts of work from her sixties to her early nineties) produce their best work after the age of 65. Younger performers and writers will get their chance, and there is already much media exposure for 'prodigies' and young stars especially in the film and music industries. If anything, an effort needs to be made to give *older* artists more exposure. The young have plenty of opportunities and exposure already.

[3] Different jobs differ in many significant ways such as pay, job security and working conditions. It is a fact of life that some jobs have a retirement age and others do not. Believing in equality does not entail everyone's jobs having to be as similar as possible in all respects.

[4] People must not be treated like children. This legislation would be an extreme measure characteristic of an overbearing 'nanny state'. We must let individuals decide for themselves whether they wish to devote their entire life to their job or prefer to follow other pursuits.

[5] In fact, such a law would be disastrous economically. The rapidly ageing population in Western countries – where people are living longer and longer – means that a greater proportion of the population are drawing pensions and a smaller proportion working to provide the money. A mandatory retirement age would only make this worse.

Possible motions:
This House calls for a mandatory retirement age.
This House would put youth before experience.

Related topics:
Term Limits for MPs
Pension (Ending State Provision of)

Museums, Entrance Fees to

Pros

[1]   Museums cost money. Significant costs include the wages of curators and other staff, the cost of purchasing new acquisitions for their collections (e.g. papers of significant politicians, writers or scientists, works of art, rare technological artefacts and other items that come to auction), and general upkeep of buildings. It is only right that this money comes from those people who benefit from the museum – those who visit it. Reduced rates can be applied to students, pensioners and the unemployed.

[2]   Museums, like cinemas, theatres or sports venues, provide several hours of entertainment. There is no reason why museums alone should be expected to provide this service free of charge. Like other forms of family entertainment, museums should be allowed to make a profit. Also, it is unconvincing to say that museums are educational but cinemas and theatres are not – the latter can be extremely educational, but are not provided free of charge by the state. Those

Cons

[1]   Society at large benefits from the increased levels of public understanding of art, culture, science and technology that museums engender. Even with reduced rates, entry fees will deter the poor and underprivileged – exactly the sort of people who would benefit most from the 'democratic' and unimposing form of education that museums offer; a form of education accessible to those who, perhaps, could not flourish in the conventional academic system of book-learning and exams.

[2]   It is arguable that some films and plays should be shown free of charge as, like museums, they are educational resources. But in general museums are more directly and explicitly educational (e.g. the Science Museum, the Natural History Museum, the Victoria and Albert Museum) than are films and plays. Films, in particular, are largely commercial and superficial forms of entertainment that it would be very hard to justify as educational. Television is no substitute: first,

who cannot afford to go to cinemas, theatres or museums can receive similar resources (plays, films, documentaries) on television.

[3]   Public money is allocated for essential educational resources – schooling up to the age of 18 for those who want it, and up to the age of 16 otherwise, and to provide loans on favourable terms for students to finance their higher education. Museums, while certainly being educational, are not a core, essential part of education, and so should not be funded publicly. If the government cannot even afford to allocate money to pay for university tuition fees, it certainly cannot afford to run museums, which are something of a luxury in comparison with higher education.

Possible motion:

This House would pay to go to a museum.

Related topics:

National Lottery (Abolition of)
Arts Funding by the State (Abolition of)
High Art v. Low Art

those people who cannot afford even reduced rates to enter museums will not be able to afford a television either – again, the poorest are those who are discriminated against; and second, seeing a documentary on television is a less participatory, active experience. Art in particular must be seen first-hand to be appreciated. These are invaluable cultural experiences, more important than mere entertainment, and they should be funded by the state.

[3]   As stated above, museums are educational resources that will appeal as much to those who have not had a university education and do not have a bookish intellectual mind as to those who do. They are important resources for continuing education of adults as well as for children. The state should be committed to funding museums *as well as* school and university education – it should not confine itself to conventional modes of education only. The fact that the state is failing to provide enough funding for universities is not an argument for its cutting back funding for other educational establishments such as museums *as well*.

Nursery Education, Free Provision of by the State

Pros

[1]   Developmental psychology has demonstrated how crucial the early education of children is for their later progress. In other words, science has shown that nursery education should be a priority for any government. Many more doors are closed in the long term

Cons

[1]   Up to the age of 4 or 5 it is right and proper that children be educated in the home. Parents (mothers in particular) are biologically adapted to be the best carers for and educators of their children. Development during this period is important but can best be fostered by

by a lack of education and stimulation at an early age than by the lack of free degree-level education. Specially trained nursery school teachers are needed to help fully to realise the development potential of all pre-school children, since most parents are not fully equipped or trained to do this entirely by themselves.

[2]   If free nursery education is not provided by the state then only the rich will continue to provide it for their children. This is particularly pernicious as it means that social and economic inequalities are being ingrained in the next generation right from the first few years of their lives. Those whose parents could not afford nursery education will be at an intellectual and educational disadvantage from the outset. Free nursery education is a crucial way for a government to fight against the perpetuation of elitism and inequality. We should not be totally fatalistic about inequality – free nursery education will do *something* to redress the balance even though it will not, of course, wipe out economic differences.

[3]   Nursery schools provide crucial social training for young children as well as preparation for academic work and school. Without free nursery education, more and more children will grow up socially underdeveloped – a real worry in our modern society where the idea of community has almost completely broken down. Socially undeveloped children can grow into anti-social and even criminal adolescents.

[4]   Nursery schools also fulfil a pastoral, social-work role. Teachers can be on the

parental attention and stimulation. Given that parents can fulfil this role, nursery education need not be seen as an essential part of an always financially stretched public sector education system. Public education spending can properly be concentrated on the school years when specialist teachers are required, rather than being stretched and depleted to cover, in addition, nursery education, university education and museums.

[2]   It is, sadly, already the case that children of the rich will already receive a better pre-school education, with or without nursery schools. It is the rich who can afford books, educational toys and technologies for their children, and who are often better educated themselves. With or without free nursery school education, socio-economic inequalities will be active in children's lives right from the moment they are born.

[3]   Again it is the home environment that is most important in the social development of children. Their most important relationships are with parents, siblings and the children of neighbours and friends. Whether or not a child is born into a well-adjusted family and pleasant community will be the deciding factor in its social development. It is important that parents take responsibility for the moral and social education of their child and do not use the absence of state-funded nursery education as an excuse for the anti-social traits of their children. Free nursery education would provide another way by which parents could abdicate responsibility for their children's development.

lookout for disturbed or abused children. It will be harder for parents to hide the neglect or abuse of their child if nursery school is compulsory and the child is in regular contact with teachers from an earlier age. Hence, as well as enhancing equality of educational opportunity, socio-economic equality and social adaptation, free nursery education is a weapon against child abuse.

[4]   It is not clear that providing free nursery education for all is the most efficient way to deal with child abuse. The money would be better spent if it were targeted at child abuse, in particular via charities and social workers. This would be cheaper and more effective than having free nursery education for all.

Possible motions:

This House believes that nursery education is a right, not a privilege.

This House believes that the child is father of the man.

Related topics:

Welfare State

Tuition Fees for University Students

Oxbridge, Abolition of

Oxford and Cambridge universities currently receive extra funding from the state in order to continue their costly systems of education. The distinctive elements of Oxbridge education are the collegiate system (everyone belongs to a particular college within the university and every student has a director of studies who oversees his or her work) and the one-on-one (or one-on-two or -three) 'supervision' or 'tutorial' method of teaching. Both of these aspects mean that an Oxbridge education costs more per student. Also, Oxbridge students, unlike students from any other university, are automatically awarded an MA (Master of Arts) degree four years after completing their BA (Bachelor of Arts). The Proposition should not argue for abolition of Oxbridge in the sense of destroying the buildings and closing the universities, but rather that their unique elements and privileges be removed, bringing them into line with other universities.

Pros

[1]   The fact that more resources per student are put into Oxford and Cambridge by the state means that the elitism of those establishments is com-

Cons

[1]   There are only a minority of students who could cope with and benefit from the more demanding and rigorous mode of teaching offered at Oxford and

pounded. The message propagated by this system is that those with inborn academic ability are worthier of the nation's investment than those born with lesser abilities. In fact, the opposite is true. Those fortunate enough to be born, by chance, with intellectual ability and/or well-educated parents who encourage them to get into Oxbridge are those least in need of the extra educational resources the state can provide. The extra money should be used to improve facilities and staff–student ratios in all other universities.

[2]   It is, as mentioned above, largely a matter of chance – the biology and sociology one is born into – who gets in to Oxford and Cambridge. It is not right that the superior resources provided at Oxbridge should compound such chance advantages. In the interest of equality of opportunity, all should have access to an equally good higher education. That means equalising the university system and removing the Oxbridge privileges.

[3]   The collegiate system is particularly iniquitous since it duplicates resources. Every college has its own library, chapel, bar and tutorial staff, even though the number of students per college is only a few hundred. These are wasteful excesses that should be curtailed.

[4]   It is a myth that Oxbridge students are hard–working academics who pay for their privileges with effort and self-sacrifice. Anyone who has been through Oxbridge or visited students there will know that the students are as alcoholic, indolent and hedonistic as those just about anywhere else. They certainly do not deserve an MA for their three years

Cambridge. This method of teaching is indeed more expensive, but it turns out excellent students with an excellent education. Forcing Oxbridge to give up the collegiate and tutorial systems would be to demand a 'lowest common denominator' higher education system in which excellence is not encouraged and all are treated as identical – spiting the intellectually gifted in an act of inverted snobbery. As for re-directing the extra resources, the amounts of money involved are a minute fraction of national higher education spending (we are, after all, talking about only *two* universities). As with private schools, the resources that allow excellence in a few centres, if spread out across *all* schools or universities, would be reduced to trivial and ineffectual amounts.

[2]   It is foolish to assert that everyone has a right to an equal higher education. Higher education, unlike more fundamental schooling, is a privilege, not a right. It is a privilege, or opportunity, that is open only to those with academic ability. And within the set of those who have academic ability, some have more than others. Liberal educationalists would ignore these basic facts. The last two governments in Britain have both fallen into the trap of advocating higher education for all (or as many as possible) regardless of the fact that this stretches resources, lowers standards, and attracts half-hearted students. Employers exacerbate the situation by demanding degrees even while acknowledging the fact that graduates are less and less well trained (because such huge numbers of students are being pumped into higher education courses). The lobby to abolish the

any more than students from other universities.

Possible motions:
This House would abolish Oxbridge.
This House would remove the privileges of Oxbridge students.

Related topics:
Marxism
Graduate Tax
Private Schools
Tuition Fees for University Students

Oxbridge method of teaching is part of this unthinking liberal drive to make everyone a graduate at the same level, regardless of academic ability.

[3]   The collegiate system is a successful and historical system, and it would be criminal to abolish it. Each college has its own strengths and traditions and caters to different sorts of students. It is true that the colleges are rich in resources (staff, libraries, etc.) – that is one of the great strengths of the Oxbridge system, one of the factors that make Oxford and Cambridge centres of academic excellence of which we should be proud.

[4]   However hedonistic some Oxbridge students may be, it is still an acknowledged and well-documented fact that Oxbridge students put in many more hours per week than students at other universities and are expected to work to a much higher level. Oxbridge arts and humanities students are required to produce up to fifteen essays per term on top of attending lectures (as opposed to three or four essays per term in other universities).

Private Schools

Pros

[1]   Freedom of choice is a fundamental principle of our democratic, capitalist society. If parents can afford to send their child to a private school, and wish to do so, why should any restrictions be put on that choice? We are, after all, allowed to buy the best car or the best stereo equipment if we have the money.

Cons

[1]   In a moral society, freedom of choice is right because it is available to everyone. If a choice is available only to the few who can afford it, then it upholds the classist, elitist society we are struggling to overthrow. Education is necessary for everyone and should be freely available – it is far more important than a car

[2]   A good education costs money. It is the government's responsibility to provide proper funding for state sector schools which are showing gradual signs of improvement. In the meantime, however, there is no doubt that private schools, with better funding raised from tuition fees, consistently achieve better academic results for their pupils – far better than any school could do if private schools were abolished. Until 1997 these schools offered places to those who could not afford the fees through the Assisted Places scheme; since the abolition of the scheme by the Labour government, schools are raising their own funding to award scholarships to the needy. Manchester Grammar School, for example, is setting up bursaries to fund places for any student who passes its entrance exam.

[3]   Many private schools offer facilities that are considered extremely worthwhile and are not found in most state schools. Many are still predominantly boarding schools, providing a secure community feeling which builds confidence in their students. Extra-curricular activities are strongly encouraged to complete a well-rounded and enjoyable education, instructing pupils in many skills useful for adult life. Several public schools exist in old manor houses in the countryside, where pupils have wider opportunities for sports and the pursuits of country life. A large proportion are single-sex with all of the benefits such a system brings.

[4]   The national curriculum has resulted in two damaging side-effects for the student. First, teachers become enslaved to the curriculum and lose their

or stereo and any comparison between them is fatuous.

[2]   The wealth of private schools, no matter how good an education they provide, causes more problems than it solves. As long as these institutions exist they will attract the best teachers, eager for high salaries, and the best resources. This means that schools in the state sector, which cater to the vast majority of students, receive disproportionately poor resources. Only when private schools are abolished will it be possible for staff and facilities to be distributed equitably.

[3]   Most of these facilities are not as welcome in a modern world. Boarding schools offer sheltered existences where outdated traditions and prejudice flourish, leaving their alumni entirely inadequately prepared for adulthood. 'Country pursuits' are an affectation of the snobbish elite, not the intelligent – most of the best modern private schools are day-schools, in cities (Manchester Grammar, St Paul's, King Edward's in Birmingham, etc.). Co-educational schools provide a better education for all sorts of reasons. Extra-curricular activities should be encouraged in the state sector; where they do not exist, it is through lack of resources taken by the private schools.

[4]   The whole point of a national curriculum and public examinations is that we can ensure that all students are given equal opportunity of education; a breakaway league of private schools would worsen the 'old school network' of academic elitism that already exists. Pupils should be judged by how successfully

freedom for imaginative, unorthodox teaching techniques suited to their particular pupils. Second, it is agreed that the standards required to pass public examinations have fallen greatly over the past few decades – which is why the grade 'A★' had to be introduced for GCSE examinations since the vast number of students attaining 'As' rendered the latter grade almost meaningless. Teachers at private schools have far more leeway in how and what to teach; and several leading private schools have discussed breaking away from the national curriculum to set their own, more difficult exams, which would challenge their brightest students more effectively.

they passed the exams, not by which exams they were privileged to take.

Possible motions:

This House would pay for its education.

This House believes that private schools are not in the public interest.

Related topics:

Capitalism v. Socialism

Marxism

Privatisation

Oxbridge (Abolition of)

Religious Teaching in Schools

Pros

[1]   Religion has been so important to history – and is so important to a vast number of people alive today, in the UK and elsewhere – that it clearly merits its place as an academic subject alongside History and English. In fact the increasing secularisation and scientific progress of the world make it doubly important that the spiritual side of humanity is not ignored.

[2]   Religious teaching can cover many faiths and denominations, outside specifically denominational schools (e.g. Roman Catholic), so it is not discriminatory against minorities. Much of it is analysis of the histories and beliefs of different religions rather than instruction in any one set of doctrines.

Cons

[1]   A large number of people also happen to regard religious belief as unimportant or wrong. Religious history, where relevant, can be taught as part of a History syllabus, but religious and spiritual discussion should be entirely optional, the choice of the student or the student's family, and conducted outside school. Too many people regard it as irrelevant to have it imposed on everyone. Compulsory morning prayers, the norm in the past, have been abandoned in many schools for this reason.

[2]   Even if religious teaching covers all faiths, it is discriminatory to the non-religious. Usually, however, it is focused largely on a small number of faiths or even the one relevant to the majority of

[3] Religious teaching is the only framework for students to discuss morals and morality. That they should form a code of morals is clearly a useful benefit to responsible adulthood. In the UK and other Western democracies, the entire legal system is founded on the basis of Christian morality, so whether or not the theology is accepted, the morality of that religion is still considered 'right' in those countries. All faiths aim to improve society and to alleviate injustice.

[4] The United Kingdom is a Christian country with an official church – the Church of England – and it is the duty of its government and society to address the falling numbers of church-goers. Religious instruction is one way to do this.

its students; this is clearly unfair on the minority who may have another faith.

[3] Just because the law is based on religious morals does not mean that it needs to be studied in that context. Atheists can have a moral code. Morals should be discussed in school, as should the law, but in a modern setting dealing with citizenship.

[4] The United Kingdom contains an increasing number of British subjects of other faiths who are being discriminated against. The Church of England should be disestablished and all religions should be accorded equal treatment – which is impossible inside a weekly religious education lesson.

Possible motion:

This House believes that religion has no place in our schools.

Related topics:

Churches in Politics
Disestablishment of the Church of England
Islam (Fear of)
God (Existence of)

School Sport, Compulsory

Pros

[1] A school education should involve much more than the simple acquisiton of facts. All sorts of skills needed in adult life should be developed. Sport provides many of these: the value of keeping fit, teamwork and discipline in particular.

Cons

[1] There are far too many 'life skills' for all of them to be satisfactorily taught in school. An alternative to sport in many schools is involvement in charity work, where students visit local residents with special needs – surely these aspects

[2]   Many children are unwilling to play sports simply because they have not been encouraged towards physical pursuits in the past: toddlers who are left to play or read in their bedrooms by their parents instead of being sent to play outside with friends. These children, when older, may choose to avoid sports if given the chance. In fact, if forced to take part, they may well discover a surprising enthusiasm and talent for certain sports. Many notable sportsmen and women started their careers this way.

[3]   Exercise is necessary to keep the body and mind healthy. While children are naturally more fit and energetic than adults, they need exercise to let off steam and to sleep properly; it is also advisable that they are prepared for a habit of regular exercise when reaching adulthood. It has been shown that academic work is generally better when coupled with exercise.

[4]   Most aspects of school life are compulsory and the enforced teaching of anything is not usually regarded as controversial. Students accept sport as part of the curriculum just as they accept mandatory subjects.

[5]   Most sports also entail social programmes and those who have chosen not to play sports miss out on these; they frequently feel excluded from events and social circles they would actually like to take part in.

of good citizenship should also be taught. When something is enforced it tends to engender resentment which undoes the benefits it may bring when voluntarily chosen. Sport should therefore be optional, although encouraged.

[2]   Students who start school sports as inexperienced, reluctant participants and then go on to shine are very few in number. Most of the resources – especially the attention of games teachers – are devoted to children who are already very sporty. Beginners are therefore ignored and lose enthusiasm.

[3]   The fitness vogue of recent years has meant that adults are certainly aware of the value of exercise whether they choose to do it or not. They are more likely to continue sports they enjoy and have chosen to play. If children are overenergetic, they will run around anyway.

[4]   Most aspects of school are compulsory only for younger ages; teenagers develop discriminatory abilities that give them clear likes and dislikes. Curricula recognise this and allow students to choose between optional subjects. Those that are enforced are frequently resented.

[5]   The competition of sport engenders an inevitable elitism and clubbiness amongst the best participants; poor sportsplayers who take part are ridiculed far more than those who do not play them in the first place.

Possible motion:

This House would make school sport voluntary.

Related topics:

Contact Sports (Abolition of)
Legislation vs. Individual Freedom
School Uniform

School Uniform

Pros

[1]   A school should encourage tidiness and discipline in its pupils. A uniform aids this whereas freedom of dress tends to make pupils too eager to express their individuality, wearing extremely messy or flashy clothes and becoming obsessed with clothes and appearance. There is also a widely accepted connection between smart dress and good behaviour.

[2]   School-teachers must manage a large number of pupils in a variety of situations. Uniforms inevitably make that task much easier when the pupils are out in public, on school trips. It is an administrative nightmare trying to monitor a group dressed casually.

[3]   Uniforms prepare students for the smartness demanded in office life.

[4]   Uniforms reduce cost for parents on their children's clothing, as they do not have to replace wardrobes every few months to follow the latest fashion trends.

Cons

[1]   Many schools do not have uniforms while still demanding certain standards of dress, such as forbidding jeans, or requiring long skirts but allowing a choice of colour. There is no reason why pupils not wearing uniform cannot still be smart. When pupils reach a certain age, they are old enough to behave responsibly while still making their own decisions. Why should they not be able to choose how to dress?

[2]   Unfortunately, uniforms also help the pupils to stand out to other people as well; fights are frequently picked between pupils from different schools who recognise each other's uniforms. Sometimes anonymity is preferable!

[3]   A relatively small percentage of jobs require suits to be worn. Why should pupils planning to be doctors not wear white coats, or future computer programmers not wear T-shirts and jeans?

[4]   Uniforms are very expensive and have no value or chance of use outside school.

Possible motions:
This House believes school uniforms are a good idea.
This House would rather go mufti.

Related topics:
School Sport (Compulsory)
Child Curfews

School-leaving Age, Lowering of

Pros

[1]   After a certain period of education, most students have attained the basic skills required by everyone in life: reading, writing, simple mathematics, and a general knowledge of language, history, science and technology. Education beyond this point starts to add specific knowledge which will be relevant to some people in life but not to many others; many of us, for example, will never need an understanding of the chemical equations we study so hard as teenagers. Second, education is simply not interesting to a large number of pupils. Surely, therefore, they should be allowed to leave school as soon as they have acquired the basic skills and have the desire and maturity to move on to paid employment – say at 15. Students who want to study further are, of course, allowed to.

[2]   Society simply does not allow for a fully educated population. For every computer scientist or industrial engineer who creates a machine, there must also be an unskilled or semi-skilled worker to operate it. Educating every person to a high level leads to over-competition for the skilled jobs and a lack of people willing to take jobs as workers. It is therefore in society's best interests that a section of the population receives only basic education. Many companies offer training courses which give everyone an opportunity to improve their skills at a later date if they so desire.

Cons

[1]   A hallmark of our advanced society is that maturity now does not begin until much later in life than when children were put to work at a very young age. It is a good thing that employment does not start until 16, and that instead we have the time and opportunity to acquire extra knowledge and skills. Options in school curricula cater for pupils' various interests, and many of them only begin to enjoy education once this is the case – and then go on to higher education.

[2]   In fact, technological advances are greatly limiting the number of unskilled workers needed. Many such workers find themselves redundant, replaced by robots, and without the skills to get a job in the new industries of information technology and computer science. It would be far better to give everyone as much training in technology as possible, at school.

[3]   Technology is an increasingly important part of school and university study; and in fact, apart from pure programming jobs, many employers will demand evidence of qualification before hiring. A-levels and degrees in computer science and similar fields are an extremely useful boost to employment prospects.

[4]   Educational resources are always stretched, and are usually a priority of any government. The answer is not to reduce the number of people taking up education – numbers that are consistently rising judging by university attendance

[3]   Technological development is usually spurred by the younger generations, the computer 'whizz kids'. Young people should begin to develop their technical and industrial skills as soon as they are able, to improve their prospects of employment in this technological age. This is better and more easily done in the workplace than in school.

[4]   School resources are stretched as it is, and became massively more so when the school-leaving age was raised to 16 in the first place. To lower it would free up valuable funding and staff for those who need and want further schooling.

– but to increase the resources, either by raising funding through general taxation or, as the Labour government did in the late 1990s, by asking the educated to share in the burden and contribute towards their education. Hence university tuition fees were introduced.

Possible motion:
This House would be allowed to leave school at 14.

Related topics:
Eighteen-year-old MPs
Voting Age (Reduction of)

Sex Education

Pros

[1]   Many social problems associated with sex – in particular sexually transmitted diseases (STDs) and unwanted pregnancies – are due to ignorance about safe sex. In this age when AIDS poses such a medical threat and only individual responsibility with condoms can prevent it, a full discussion is essential. Sex education must form a significant part of the curriculum.

[2]   There is also a need to understand sex and its role in society, whether in a stable relationship or outside it: to ensure it is treated responsibly and with respect. Too much distress is caused by sexual encounters where the two partners have different expectations. The media glamorise meaningless sex and yet are appalled by the rise in casual sex and date rape

Cons

[1]   Yes, awareness of the need for safe sex is important but teachers are not the right people to raise it. Clearly the current strategy for sex education is not working if so many pupils are still careless. Safe sex (i.e. the use of condoms) is seen as unfashionable, and its espousal by teachers will only confirm that view. It is better to promote it through style magazines, television programmes and other sources that will emphasise how acceptable it is.

[2]   Again, school is not an arena in which teenagers take such things seriously. Any discussion of sex in a classroom is likely to lead to ridicule, especially in co-educational classes. Respect for sex can only be encouraged on a one-to-one basis, probably in the family by older

which surely they play a part in causing. Again, classroom discussion can engender a more responsible attitude among students.

siblings or parents. To try to teach it in school can only be detrimental.

Possible motion:
This House would keep the bedroom out of the classroom.

Related topics:
Censorship by the State
Population Control
Co-education
Contraception for Under-age Girls

Sport, Commercialisation of

Pros

[1]   The commercialisation of sport directly harms the sports themselves. The team loyalties that were once a major factor in many sports have been replaced by modern transfers, by which sportsmen and women move from one team to another in pursuit of a higher salary. Often they abuse the system by not competing for significant stretches of time owing to 'injuries,' confident in the knowledge that they are nevertheless being paid seven-figure sums. Some absurd events are staged for purely commercial purposes, especially in boxing, where aged fighters are brought out of retirement and mismatched against younger opponents. Other sports are under pressure to alter their rules to make them more 'watchable'. These monetary considerations undermine the ethos of sport.

[2]   The sheer cost of high-profile

Cons

[1]   Far from harming sports, commercialisation aids them. With new money come better facilities and better training for sportsmen and women, allowing them to perform at their very best and fulfil their potential. Better competitors make for better events; therefore increasing investment in sport can only be a good thing for the sports themselves. Although there are occasional abuses, the spirit of sport – and the desire to win on the field as well as in the bank-balance – is as vibrant as ever. Indeed, major sports bodies such as the Football Association have chosen to resist reforms that would damage the sport in pursuit of greater profits.

[2]   Less high-profile sports have never been highly funded. It may be true that increased investment in popular sport has not been accompanied by more direct investment throughout the sporting

sports is squeezing out less well-known ones. The potential commercial returns from sponsoring the likes of the Premier Division, or Rugby Super League, and the massive amount of money involved, starve other sporting activities of investment. Those that remain amateur – in which it is truly the talent of the competitor rather than the price of his or her training that is being tested – are particularly hard hit.

[3]   Commercialised sport is also bad for the viewer. As covering major events has become more expensive, rights to do so have been bought by subscription-only and pay-per-view channels; public broadcasting can compete only with the aid of state intervention, which is heavily opposed by sporting bodies greedy for more cash, leaving fans out of pocket. Coverage is in danger of becoming ever more revenue-led – football in particular is under pressure to become a game of four quarters to allow more advertising. As sports clubs become money-making machines, their ability to hire the best players and the best coaches makes team sport increasingly predictable, as with the NBA in America.

[4]   Sportsmen and women simply do not deserve the inflated salaries they earn. For basketball players such as Michael Jordan to earn some $80m in a year is obscene when teachers and nurses are paid barely enough to make a living.

[5]   Modern sport sets a bad example. Commercial interest in the investment made in major sporting figures ensures that even the most horrific behaviour goes excused. Mike Tyson is a case in

world, yet even amateurs engaged in minority pursuits have gained indirectly from better training facilities, equipment and stadia. That the so-called 'amateur ideal' is disappearing from high-profile sport is simply the dispelling of a hypocritical illusion – for many years, those at the top have enjoyed highly paid yet low-commitment jobs provided for them by sporting clubs.

[3]   The extra money in sport is in fact good for the sports fan. Obviously, the more highly trained athletes result in a more exciting spectacle. Also, major sporting fixtures have become national events. For those dedicated enough to attend in person, expensive new stadia provide room for more fans in more comfort and safety than ever before; for others, well thought-out comprehensive coverage is provided on television and radio. Even though rights are increasingly bought up by satellite and cable channels, deregulation of the broadcasting market means that ever more people have access to these. Finally, events of national significance – for example the Wimbledon finals, the Cup final, the Olympic Games – have, since 1990, been protected by parliament from becoming 'pay-per-view'.

[4]   Modern sportsmen and women deserve the money they are paid. Their activities entertain millions worldwide, yet their professional lives are often short. Recognition should be given to those who have given their all in pursuit of a sporting ideal, and who are often heroes to many members of the public.

[5]   Although it may be a cliché, sport

point: in the two years after being released from prison for rape, he made some $142m. Despite biting off an opponent's ear on live television, his ability to bring in revenue suggests that vested interests will not allow his career to end. Moreover, the pursuit of sports-star salaries tempts many children to abandon their education, despite the fact that only a handful can succeed. These are not the role models our society needs.

does provide a route out of the ghetto for many poor children. Sportsmen and women can become powerful symbols for the victory of talent over background, and of racial and social integration. Many people bemoan the commercialisation of American sports, yet the fact that seven of the top ten earners in sport in the US are black (1998) provides a set of role models for disadvantaged children to look up to. Although some do behave inexcusably, the vast majority are successful, respectable and even admirable people. Compared with the alternatives, they are some of the finest role models we can have.

Possible motions:

This House believes that there is too much money in sport.

This House applauds the Olympic ideal.

Related topics:

Capitalism v. Socialism

Broadcasting (Ending Public Control of)

Contact Sports (Abolition of)

School Sport (Compulsory)

Tuition Fees for University Students

John Major's government froze university student maintenance grants (for accommodation, food, living expenses) and partially replaced them with 'student loans' to supplement the grant. These loans were to be repaid after graduation when the ex-student's income reached a certain level. Tony Blair's government scrapped the maintenance grant completely and replaced it with a loan for the whole amount required for maintenance over three years. In addition they have introduced tuition fees for university students – initially a contribution of £1,000 a year for each student. Students have never before had to make contributions to their university tuition costs in Britain. The system is much the same as with maintenance loans. Those who cannot afford the tuition fees can pay them after graduation when their income reaches a certain level.

Pros

[1] There is always only a finite amount of money available that can be

Cons

[1] As developed countries become more technologically advanced and

spent on education by the government. It is right that the focus should be on schooling for children from the ages to 5 to 16 – this is the core period of education to which everybody is entitled. Higher education is not part of the core education which the state must provide free of charge for all. University education, like nursery education, is a bonus, a privilege rather than a right. It is therefore acceptable to raise money for higher education by charging fees.

[2]   It is right to follow the principle that the consumer pays. It is the students themselves who benefit most directly from their university education – earning as much as 50 per cent more, on average, than a non-graduate in later life. It is therefore they themselves who should pay for their university fees.

[3]   The important consideration is equality of access and opportunity – a system that discriminated against the poor would be elitist and unacceptable. Such equality is guaranteed by the fact that those who cannot afford fees will not have to pay them until they are earning enough to pay them back. This system has worked well for maintenance loans, without discouraging poorer students from applying, and should work well for tuition fees too.

[4]   In fact, in the first two years of this system, there has been an *increase*, not a decrease, in the number of young people applying to universities. Charging tuition fees is not a disincentive when the above allowances are made.

[5]   In any case, it would not necessarily

richer, there is a need for a fuller education for young people, and there are the resources to pay for it. If there was the political will, university education could still be free – even if that might involve raising taxes by 1 per cent or 2 per cent. We should campaign for free university education for all as part of the education the state provides to each citizen as a right.

[2]   This is a falsely individualistic argument. Individuals do not exist in a vacuum – we are all part of one organic society. Just as students are dependent on the work of others (e.g. parents, teachers, cleaners) for their educational opportunities, so society is dependent on well-educated graduates (e.g. academics, scientists, economists, bankers, doctors) to prosper and flourish. Society at large benefits from the skills and wealth generation of graduates and so society at large (i.e. the state) should pay. There should be no tuition fees for university students.

[3]   Charging tuition fees will discriminate against the poor and perpetuate elitism in the university system. Those from poorer backgrounds will be particularly unwilling to take on further debt in order to gain a university education, so those young people who happen to have rich parents will, on average, get a better education. We do not (and cannot) know how many people were deterred from going to university by the introduction of student loans in place of maintenance grants. It is mere assertion to say that because numbers did not drop no poorer students were deterred. If grants had not been scrapped, numbers of students from

be a bad thing if fewer people applied to university. Not everyone is suited to an academic degree, and it is questionable whether so many people (currently around 35 per cent) should be encouraged to go to university. Politicians often boast of the increasing numbers of people going to university but this, in fact, means that standards drop, resources are stretched to breaking point and many young people find themselves spending three more years studying for little long-term gain when they could have been working. Introducing tuition fees will teach people to value a university education as a privilege rather than a right – if this means a drop in numbers and a raising of standards, that is no bad thing. It is false to say that universities currently decide who can get in – they are forced by the way in which the government finances them to admit as many students as possible if they want to survive – they are funded *per student*.

poor backgrounds might have risen much more rapidly.

[4]   If tuition fees had not been introduced, even more young people might have continued to apply to university. Also, the figures so far are only for a couple of years. In the long term we will almost certainly see a levelling off of university applications because of this policy, so in the long run our young people will be less well educated and the nation will suffer.

[5]   It is patronising and elitist to say that some people who go to university are not really up to it. It is up to the students and the universities to decide whether these people have the ability to do a degree. Employers continue to prefer graduates over non-graduates and so in the interest of equality, free university education should be available for all. University education is a right, not a privilege.

Possible motions:
This House would charge university tuition fees.
This House believes that the consumer should pay.
This House believes in a 'graduate tax'.

Related topics:
Capitalism v. Socialism
Ideology v. Pragmatism
Privatisation
Welfare State
Graduate Tax
Oxbridge (Abolition of)
Private Schools

SECTION G

Law and Crime

Capital Punishment

Around 90 countries retain the death penalty (including China, Islamic countries, and 37 states of the US). Like the debates on Prison v. Rehabilitation, Mandatory Prison Sentences and Zero Tolerance, this debate calls into question what the purpose of punishment should be – is it purely for retribution or should there be an element of rehabilitation of the offender too?

Pros

[1] In any country – democracy or dictatorship – one of the roles of the state is to punish criminals. In the case of serial murderers, terrorists, 'cop killers', etc., they should be punished by death. Our human rights are given to us as part of a contract – which says that we can do anything we want as long as it does not hurt anyone else – and so if we take away the life of another person, then surely we forfeit the right to our own life.

[2] Use of the death penalty deters criminals from murdering. Numerous studies in the US (e.g. Utah from 1976 to 1988) showed a noticeable drop in murder rates in the months directly following any execution. One study concluded that each execution prevents, on average, eighteen further murders. Since capital punishment was abolished in the UK in 1965 (for all crimes except treason) the murder rate has doubled.

[3] Executing murderers prevents them from killing again. In Britain over seventy-five murders have been committed by released killers since the abolition of capital punishment. Serial killers – those who are so 'evil' or hardened as to be incapable of reform — can be removed permanently from society.

Cons

[1] If killing is a crime and immoral in the eyes of society, then for the state to kill its citizens is equally barbaric. Two wrongs do not make a right, and it is never right to put someone to death no matter what the crime. The death penalty is a 'cruel and unusual punishment', especially in view of the psychological torture inflicted on those on Death Row who know that they are going to be executed but do not know when.

[2] If the death penalty is such a deterrent, then why is the murder rate so high in the US where it is employed in many states? There has been virtually no change in the overall rate since 1976 when the death penalty was reinstated, despite an enormous increase in the number of executions. Also, death penalty states often have a higher murder rate than their neighbouring non-death penalty states. A distinction also needs to be made between local short-term deterrents (immediately after executions in particular places) and long-term deterrents that have an effect on national crime rates, for which there is less evidence.

[3] Execution may remove some killers from society, but in return it brutalises

[4]   The other possibility of removing killers from society – life imprisonment without parole – imposes an immense financial burden on the public purse. A study by TIME magazine estimated the cost of keeping a prisoner for fifty years in the US at about $4 million, more than twice the cost of a death penalty case. If the prisoner has to be kept in a maximum security cell, this figure would be over $2 million more.

[5]   The death penalty is only given when the facts are certain and the jury has no doubt whatsoever, and only carried out when every right to appeal has been exhausted. There have admittedly been some cases of wrongful conviction leading to execution in the UK (notably Timothy Evans and, probably, James Hanratty) but, although it may seem harsh, this is negligible when compared with the number of murders prevented by the death penalty. The discrimination between various degrees of homicide or manslaughter allows the jury plenty of opportunity for clemency, and insane murderers are never executed.

[6]   If there is no death penalty then there is no incentive for prisoners sentenced to life without parole not to commit crimes while in prison – to kill warders, other prisoners, or to try to escape and kill again. Nothing they can do can result in further punishment.

[7]   The death penalty is a harsh but fair punishment and an effective deterrent. That criminals fear the death penalty more than life without parole is shown by the fact that, when it comes to the punishment phase of their trials, 99.9 per

society and invests killing with state-sanctioned acceptability. Not only is capital punishment not a deterrent but it can even increase the murder rate; California's rate showed its biggest increases from 1952 to 1967 when executions occurred every two months on average.

[4]   We cannot kill prisoners because it is too expensive to imprison them, or we would start executing burglars to pay for tax cuts. More money must be found for prisons if the funding is currently insufficient; law and order should be a priority in any government's budget. It is also arguable whether life without parole is cheaper than death penalty cases, which can cost $1.5 million or more because of the lengthy and complex appeals procedure.

[5]   A single mistaken execution of an innocent person, among no matter how many thousands of cases, is utterly unjustifiable and is enough to destroy our trust in the death penalty and in any judicial system that uses it. Second, rehabilitation is part of the purpose of punishment, and who is to say that any guilty criminal cannot be reformed? Any prisoner must be given every chance to come to terms with the wrongdoing and perhaps be rehabilitated into society – a chance that execution denies.

[6]   There are several ways of dealing with misbehaving prisoners: revoking of privileges if their disorder is minor, and solitary confinement in a maximum security cell if they are violent. There will always be psychopaths who need to be confined in this way. Those who are not should not be sentenced to life without

cent of convicted defendants argue for life rather than the death penalty. The appropriate punishment for murder is execution, not life imprisonment.

Possible motions:

This House would bring back the rope.

This House supports the death penalty for murder.

This House believes that life without parole is too good for a murderer.

Related topics:

Ends v. Means

Legislation v. Individual Freedom

Bill of Rights

Mandatory Prison Sentences

Prison v. Rehabilitation

Zero Tolerance

parole – if they have the chance of parole, they have an incentive towards good behaviour.

[7]   Life imprisonment can be a worse punishment than execution, and therefore a more appropriate one and also a better deterrent. The prisoners who argue for life imprisonment have not begun to experience a lengthy stay in prison yet; many later argue to be allowed to die. If we want to punish killers, then execution is too lenient.

Child Curfews

Pros

[1]   There is a worrying increase in anti-social and criminal behaviour among young children. There have been extremely horrific cases of crimes perpetrated by children under the age of 13, such as the Jonesboro school massacre in Arkansas, US, and the Jamie Bulger killing in England. We need to take action to stem this tide of young offending. Children pick up anti-social and criminal behaviour and habits from older children with whom they associate. Much of this crime (car theft, drugs, vandalism, gang fights) takes place at night, and child curfews will give the police an additional weapon with which to fight young

Cons

[1]   The sort of children who would murder, or even those who would get involved in gangs, drugs and car theft, will not take the slightest bit of notice of a curfew. The sort of children who behave in these criminal and anti-social ways are well past taking notice of bedtimes. Youth crime is a radical and alarming problem that calls for a more radical solution. The age of criminal responsibility should be lowered to 8, and sentences for young offenders should be more severe, and imposed after a single 'final warning' rather than children receiving several 'cautions' before any punishment is dished out.

offending. We propose that children under the age of, say, 10 or 12 be not allowed out without their parent or guardian after 11pm. This measure would serve as a deterrent to some and simply function as an enforcement tool in more difficult cases.

[2]   Parents would also have a responsibility to enforce the curfew. Any policy to combat youth crime must include an important role for parents who must be made to take responsibility for their children. They, along with their child, will be liable to punishment if the curfew is broken. This will serve as an incentive to better and more responsible parenting.

[2]   Most young offenders learn violent behaviour, lack of respect for property, indiscipline and dishonesty from their parents. Others learn it from their peers, and the need to impress these peers and be included by them outweighs any worthy parental entreaties. In the first case the parent would not care whether a curfew was enforced and in the second case they would be powerless to see that it was. So introducing a curfew would be an empty and futile gesture.

Possible motions:
This House would impose a curfew on children under 10.
This House blames the parents.

Related topics:
Legislation v. Individual Freedom
School Sport (Compulsory)
School Uniform
School-leaving Age (Lowering of)
Zero Tolerance

Drugs, Legalisation of

In Britain, illegal drugs are classed as 'Class A' or 'Class B'. Class A, or 'hard', drugs include cocaine, crack, acid (LSD), ecstasy (E) and heroin. Class B, or 'soft', drugs include cannabis and amphetamines such as 'speed'. The most balanced debate on this subject is the legalisation of *soft* drugs, and the arguments below are designed for such a debate. It would be possible to take a more extreme line and argue for the legalisation of all drugs, hard as well as soft. The Proposition in that case would rely heavily on the defence of the individual's freedom to do whatever he likes to himself.

Pros

[1]   The role of legislation is to protect society from harm, but not to protect people from themselves. We do not

Cons

[1]   It is right that governments should legislate in a way that overrides personal freedom to protect people from *themselves*

legislate against fatty foods or lack of exercise, both of which have serious health implications. The individual's freedom is paramount unless serious harm is done by a particular act. Taking soft drugs does not harm anybody else and has only minimal negative effects on the person taking them – it is a 'victimless crime'. As such, it should not be a crime at all.

[2]   Individuals should be left to choose their own lifestyle and priorities. If that includes using drugs for pleasure and relaxation then that is a perfectly valid decision.

[3]   The law is currently inconsistent. Cannabis and speed have comparable physical and mental effects to those of alcohol and tobacco, which are legal drugs. If anything, alcohol and tobacco have more seriously damaging effects. Tobacco-related diseases kill millions each year, and alcohol is responsible for deaths on the road, civil disorder and domestic violence on a huge scale. Cannabis and speed make people 'spaced out' or hyperactive respectively for short periods in social situations and are relatively harmless. If alcohol and tobacco are legal then soft drugs should be too.

[4]   Speed and cannabis are widely used, not just by stereotypical 'drug users', but by a large minority of middle class and professional people. The current law makes criminals of many otherwise 'respectable' citizens. The government should listen to society.

[5]   Soft drugs are not physically addictive, and even if they were that would not be a reason for them to be illegal

as well as from each other. That is why bare-knuckle boxing is banned and seat-belts are compulsory in some countries (e.g. Britain). These are ways in which personal freedom is overridden by legislation designed to protect personal safety. Soft drugs *are* harmful: cannabis smoke (as well as the tobacco with which it is often mixed) is carcinogenic, and prolonged cannabis smoking has been shown to cause brain damage and significant loss of motivation and short-term memory. Amphetamines interfere with the nervous system in a potentially damaging way. Drug-takers also put others at risk by taking mind-altering substances that can lead to unpredictable and dangerous behaviour.

[2]   The government should provide moral leadership as well as legislating to protect the health of the individual and the safety of others. The drug-using lifestyle is a shallow, hedonistic, apathetic, inward-looking, uncreative form of escapism. Governments should legislate and speak out against drugs to discourage young people from this lifestyle and encourage them to engage in healthier and more creative pastimes.

[3]   The effects of soft drugs may be 'comparable' with those of alcohol and tobacco but there are important differences. Cannabis and speed are mind-altering in a way that alcohol and tobacco are not. In any case, the fact that harmful and dangerous substances (tobacco and alcohol) are already, regrettably, socially entrenched is not a good reason to allow two more such substances to become more widely used and socially acceptable.

– caffeine, alcohol and nicotine are physically addictive and still legal. And being psychologically addictive is even less of a reason to ban something. Many things, such as shopping, sex, jogging or gambling may be psychologically addictive, and many people are innately susceptible to psychological addiction. We cannot ban all things that a minority might come to depend upon – we should instead provide counselling for addicts.

[6]   Legalising soft drugs, and allowing them to be sold in licensed premises, perhaps like the 'coffee houses' in Amsterdam that sell cannabis, will separate them from the criminal underworld associated with drug dealing. The 'slippery slope' would then no longer exist. People could purchase soft drugs without having to come into contact with dealers who might cut their drugs with harder drugs or try to get them onto harder drugs in other ways. (In any case, only a tiny minority of cannabis users ever go on to use harder drugs.) Finally, the government could use the sale of soft drugs as a source of revenue through excise duty, as is already done with alcohol and tobacco.

Possible motions:
This House would legalise all drugs.
This House would legalise soft drugs.
This House believes in the right of the
   individual to choose which drugs to use.

Related topics:
Legislation v. Individual Freedom
Prohibition of Alcohol
Zero Tolerance
Smoking (Banning of)

[4]   Our aim is to minimise drug use, since it is a destructive, dangerous and anti-social activity. Legalising soft drugs will inevitably mean that there is an increase in drug use. Therefore we should not legalise soft drugs, even if an alarming number of people already use them.

[5]   It is hard to draw an exact line between physical and psychological addiction – they are two sides of the same coin. We should be concerned about any addictive substance. Recent research has demonstrated that cannabis is highly addictive – in the US in particular, many self-help groups for cannabis addicts have recently been formed, with rapidly growing membership. Whether we call that addiction 'psychological' or 'physical' is immaterial. While it would be impractical to ban many psychologically addictive things (like coffee or shopping), in the case of soft drugs they are already banned and there is no reason to reverse that situation.

[6]   Soft drugs are dangerous because they start people down the 'slippery slope' to using ever-harder drugs. The same dealer will try to push harder drugs onto his clients who use soft drugs, by cutting cannabis or speed with cocaine or heroin or offering free samples to get them hooked. Legalisation of soft drugs would, ironically, provide a whole new market for hard drug pushers, who would be able to undercut the prices of duty-inflated market goods.

Handguns, Ownership of

The ownership of handguns is still upheld as a basic right of the private individual in the United States. In the UK, the private ownership of handguns was banned in 1997, partly in response to the Dunblane tragedy of 1996, when Thomas Hamilton, armed with handguns, massacred a roomful of infant schoolchildren and their teacher in a small Scottish school.

Pros

[1]   Ownership of handguns must be allowed because the right to keep and bear arms is a basic human right. That is why it is incorporated as the second amendment to the US constitution (1791) as part of the 'Bill of Rights'. Banning handguns is a violation of this basic individual right.

[2]   In the modern world, with gun crime on the increase, especially in the United States, and increasingly in Europe, a handgun is an essential weapon of self-defence for the law-abiding citizen. However strong our distaste for violence, we must be practical and seek to protect life. Until the government and police succeed in cutting down the possession and use of firearms by criminals, it is unreasonable to expect citizens to remain defenceless. If handguns are banned, criminals will know that they can hold any law-abiding citizen to ransom in the street or in their own home by using a firearm without fear of effective self-defence. Handgun ownership must be allowed unless we want to give criminals the upper hand.

[3]   Tragedies involving the use of handguns by criminals and by psychopaths and other unbalanced individuals will,

Cons

[1]   Ownership of handguns is not a basic right. First, it is only in the American Bill of Rights, not in the UN Universal Declaration of Human Rights (1948) or the European Convention on Human Rights. Second, rights are not immutable and timeless but must be open to criticism and change over historical time. Even in the US where the right to bear arms has historically existed, it must be reconsidered in the light of the escalation of gun-related crime. Allowing ownership of handguns will inevitably increase the number of people who use and misuse firearms. Banning handguns will reduce the number of deaths from firearms-related incidents, accidents and crimes. For that reason the old 'right to bear arms' must be abolished.

[2]   Violence is always wrong, no matter what the circumstances. In cases of mugging or even racial oppression, non-violent resistance and protest is the only morally acceptable response. Self-defence is, of course, important, but handguns are not the answer. When an assailant or intruder is armed with a gun, pulling a gun oneself is merely dangerous and inflammatory, greatly increasing the chance that one or both parties will be injured or killed. Allowing the ownership

sadly, always occur. Such people will not be deterred by legislation any more than they are by reason, humanity or conscience. The incidence of such tragedies will not be affected by banning handguns.

Possible motions:

This House believes in the right to bear arms.

This House demands the right to own a handgun.

This House believes that banning handguns gives criminals the upper hand.

Related topics:

Legislation v. Individual Freedom

Armaments (Limitation of Conventional)

of handguns (rather than teaching unarmed forms of self-defence) will engender a mentality of vigilantism, encouraged further by rhetoric about 'criminals getting the upper hand'. It is the job of the police, not of private citizens, to be armed and capable of tackling armed criminals.

[3]   Tragedies such as the massacres at Hungerford in England, Dunblane in Scotland and Jonesboro in Arkansas, US, are the indirect result of the ownership of handguns. One of the young boys responsible for the shootings at the school in Jonesboro, in 1998, had been trained in using firearms by his family from a very early age. If that had not been allowed, he would not have even been able to use a gun and the tragedy would most likely not have occurred. Banning handguns will not eliminate such tragedies altogether, but will significantly reduce their incidence. There will simply be fewer guns in circulation and fewer people capable of using them.

Judges, Election of

Most judges in the US are currently elected (but not Supreme Court judges). In the UK no judge is elected.

Pros

[1]   Being a judge is a crucially important job – implementing fairly and firmly the laws of the land. The incumbent must be answerable to and removable by the people. The job also brings with it power, prestige and influence, and as with MPs or prime ministers the people should

Cons

[1]   Just because a post is important and influential does not mean its holders must be democratically elected. CEOs of international corporations, Secretaries General of the UN, university professors and Nobel prize-winners, are all powerful and influential people who are

have a say in who it is that gets the power and influence. Appointed judges gain power through unaccountable processes of networking and politicking and are not answerable to anybody.

[2]   It is idealistic and naive to believe that anyone is ever genuinely politically neutral. Every judge will have some political leaning or other and some particular biases. It is better that these political and juridical leanings be known and voted on than that they be concealed through the system of appointment.

[3]   If judges are appointed, then the government of the day will be able to appoint judges who are sympathetic with their legislative programme and policies. If judges are elected, on the other hand, they will often be figures who are critical of the government of the day, just as happens in mid-term local government elections, which almost always favour the opposition parties over the governing party.

[4]   It is right that the law should be open to indirect influence over time by public opinion, rather than being entrusted entirely to an often out-of-touch, elitist, establishment-appointed judiciary. Electing judges with known views on crime and punishment (e.g. for or against the death penalty, in favour of retribution or rehabilitation, tough or lenient on drugs and prostitution, etc.) means that the judicial process is democratised, and figures can be elected in order democratically to shape the way that law is interpreted, implemented and evolved.

selected not by national election but are appointed by well-informed peers in the relevant institutions. Similarly, judges should be appointed by fellow-experts in the legal profession on the grounds of their understanding of the law and ability to analyse a case expertly, fairly and lucidly. The general public cannot be expected to be able to discriminate between two candidates except on largely irrelevant matters of presentation and politics. Electing judges may be democratic but it is anti-meritocratic.

[2]   Judges should be apolitical figures. One of the great features of the British constitution is its independent judiciary which is answerable to parliament (the legislature) but is apolitical. Interpretation of the law is not a political matter and when sitting in court judges should not be seeking to fulfil the mandate of any one political lobby, just to apply the law fairly and neutrally.

[3]   Judges are appointed in Britain by the Lord Chancellor, on the advice of a panel of experts (judges) and laypersons, not by the government itself. The exceptions are 'Law Lords' who are nominally appointed by the prime minister, but are in fact selected on the advice of existing Law Lords, not on political grounds. It would, in any case, be just as objectionable to have judges selected because they were allied with an opposition party that was popular mid-term, as it would to have them appointed by the government on political criteria, if that were the case.

[4]   First, we should seek, in a civilised society, to minimise the rule of 'lynch law'. The   democratic   and   judicial

Possible motions:

This House believes that judges should be elected.

This House calls for a democratically answerable judiciary.

Related topics:

processes are set up specifically to remove important judicial decisions from emotive public pressure and prejudice. Elected judges will pander to public opinion (e.g. turning down appeals against death penalty sentences) seeking votes rather than justice. Second, public opinion already has enough influence on the judicial process. The Home Secretary (a politician) sets the 'tariff' of those given life sentences (at, say 20, 25 or 30 years or, occasionally – as in the case of the moors murderer, Myra Hindley – for life). The Home Secretary also makes the ultimate decision, on the advice of the parole board, about who is released on parole. Thus important judicial decisions are politicised and subject to lobbying by the public and the popular press. Home Secretaries will often try to be seen to be harsh to garner public political support. The Lord Chancellor is also a political figure, and legislation is introduced through the House of Commons, the chamber of elected representatives. This is sufficient democratic representation of public opinion.

Jury System, Reform of

Pros

[1] In the modern world, there is no longer any need for protection against unscrupulous or politically biased judges. Therefore we do not need a jury, which used to provide this safeguard.

[2] Jurors are unreliable lay people, uninformed about the law and with no training, and no proven skills of attentive-

Cons

[1] In Britain judges are appointed by the Lord Chancellor (himself a political appointment made by the prime minister of the day) and in the US judges are elected. In other words judges are already political figures and it is still appropriate to have a jury to guard against their potential prejudices. The jury system ensures that judicial decisions must be

ness, analysis or fairness. They, unlike legal experts, will be swayed by prejudice and preconception (e.g. judging defendants by their appearances). It is not in the interest of justice to have such people decide the fate of those accused of serious crimes whose futures, or even their lives, hang in the balance. Particularly in the case of fraud trials which last months or years and are full of complex legal technicalities, juries cannot be expected to follow the case or know how to reach a verdict. Juries should be replaced by panels of lawyers (as already happens with appeal court judges who always sit in panels) or magistrates, the latter being a compromise between the totally untutored lay person and the professional lawyer. Other alternatives, particularly for civil cases, include a panel of three judges, or a single judge assisted by two 'qualified lay judges' – for example, professional bankers in cases regarding banking fraud, or insurers in cases of insurance fraud. Industrial tribunals, for example, are decided by a panel composed of a lawyer and two lay people, one with experience representing employers and one with experience in the union movement, representing employees.

[3]   In effect, most jurors, especially if they have not understood or followed the case closely, will be swayed by the summing up of the judge. A panel of lawyers or magistrates would have their own understanding of the case to balance that of the judge. So replacing jurors with an expert panel will in fact provide a more efficient check on the influence a single judge can bring to bear on the outcome of a case.

seen to be reasonable to the lay person and are not the preserve of a legal elite.

[2]   The jury system forces lawyers and judges to make the law lucid and comprehensible. Without a jury, barristers and judges would have no obligation to make a comprehensible case, and the courtroom would become an alienating and incomprehensible preserve of legalistic jargon in which defendants were left not understanding the accusations made against them and the process by which they were acquitted or convicted. While they are, indeed, untrained in legal matters, jurors bring an open mind and common-sense judgement to bear that expert panels would lack. Expert panels would tend to become 'case-hardened' and cynical, disbelieving often-heard defences simply because they were frequently encountered, not judging them on their merits.

[3]   There is already the appeals process to deal with cases where judges have misdirected the jury. And expert panels would be inclined towards the opposite danger – trusting too much to their own ability at legal interpretation and tending, arrogantly, to ignore the judge's direction as inferior to their own analysis.

[4]   Expert panels might be less open to emotive appeals, but barristers would soon learn to manipulate them in different ways – perhaps artificially multiplying precedents and jargon to appeal to the panel's own inflated admiration for legalism over plain facts and emotions.

[4]   Expert panels are less likely than jurors to be swayed by the emotive rhetoric of barristers, and more likely to be able to weigh up objectively the true legal merits of a case.

Possible motions:
This House would reform the jury system.
This House would not trust a jury.

Related topics:
Judges (Election of)

Licensing Laws, Relaxation of

A government working party recommended in 1998 that Britain should adopt 24-hour licensing laws common in many European countries. It remains to be seen whether these proposals will become law and if so how successful they will be. Small experiments in relaxing restrictions temporarily have occurred with the Euro '96 football championships and the Millennium celebrations.

Pros

[1]   Britain's licensing laws, and in particular the opening times for public houses, are some of the most eccentric in the world. They are the result of legislation passed during the First World War to ensure the sobriety of munitions workers, part of the puritanical attitude of those in power regarding the dangers of drink among the working classes. As conditions and attitudes have changed, so the basis for these laws has disappeared.

[2]   A move towards more relaxed licensing laws is not an isolated change but part of a wider shift in British legislation. Other needless regulation – such as the restrictions placed upon Sunday trading – is gradually being removed to allow retailers and consumers a greater degree of choice; the same should apply to opening times.

[3]   Inflexible drinking hours can result

Cons

[1]   Even if the reasons that created the current laws are outdated, this is in itself no reason to replace them if they work. Especially with recent modifications to allow all-day drinking, the British laws are by no means harsh, and there is no great public demand for them to be changed.

[2]   The loosening of restrictions on Sunday trading has substantial support from retailers and consumers alike. The loosening of licensing laws has no such clear mandate. Licensees already work a full day, from the morning until past midnight; there is little pressure from them to extend opening times. With no limitations upon the right to drink at home at any hour, there is also little pressure from drinkers.

[3]   There is no evidence to suggest that more liberal licensing laws would

in dangerous drinking. Strict rules in parts of Australia, enforcing a 6pm closing time, caused substantial problems and had to be relaxed; similarly, the rush before last orders is familiar in Britain. Were time pressure to be removed, people would drink more slowly. This is healthier, and also lowers consumption – while the combined effect of several rapid drinks is felt only some time later, slow drinkers have time to absorb the alcohol from each drink into their bloodstream before starting the next, and are more likely to know when to stop.

[4]   Current opening times can lead to violence as drinkers are ejected onto the streets at closing time; flexible closing times would circumvent this problem. The Scottish experience of wider opening times and curfews has been a success in this respect, as well as reducing levels of alcoholism.

[5]   British cities often have nightlife restricted to the young. In contrast, the centres of European cities are often alive with people of all ages and social groups well into the night. This is in part the result of more relaxed licensing laws: as so many social activities involve drink, they stop when drink can no longer be served. A more continental attitude would be desirable from a social point of view, might help to make cities safer at night, and would boost tourism.

lead to safer drinking habits. The relaxed attitudes of continental Europe have not led to lower rates of alcoholism, or fewer deaths from alcohol. While overly strict legislation may be harmful, as was the case in Australia, the current British laws strike the right balance, especially with the introduction of the twenty minutes 'drinking-up time.'

[4]   The Scottish example may be misleading; the laws that were enforced there before reform were overly strict. Although a wider distribution of closing times might make the introduction of drunk patrons onto the streets less visible, it would not necessarily lower the risk that they might commit a crime. It might also create further problems by funnelling patrons towards establishments with later and later closing times, eventually bringing all the most serious drinkers together in one place.

[5]   There is substantially more to a nation's social – and drinking – habits than its licensing laws. Pubs, and pub opening times, are a unique part of British life; relaxing the law would not substantially change our cities.

Possible motions:
This House would drink all night.
This House believes that Britain's licensing laws are outdated and draconian.

Related topics:
Legislation v. Individual Freedom
Sunday Entertainment and Shopping
Child Curfews
Prohibition of Alcohol

Mandatory Prison Sentences

Currently in Britain a murder conviction carries a mandatory life sentence. In the early 1990s the Conservative Home Secretary Michael Howard brought in legislation to provide mandatory prison sentences for third convictions for burglary and for violent and sexual crime. The courts are still left a minimum degree of discretion to over-rule these mandatory sentences if they feel justice demands that they do so. In California there is a 'three strikes and you're out' policy. A third conviction for a felony (serious crimes against property and violent or sexual offences) carries a mandatory life prison sentence of three times the normal sentence for the offence or twenty-five years, whichever is the longer. The arguments below are for and against a system something like the Californian one with minimal judicial discretion.

Pros

[1]   Governments need to be tough on crime to counteract the alarming increases in crime that characterise modern Western societies. Mandatory prison sentences of, for instance, five years for third burglary convictions and mandatory ten year (or life) prison sentences for a third conviction for serious violent or sexual crimes are powerful and effective deterrents in the fight against crime.

[2]   Political gestures are important for public confidence. The government must be *seen* to be tough on crime. Mandatory sentencing will increase public confidence in the judicial process and make people feel safer in the face of the threat of serious crime.

[3]   It is particularly important for more serious crimes that there is consistency of sentencing. For prison sentences to be effective deterrents and for them to be seen to be justly and uniformly imposed, they must be imposed at the same level for the same crime by all judges. If repeat offences against property (theft and

Cons

[1]   First, the fact that mandatory sentences *may* have a deterrent effect does not begin to compensate for the injustices that such a system produce. A third offence in exceptional extenuating circumstances can technically qualify for a mandatory ten-year or life sentence despite clearly not deserving it. In an infamous case in California, the third felony that carried the mandatory life sentence for one unfortunate young man was the theft of a slice of pizza from a child on a beach. In another case a man was sentenced to fifty-one years for owning a forged driving licence, because it was his third felony. Judicial discretion must be allowed to decide each case on its merits. Second, prison sentences are an expensive way to make bad people worse and we should not be seeking to increase them. The Californian system has seen the prison population increase by 60 per cent in eight years. Probation and rehabilitation through community work and social reintegration (through measures such as help to return to employment) are the really effective ways to tackle crime.

burglary) are given substantial custodial sentences by some judges and not by others, then the sentence will not serve as a deterrent, but instead the criminal will be tempted to chance his or her arm. Allowing judicial discretion will result in too many freak verdicts of over-lenient sentences, and hence an erosion of the deterrent effect. The sentence received should be determined by the crime, not by the biases of the judge.

[4]   It is already the case that a criminal's previous convictions are taken into account when a judge passes sentence. A first-time offender is always sentenced more leniently and a repeat offender will be treated more harshly. Mandatory sentencing for third-time burglars, sexual and violent offenders is simply a formalisation and standardisation of this existing judicial procedure.

[5]   It is, of course, a concern that crackdowns on crime often seem to have harsher consequences on black, Hispanic and Asian individuals than on white members of the community. But mandatory sentencing is not the cause of this discrepancy – it is an endemic problem for the judicial system and for society as a whole, and has complex socio-economic causes. Black communities are often poorer than white – a hangover of centuries of discrimination and inequalities – and poverty causes crime.

[2]   Mandatory sentencing is an unnecessary political gesture, and an inappropriate meddling by politicians with a judiciary that should be kept apolitical and independent. There are already sentencing guidelines laid down by the Court of Appeal, and prosecutors have the power to appeal (often successfully) against sentences they consider to be too lenient. There are already mechanisms in place to ensure that appropriately severe punishments are meted out.

[3]   The whole problem with mandatory sentencing is that it makes sentencing *artificially* 'consistent', whereas every crime and every criminal is in fact unique. The punishment should fit the crime. That is why we should rely on judges to use their experience, expertise and discretion to apply sentencing guidelines in a fair and appropriate way. Governments legislating for mandatory sentences send out the message that the judiciary cannot be trusted to pass the correct sentence. Far from bolstering public confidence, this will undermine confidence in the fairness and reliability of the judiciary.

[4]   Exactly. There are *already* mechanisms and guidelines that ensure that a criminal's previous convictions are taken into account in the appropriate way. Mandatory sentencing is an unnecessary and unwelcome political gesture.

[5]   Mandatory sentencing – e.g. in the Californian experience – has been seen to hit ethnic minorities disproportionately hard. It is a worrying fact that law and order crack downs are often used by law enforcement officers and the judicial

Possible motions:

This House calls for mandatory sentencing for repeat offenders.

This House believes in 'Three strikes and you're out'.

Related topics:

Capital Punishment

Prison v. Rehabilitation

Zero Tolerance

system as an occasion for racist oppression of non-white communities.

Prison v. Rehabilitation

Pros

[1]   Prison is the right punishment for all crimes against property and all violent crimes. The primary purposes of punishment are deterrent, retribution and prevention. Prison serves all of these purposes well. The threat of the complete loss of liberty in a prison sentence deters potential criminals, criminals who are in prison are prevented, for that period, from committing further crimes, and prison is also society's way to gain retribution from an offender for what he or she has done. Rehabilitation is not part of the purpose of punishment and is very much a secondary concern of the justice system.

[2]   Prison works. Rehabilitation (counselling, psychiatric treatment, work in the community) is a soft option for criminals who will simply feel that they can continue to offend with virtual impunity so long as they volunteer for counselling and community work. The justice system must be seen to be strong

Cons

[1]   Prison is the wrong form of punishment for all but the most serious crimes (e.g. rape, murder). If we really want to reduce crime and live in a safer society we need to *understand* criminals as well as having our retribution against them for the wrongs they have done. Punishment without rehabilitation is merely dealing temporarily with the symptoms rather than addressing the root causes. A criminal who is put in prison cannot offend for that period of time, but when he comes out he will be the same person – or worse – and will simply go straight back to a life of crime. Rehabilitation must go together with deterrence, retribution and prevention as an integral primary concern of the justice system.

[2]   Prison does not work. As the British politician Douglas Hurd once said, 'Prison is an expensive way to make bad people worse'. Centuries of reliance on the retributive imprisonment system have

in its imposition of punishments if the fight against crime is to be won. Prison is the best form of punishment to send out this strong message.

[3]   For society to function we must maintain a strong sense of individual moral responsibility. We cannot allow people to absolve themselves of moral responsibility on the grounds of 'medical', 'psychological' or 'social' dysfunction. People have even claimed in their defence that they are genetically predisposed to crime and so should be treated leniently. These excuses are simply ways of hiding from the fact of moral transgression. A culture of rehabilitation denies individual responsibility and thus erodes the moral fabric of society. Prison sentences, enforced strictly, reinforce the crucial notion of individual responsibility for actions.

Possible motions:

This House would condemn more and understand less.
This House would be tough on crime.

Related topics:

Capital Punishment
Mandatory Prison Sentences
Sex Offenders (Chemical Castration of)

failed to stem the increasing crime rate. The way to reduce crime is to change people's beliefs and habits of behaviour – this is most effectively done by counselling and especially by integration into the community. If young people can be set to work on community regeneration projects rather than sent to young offenders' centres – which in effect are often little more than academies of crime – they will have a greatly increased chance of living a life free of crime in the future. In one American study, drugs offenders who spent twelve months in prison followed by six months drugs rehabilitation and training in skills for future employment had a 50 per cent lower re-offence rate than those imprisoned for similar offences for the whole eighteen months.

[3]   The autonomous morally responsible self is a myth. The victims of sexual abusers do not go on to become sexual abusers themselves just because, by coincidence, they are morally wicked people too. Children brought up with poverty, drugs and violence do not grow up to be criminals or drug users because they are just morally bad individuals. The advocate of radical individual responsibility is peddling an ineffective, simplistic and vindictive myth. In truth criminal behaviours have complex psychological and social causes that stretch well beyond the boundary of the individual. Parents, teachers and society at large must be responsible for teaching by example and understanding and healing disturbed individuals. Social regeneration through employment, reintegration of offenders into communities, the renewal of the family, counselling and psychiatry, rather than blank retribution through imprisonment, are the ways to reduce crime.

Prohibition of Alcohol

Pros

[1]   Statistics show undeniably that alcohol plays a role in many crimes. In the UK it is a factor in 65 per cent of murders, 40 per cent of cases of domestic violence, and a third of all cases of child abuse; the Association of Chief Police Officers puts the proportion of violent crime that is alcohol-related at about 70 per cent. Studies state that eight out of every ten people treated in accident and emergency departments are there because of alcohol use, with ten people killed through drink-driving every week and thousands permanently scarred every year by drunken fights. The government must intervene in response to these horrifying statistics by banning alcohol consumption.

[2]   As well as posing a risk to others, alcohol also harms the user, increasing the likelihood of liver failure, some forms of cancer, and involvement in accidents. Alcohol abuse can also have serious psychological effects. It is a common misconception that alcohol is not physiologically addictive, but regular use can result in a physical dependence, with all the problems that implies. As an addict cannot truly be said to be exercising 'free choice', the state has an even stronger right to intervene.

[3]   As a harmful and addictive drug, our treatment of alcohol should be the same as our treatment of cocaine or heroin. Moreover, alcohol is for many addicts the first drug on the path to ever harder drugs.

Cons

[1]   Alcohol is a factor in crime and can cause social problems. However, the vast majority of those who consume alcohol do so responsibly – for them, drinking is a harmless and pleasurable activity, which adds to their enjoyment of social events. Alcohol *abuse* should be tackled; to penalise the majority for the actions of a minority is not the solution. Prohibition would be a ham-fisted and over-simplistic way to deal with a complex issue.

[2]   While the state has the right to act against citizens when their actions are causing harm to others – as it does at the moment when drinking leads to violence or public nuisance – it does not have the right to interfere in their private lives. Drinking may carry a health risk for the individual, yet so do many legal activities, including most forms of sport; moreover, alcohol is different from most illegal drugs because responsible usage in moderation is neither addictive nor harmful (indeed, some medical research implies that it can do good).

[3]   Alcohol cannot be treated in the same way as other drugs. After thousands of years, drink plays an important role in our social lives, and even in religion; many of our social structures have been built up around it. As Prohibition in America (1919–33) demonstrated, this means that any such legislation cannot work – instead, it drives ordinary citizens into the hands of criminals, and in fact encourages experimentation with other drugs.

Removing this first link in the chain may be an important step to solving the drug problem altogether.

[4]   A great deal of money and effort is directed towards solving the problems caused by drink. Surely it would be wiser to focus efforts on eradicating the root cause of these problems.

Possible motion:

This House would ban all alcoholic drinks.

Related topics:

Legislation v. Individual Freedom
Drugs (Legalisation of)
Licensing Laws (Relaxation of)
Smoking (Banning of)

[4]   To say that alcohol is the root cause of many social ills is a dangerous over-simplification – rather, it is the *result* of those ills. Throughout history it has been convenient for politicians and moralists to blame drink for 'corrupting' citizens. From the time of Hogarth's *Gin Lane* through Victorian England, it was seen as one of the most significant dangers facing society, yet this was simply to ignore the fundamental injustices that drove the poor and the desperate to alcoholism. It is these which we must tackle: the Victorian hypocrisy of prohibition has no place in the modern world.

Prostitution, Legalisation of

The actual act of prostitution – exchanging sex for money – is legal in many countries, although other practices associated with it are not. In Britain, for example, solicitation (i.e. negotiating with potential customers), advertising, 'kerb-crawling' or running brothels (where two or more prostitutes work) are all illegal while prostitution itself is not. In the United States it is a misdemeanour, except in parts of Nevada. But that is not to say that Britain encourages prostitution – the act is legal because it happens behind closed doors and any law against it is unenforceable. This debate is therefore about the principle of tolerating open prostitution, and legalising *all* of its associated practices. It is assumed that child prostitution would remain illegal.

Pros

[1]   It is an adult's right to do with his or her body as he or she chooses, and this must include having sex with a consenting partner. The exchange of money does not invalidate the right to have sex. If two individuals have no moral problem with selling sex, they should be left alone to do

Cons

[1]   There is no parallel between the use of bodies by actors or builders and by prostitutes. The latter do not have the choice whether to sell their body or not; it is a male-dominated world and many young women are locked into a life of dependency, on customers and pimps.

it – no-one is suggesting that prostitution should be made *mandatory* for everyone else. Athletes, construction workers, models and actors all sell their bodies in a way and we have no problem with that.

[2]   Prostitution is a method whereby people who want sexual relations can easily have them. There are many people who are too busy, too unattractive, too shy or too lazy for the considerable effort of starting and maintaining a successful relationship. Some want variety or the fulfilment of specific fantasies. Unless it can be proved that prostitution is immoral in an absolute sense, then clearly it performs a valuable and popular function.

[3]   Whatever moral position is taken, it is clear that legalising prostitution would bring the many benefits of open regulation. In particular, the spread of AIDS and sexually transmitted diseases (STDs) demands that all prostitutes should be issued with licences, regularly renewed on the completion of a negative test for diseases.

[4]   Many prostitutes are forced into the profession because they have no skills or opportunities for other careers. Once involved in the black market, they are abused by pimps, susceptible to drugs and other crime, and at the mercy of violent customers, with no legal rights of redress. Bringing prostitution into the open allows these men and women to pursue a career safely, outside the black market, with none of its dangers.

[5]   The stigma attached to prostitution as it stands is immense, and a woman with one conviction is unemployable and

Consensual sex implies that both partners approach the act from an equal footing, with the same opportunities; this is clearly not the case with prostitution.

[2]   The sale of sex debases an activity that is fulfilled only in loving relationships. In particular it encourages infidelity by offering easy opportunity for conscience-free, extra-marital sex. The loving relationship is an ideal that should be encouraged, and people who are less attractive or too shy should be made to see that they can have such a relationship, rather than being relegated to a lifetime of visiting prostitutes.

[3]   At the moment, the spread of STDs among prostitutes is very low. They are well versed in spotting symptoms in customers, and insist on the use of condoms just as dentists use rubber gloves. Also, the sort of customer who might break the law in visiting prostitutes now is unlikely to be conscientious about demanding recently renewed licences.

[4]   Prostitutes are forced into the black market because they are usually homeless and need the rewards that crime can offer. Legalised prostitution, in the free market, will inevitably lead to loss in prices and profits due to competition. Prostitutes – and especially pimps – will merely move onto other criminal methods for lucrative profit: drugs, child prostitution, theft, and so on.

[5]   There should be stigma attached to a crime. We might as well legalise robbery to avoid endangering the future employment prospects of burglars.

trapped into a life of crime. This stigma would recede with legalisation, as it did in France until the Second World War when it was common and tolerated for girls to work in brothels for a few years, saving up for marriage dowries.

[6]   As has happened with New York's sex stores and strip clubs in the late 1990s, the legalisation of brothels would allow their location to be dictated by local authorities. They could be situated in industrial areas, away from residences and from each other, thereby avoiding the ghettos of illegal establishments spilling into residential areas which develop at the moment.

[6]   The location of brothels can already be dictated by authorities: namely, by shutting them down. The only reason why areas such as King's Cross and Soho in London, for example, are full of them is because they have traditionally been ignored by a police content to keep them under supervision. Far more concerted efforts could be made against the prostitution industry, and the fact that they have not been made is not an argument for legalisation.

Possible motions:
This House would lift all restrictions on prostitution.
This House believes that sex is sacred.

Related topics:
Legislation v. Individual Freedom
Feminism (Devaluation of Parenthood by)
Pornography
Zero Tolerance

Sex Offenders, Chemical Castration of

Castration means the removal of sex glands (ovaries or testes) in the male or female of any animal. It is used here in its most common sense of the removal of the *male* sex glands. 'Chemical castration' is a process whereby the effects of the sex glands are removed not by removing the glands themselves but by administering the appropriate hormones to the individual in question.

Pros

[1]   One of the principal purposes of the punishment for any crime is prevention of re-offence. Chemical castration would take away the sex drive of sex offenders and thus guarantee that they would not re-offend. It would also be a

Cons

[1]   Chemical castration is not an acceptable form of punishment. In a civilised society we do not permanently physically alter people as a form of punishment, but always allow for rehabilitation of some kind after a prison sentence has

strong deterrent. It is therefore an effective and appropriate punishment.

[2]   Sex offenders currently pose a problem for the criminal justice system. They are often victimised in prison and subjected to a witch-hunt and hounded out of each new community by concerned members of the public on their release. Chemical castration would make these people safe – they could live in the community without posing a threat. This would avoid their abuse in prisons, would help reduce the ever-increasing prison population and would allay the fears of concerned members of a community.

[3]   For the sake of the offender himself, chemical castration is the best solution. Offenders often feel that they are ill, or possessed by a physical force outside their control from which they long to be freed. Chemical castration would liberate them from the mental torture and resulting crimes of their condition by removing their sexual drive.

[4]   Sexual offending is caused by physical and mental disturbances working together. The psychological cannot be separated from the physiological. Chemical castration will get to the heart of the problem. Opposition to this view, and the tendency to 'psychologise' sex offending is often motivated by the desire to demonise the offender rather than to understand his medical condition. Chemical castration is humane and characteristic of an approach that seeks to understand rather than merely condemn.

been served. Also, as with the death penalty, miscarriages of justice would have disastrous permanent consequences if chemical castration were the sentence for all sex offences. Would first-time sex offenders be chemically castrated? The punishment is extreme and unsophisticated. Prison sentences and psychiatric treatment are to be preferred.

[2]   We cannot be confident that chemical castration would be such a magical cure. If sex offending really is just the result of chemical drives, then whatever the punishment, it will not work as a deterrent. Prison would still be needed as a form of deterrent and also to protect society even from those who have been chemically castrated. As for the public's response, the fear of parents and other members of the community will not be allayed by a chemical procedure – sex offenders will still be feared and hated and the subjects of witch-hunts.

[3]   First, our first thought should be to *punish* the sex offender. Second, when it comes to treating the sex offender himself, a more subtle form of counselling and rehabilitation is required rather than just putting our faith in a one-off physical treatment.

[4]   This is a simplistic view of sexual offending. It is not just a *chemical* problem. Sex offenders are psychologically disturbed in a way that cannot be cured by a 'magic pill'. The sexual abuse that often caused their own sexual offending is deeply mentally engrained. Sex offenders need psychological and psychiatric help.

Possible motions:
This House would chemically castrate sex
  offenders.
This House believes that sex offending can be
  chemically cured.

Related topics:
Ends v. Means
Bill of Rights
Prison v. Rehabilitation
Sex Offenders (Registration of)

Sex Offenders, Registers of

Since 1996 in the US it has been compulsory for enforcement agencies in all states
to release information concerning convicted sexual offenders residing in the area. This
is known as 'Megan's Law', named after 7-year-old Megan Kanka who was brutally
sexually assaulted and murdered in New Jersey.

Pros

[1] Society at large needs to be
informed of the whereabouts of sex
offenders after they are released from
prison so that it can take appropriate pre-
cautions and be fully informed. Parents,
in particular, will be concerned to have
this information available. Therefore sex
offenders, after their release from prison,
should be obliged to register with a local
police station whenever they move to a
new area, so that their details can be kept
up to date on a national register. Police
will inform local residents, schools, and so
on, when an offender from the register
moves to a new area.

[2] Sexual crimes are particularly
destructive and repugnant and there is a
worryingly high rate of reoffence. So,
although sex offenders cannot be kept in
prison indefinitely, and some will be successfully rehabilitated there is a need for
more vigilance and caution than with
released criminals whose offences were
petty or whose risk of re-offence is low.
Sex offenders are therefore a special case

Cons

[1] If sex offenders are ever to be rehabilitated we cannot treat them as social
outcasts and subject them to witch-
hunts. Whatever the good intentions of a
register, it inevitably means that the
whereabouts of sex offenders become
known and they are hounded out of
one neighbourhood after another. Community notification is a new punishment
imposed on people who have already
served their sentence. Already in some
parts of the US the information made
available has led to physical attacks on
convicted sex offenders who have served
their prison term and been released.

[2] If they are still a real risk to the
community they should not be allowed
out of gaol and prison sentences should
be increased. But if they are not, then
paranoia and loathing should not be
whipped up by introducing a register of
sex offenders. Any version of 'Megan's
Law' fails to discriminate between those
past offenders who still pose a risk, and
those who do not.

which demands a special measure – a national register.

[3]   Sex-related offences are often the most disturbing crimes and those that need most urgently to be solved to prevent a repeat offence. A register of past sex offenders will enable the police massively to increase the speed with which they can pursue leads and eliminate suspects. The register would be even more effective if it contained DNA samples as part of the information held on registered offenders.

[4]   The offenders themselves will benefit from being on such a register. With their whereabouts and employment always known, resources for continued monitoring and rehabilitation will always be available.

[3]   Probation and intelligence services already exist to keep tabs on high-risk individuals. The existence of a register merely serves to stigmatise unnecessarily those who have been successfully rehabilitated and to make social and familial re-integration impossible for all past offenders regardless of the real level of risk involved.

[4]   Resources for rehabilitation – such as counselling and psychiatric treatment – should be available to all past offenders with or without the existence of a register.

Possible motions:
This House would introduce a register of sex offenders.
This House would publicise the whereabouts of sex offenders.

Related topics:
Legislation v. Individual Freedom
National ID Cards
Privacy of Public Figures
Sex Offenders (Chemical Castration of)

Trials, Televised

Pros

[1]   The judicial process is currently mysterious and threatening to most ordinary people. If they find themselves in court they will be baffled and intimidated by the strange language and procedures of the court. The televising of trials and other judicial proceedings will demystify the process and serve to educate the

Cons

[1]   Mock trials in films and soap operas are often realistic and give everybody a very good idea of what happens in a courtroom. Increasingly great attention is paid to detail in historical and popular films, and the picture of the judicial system portrayed is reliable and accurate. If this is not considered enough, public

public about the judicial process. Only real court proceedings can truly perform this educative function – TV and film portrayals are over-dramatised, glamorised and unrealistic. Nobody will watch a public information film, but people will watch a real trial.

[2] Currently judicial proceedings are only accessible to the public at large via news reports in the media, which are partial and potentially biased. The television camera does not lie. Allowing TV cameras in courts will provide full, accurate and honest coverage of exactly what happens in any given case. Whatever media spin or reportage is laid over the TV coverage, the proceedings will be in full view of the public, which at the moment they are not.

[3] It is democratic to allow cameras in courts. The scrutiny made widely possible by television coverage of court proceedings will create healthy criticism of the process and personnel of the judicial system, and will make them answerable. Unfair laws, prejudicial practices and incompetent lawyers and judges will be exposed to a wide public.

[4] If trials are televised, a huge audience is made aware of the case and the evidence, and crucial witnesses may come forward who would otherwise have been ignorant of the case and their potential role in it. Televising trials will thus increase the chance of a fair trial.

information films of mock trials, or reconstructions of famous past trials can be shown – television coverage of actual trials is not necessary.

[2] There are already full and accurate records of court proceedings available to anyone who is interested in them. Legal reports in reputable newspapers are reliable and objective. Anyone truly interested in the judicial system can also sit in the public gallery of most courts. The TV media will in fact invariably create a much *more* distorted picture of a trial – as in the famous case of the O. J. Simpson trial which became a media zoo. Most people will not have the time or inclination to sit and watch every last boring minute of the process of a trial but will rely on 30-second 'soundbites' in the evening news with the biased spin of the TV journalists presenting the case. Cameras in courts will *increase* media distortion of trials.

[3] Injustices in the judicial system and incompetence of judges and lawyers are already fully reported in the press and broadcast media. There is no need to see actual pictures of scenes in a courtroom to believe these news stories or to act upon them. Judges have been forced to resign for widely publicised incompetence in Britain despite the lack of television cameras in courts. There are also many groups campaigning for fairer legal status, for instance for lesbians and gay men, despite the lack of televised judicial proceedings. Unfairness and incompetence will be reported on and campaigned against with or without cameras in courts.

Related topics:

Broadcasting (Ending Public Control of)

Privacy of Public Figures

Possible motions:

This House would put cameras in the court-room.

This House believes that justice should be blind.

Related topics:

Broadcasting (Ending Public Control of)

Privacy of Public Figures

[4]   Far from creating fairer trials, TV coverage will create more miscarriages of justice. Jurors will inevitably be swayed by high-profile TV reporting of cases and people will come forward as witnesses not because they have crucial evidence but because they want to become TV stars. American TV talk shows demonstrate that people are prepared to do and say absolutely anything to get on television – the same cannot be said about getting into the legal pages of *The Times*. Also, in countries such as the US where judges are elected, the televising of trials will lead to judges performing to the electorate by, for example, imposing harsher sentences than they otherwise might.

Zero Tolerance

'Zero tolerance' is a phrase that first came to light as a description of the crackdown on petty crime in New York City by William Bratton, police commissioner for that city, appointed by Mayor Rudolph Giuliani in January 1994. The aim of zero tolerance is to prevent petty criminals graduating to serious crime by imposing immediate and harsh sentences for petty offences such as under-age drinking, small-scale drug use and dealing, shoplifting or vandalism (rather than using cautions or fines). It is this particular law and order policy that the arguments below are about. 'Zero tolerance' is, however, a phrase that has come to be used in a panoply of other contexts to mean, for example, a tough and uncompromising approach to racism, fascism or violence against women.

Pros

[1]   We need to find innovative and effective new weapons in the ongoing fight against crime. Zero tolerance is just such a weapon. It sends a clear, tough message that the state will condemn and punish rather than be soft and 'understanding'. This stance functions as an

Cons

[1]   Zero tolerance is precisely the wrong way to approach crime. Understanding and rehabilitation rather than macho rhetoric of punishment and condemnation is the key to reducing crime. And far from raising public confidence in the police and judiciary, it makes them

effective deterrent to potential offenders, especially potential young offenders, and also raises public confidence in the police and judiciary.

[2] Zero tolerance works. Murders in New York City fell by 40 per cent between 1993 and 1997, while robberies and shootings fell by 30 per cent and 35 per cent respectively. These are phenomenally impressive results. Cities in Britain (e.g. Coventry) and Australia (e.g. Melbourne) have achieved similar impressive results through implementing zero tolerance of the use of drugs and alcohol in public places. Racism in police forces and in society at large is a problem but it is long-term and endemic, not the result of this particular policing initiative.

[3] Zero tolerance not only prevents young offenders from graduating to serious crime, it also breaks the back of organised crime by depleting the ranks of the 'foot soldiers', especially small-time drug dealers who together provide the power base and financial resources for drugs barons and Mafia bosses. Without these petty criminals on the streets, organised crime ceases to flourish.

[4] Zero tolerance is a policy developed by police on the streets for implementation by police on the streets. It will appeal to and motivate the police in a way that integrates them with the judicial system from which they often otherwise feel alienated. This is a crucial step in the fight against crime.

alienating and inflexible figures set over against society, rather than agencies that can work with and for members of their community.

[2] First, New York's gain is its neighbours' loss. A high-profile crack down on petty crime in one place simply makes the petty criminal move elsewhere to ply his trade. Second, these results are bought at a heavy cost. Brutality complaints against the New York Police Department have soared since the introduction of zero tolerance. Some police seem to have used the initiative as an occasion to oppress black communities. Zero tolerance may not cause racism but serves to increase and exacerbate it. Also, like mandatory sentencing, zero tolerance necessarily reduces judicial discretion in individual cases. A harsh fine or prison sentence may be inappropriate and counter-productive in many cases, but zero tolerance insists that no leniency, subtlety or professional judgement be shown by judges.

[3] Small-time drug dealers and petty thieves are not the real criminals. They are unfortunates trying to escape from poverty and deprivation through the income they can make through petty crime. Not only are they not the real criminals, they are also indefinitely replaceable from among the ranks of the poor and deprived. Once one set of petty criminals is locked up, a new set will emerge to replace them. The multi-million dollar fraudsters, money-launderers and drugs barons are the ones that must really be removed to bring down the system.

[4] Zero tolerance will encourage

Possible motions:

This House would have zero tolerance.

This House would crack down on petty crime.

This House would be tough on crime.

Related topics:

Legislation v. Individual Freedom

Beggars (Giving Money to)

Corporal Punishment

Capital Punishment

Child Curfews

Drugs (Legalisation of)

Mandatory Prison Sentences

Prison v. Rehabilitation

Prostitution (Legalisation of)

Sex Offenders (Chemical Castration of)

brutal and repressive policing. The de-humanising and extreme rhetoric associated with zero tolerance engenders a dangerous witch-hunting attitude towards the petty criminal, which will inevitably increase police heavy-handedness and brutality.

SECTION H

Health, Science and Technology

Alternative Medicine

Pros

[1]   Alternative Medicine is an umbrella term that covers relatively well accepted treatments (such as acupuncture) through to such controversial methods as faith healing and homeopathy (medicines diluted so many times that none of the original substance remains). Alternative medicine works for many millions of people across the world. Even if some scoffers would say their success was down to psychosomatic effects (or the 'placebo effect'), that does not change the fact that one way or another they improve people's health and as such should be welcomed, and made more widely available, e.g. on the NHS.

[2]   There have been studies of alternative medicine that show a beneficial effect not only on people but also on animals (in one case, horses were successfully treated using homeopathic remedies) – it can hardly be said that animals are being irrationally swayed by superstition. It is rather far-fetched to suggest that horses can pick up on the fact that their vet is confident the treatment is going to work.

[3]   Conventional medicine treats symptoms rather than causes. Alternative medicine treats the whole person and works in harmony with nature instead of fighting it. Too often, the side-effects of 'scientific' medicine can be as dangerous as the disease it supposedly fights (e.g. chemotherapy). Also, a surprisingly small percentage of traditional medical techniques are 'evidence-based' – that is to say

Cons

[1]   Some 'alternative' medicine (such as acupuncture) is clearly beneficial, even if the reason is unclear. But much of the rest, such as faith healing and homeopathy, has had no significant success. We must understand what is meant by a medicine 'working'. If a hundred migraine sufferers are given a tablet made of salt, some, perhaps the majority, will be 'cured'. This is the well-understood 'placebo effect', where an initial mis-diagnosis or the natural waning of an illness appears to be caused by a treatment, or where the patient's belief in a cure is so strong as to have a psychosomatic effect on the body. The only useful evaluation of a proposed medicine is by comparing its effects with that of a placebo. Homeopathy and similar quackery have never passed such an evaluation.

[2]   The study referred to (like several others purporting to show homeopathy working) was flawed in that it did not involve 'double blind tests'. For fifty years, medical evaluation procedures have ensured that not only is the patient ignorant of whether their treatment is the placebo, but the physician is also in kept in the dark. If the person administering the treatment knows whether or not it will work, with the best will in the world, their 'bedside manner' and general pastoral care will be affected – even with animals.

[3]   All this talk of 'holism' and working 'with nature' is no more than mystical

that many treatments are the result of *ad hoc* prescription of drugs and physical treatments that may or may not work but have never been proved to work in scientific tests. The dichotomy drawn between 'scientific' conventional medicine and 'unscientific' complementary and alternative therapies is a totally bogus one.

Possible motions:

This House would provide complementary medicine on the NHS.

This House believes that alternative medicine is bunkum.

Related topics:

Tradition v. Innovation

National Health Service (Privatisation of)

Animal Rights

Experimentation and Vivisection (Banning of)

Vegetarianism

Science: a Menace to Civilisation?

mumbo-jumbo. Medicine has sought to find the true causes of disease for hundreds of years. When faith healers claim someone's headache is caused by a 'bad aura' is that really going to help solve the problem? Conventional medicine can be complemented by conventional psychology and psychiatry to look at mental aspects of disease. Encouraging the use of faith, crystals, oils, herbs, homeopathy or aromatherapy is simply to give false hope to those who are ill and open up the market for charlatans and pseudo-mystics to exploit the aged, terminally ill, impressionable and credulous. In many cases patients are persuaded that they can dispense with their conventional medicine, and die.

Contraception for Under-age Girls

Pros

[1]   Young people will experiment with sex regardless of what the state, their doctor or anyone else says. One in three teens has intercourse before the age of 16, and Britain has a rate of teenage pregnancy twice the European average. The relative difficulty of access to free contraception is one of the most obvious reasons for this difference. To suggest that access should be restricted further is ludicrous.

Cons

[1]   Since 1985, doctors have been allowed to prescribe contraceptives for under-age girls without their parents' consent. Indeed the British Medical Association has said that any doctor who did inform the parents would be guilty of professional misconduct. As a direct result, 90,000 under-age girls were prescribed contraceptives in 1997. This is astonishing state-sanctioned immorality. If it is illegal for an under-age girl to have sex, it should surely be illegal for anybody

[2]   Young women should be given the information and resources to stand up for themselves and make informed choices. Not all parents are able or willing to give their daughters these resources. Contraception must be just one facet of a comprehensive sexual health and education programme, encompassing schools and society at large. And both research and comparisons with continental Europe show that such programmes delay sexual activity rather than promoting it.

[3]   Children should not be kept ignorant and in the dark, and then expected suddenly to be 'grown up' when they hit 16. Delaying problems is no substitute for solving them. Parents often find it difficult to raise issues of sex with their children – and yet under 5 per cent of parents opt out from optional sex education lessons for their children. Far from fighting against sex education, parents are crying out for it.

to aid and abet her in that activity. Moreover, the apparent official sanctioning of such behaviour can only encourage it.

[2]   We should not be encouraging young people to have sex at an early age. Contraception is far from being 100 per cent effective, and failure can lead to unwanted pregnancy or even AIDS. Rates of teenage pregnancy and abortion are rising all the time. And most contraception can not prevent sexually transmitted diseases (STDs) such as chlamydia or protect young women from the increased risk of cervical cancer that results from starting intercourse before the age of 17. Our resources would be better targeted at discouraging under-age sexual intercourse.

[3]   Children already have to cope with a barrage of sexual images from a multitude of sources (pop videos, magazines, films, the Internet); the state should not be joining in the assault. It is parents who should be empowered to provide a moral framework for their children, rather than doctors or the Government.

Possible motions:

This House would make contraception freely available.

This House believes that if you are old enough to be having sex then you are old enough to use contraception.

Related topics:

Population Control

Abortion on Demand

Sex Education

Eugenics: IVF and Genetic Screening

'Eugenics', meaning 'good breeding', was first used by the English scientist Francis Galton in 1883 to refer to the study of ways to improve the mental and physical characteristics of the human race through targeted mating. It did not then have the sinister overtones that it has since acquired through association with the attempts in Nazi Germany to exterminate entire racial and social groups. Modern techniques such as genetic engineering and in particular the genetic screening of embryos created by *in vitro* fertilisation have again raised the question of whether we should intervene to determine the biological make-up of our children.

Pros

[1]   Scientists predict that in the future *in vitro* fertilisation will be the normal way to make a baby, and sex will be merely a leisure pursuit. Using IVF, a large number of embryos can be made from the sperm and eggs of the parents. A cell biopsy can be done on each embryo and the DNA from the cell can be screened. This will tell the parents which of the embryos has the lowest risk of heart disease, cancer or diabetes and which will contract genetic diseases such as Alzheimer's, muscular dystrophy, haemophilia or cystic fibrosis later in life. This technology already exists, and it is inevitable and understandable that parents will want to use it to ensure their baby is as healthy as possible. Modern 'eugenics' is already occurring.

[2]   It is also *right* that the technology should be used. If we have the power to decide whether we bring a baby into the world with or without cystic fibrosis, with or without a genetic neurological disease such as Huntington's chorea (which brings on rapid and extreme mental dementia in middle age), then we surely have a duty to choose the latter. This is not genetic *engineering* – it is merely a case of choosing which of the embryos 'naturally' created from the parents' sperm and egg should be implanted in the womb.

Cons

[1]   It is right that those couples using IVF because they cannot conceive by other methods should be told whether their embryos have certain serious genetic defects, but a line must be drawn between this and the widespread use of genetic screening to make 'designer babies'. Apart from its being an affront to disabled people to suggest that those born with physical or mental impairments should be 'bred out' of the human race, to use genetic screening is to open up existing technology to widespread abuse. It is not inevitable that genetic screening will become widespread, but it *is* inevitable that if there is not an international moratorium on this development (as there should be) people will use it to select embryos conforming to stereotypes of intelligence, physical beauty, athleticism and so on. The modern eugenics of genetic screening will open the door to the creation of a new 'master race', narrowing down the human genetic pool in perpetuity according merely to current ephemeral and arbitrary standards and beliefs about ideal human mental and physical traits.

[2]   This is objectionable for three reasons. First, it envisages the use of human embryos as commodities and as resources of medical technology – as mere things rather than potential people.

[3]   Healthy embryos not chosen after screening can be frozen (as surplus IVF embryos often are) and offered up for 'adoption' by childless couples. Government agencies can be set up (as opposed to the private clinics that trade in these embryos in some states of America), analogous to adoption agencies, to administer and oversee this process. Couples will not be allowed to dictate the genetic make-up of the embryo but could be offered a selection of healthy embryos from which to choose. This method has two principal advantages over traditional adoption: first, the parents have an assurance that the embryo is genetically screened and so their child will be healthy, and second the mother will carry the child to term herself, thus forming an important additional physical and emotional bond with her child.

Possible motions:

This House calls for universal genetic screening.

This House would choose its babies.

Related topics:

Ends v. Means
Population Control
Abortion on Demand
Surrogate Mothers
Euthanasia
Genetic Engineering
Science: a Menace to Civilisation?

Those embryos that are rejected will be disposed of or indefinitely frozen. This is a dangerously cavalier attitude to take to human life. Second, it perpetuates the idea that those with physical 'defects' are inferior human beings. This is a narrow and discriminatory approach. Who are we to decide what physical traits are 'defects'? Those who are blind, deaf or impaired in other ways often develop quite exceptional talents that they would not have done had they been chosen for being genetically 'normal'. Third, we should be wary of artificially selecting against certain genes. Our genes survive, in general, by conferring some advantage. Even though the mapping of the different elements of the human genome is progressing rapidly, we have little understanding of how the different genes interact to form complex human traits. Many genes and groups of genes confer advantages as well as disadvantages (such as the gene for sickle-cell anaemia that protects against malaria). Selecting out genes for supposed 'defects' will narrow the human gene pool in a potentially dangerous way. Even though this form of genetics differs from genetic engineering, it shares many of the dangers.

[3]   This is a nightmarish scenario. The ghoulish predictions of Huxley's *Brave New World* and Orwell's *1984* are coming true. This proposal would make embryos into commodities to be chosen between like objects on a supermarket shelf. Second, it is a fallacy to assume that everyone has a fundamental right to be a parent. Those who cannot have children should foster or adopt children without homes of their own, or accept that parenting will not be a part of their life.

There is no need for this alarming use of screening and freezing embryos, since traditional adoption is available.

Genetic Engineering

One must be careful to distinguish between *genetic engineering* – actual tampering with the genetic code of a being or embryo – and other forms of intervention in the natural process. Some of the latter are grouped together in the topic 'Eugenics: IVF and Genetic Screening', which affect the 'natural way of things' but which do not involve changing or substituting DNA cells.

Pros

[1] There are myriad benefits to genetic engineering in the plant world, of immense significance to the world's starving millions. Perhaps the most immediate will be the creation of crop varieties that are resistant to disease, thereby requiring less pesticides and safeguarding the environment. Even more importantly, the development of varieties that require little in the way of expensive chemical treatments will be a boon to the developing world.

[2] Genetic engineering is nothing new. Man has been 'genetically engineering' crops and livestock by artificial selection for thousands of years. Wheat could never have evolved in the wild; the domestic cat is an artificial animal, the result of 4,000 years of 'unnatural' breeding. But in the past we had to genetically engineer indirectly, by painstaking cross breeding and hoping to keep certain genes. Genetic engineering allows us to transfer genes one at a time, and with a far greater degree of certainty. It is a revolution only in technique.

Cons

[1] Genetic engineering involves man acting in a sphere that should be the preserve of God, or at least natural evolution. In the quest for ever greater profits, we are fiddling with workings that we barely understand.

[2] The promises made now about genetic engineering are reminiscent of those made about pesticides in the 1950s and 1960s (e.g. DDT), which proved disastrous for the food chain. Like all science from nuclear power to the 'green revolution', we can be sure genetic engineering will promise far more than it will deliver, and create problems no-one can predict.

[3] Genetic engineering poses serious risks which we barely understand. For example, a soybean variety which had been engineered to resist a herbicide was withdrawn from sale after it was discovered that a brazil nut gene inserted into the soybean DNA caused an allergic reaction in people allergic to nuts. A genetically altered cotton plant, designed

Internet is no different. Freedom of speech is not an absolute but a right that our society gives us; when, however, freedom of speech conflicts with another individual's right to privacy, quality of life or even life itself, censorship is not only justified but a duty of any society. Racist and terrorist propaganda and hardcore pornography on the Internet should be censored. The landmark Communications and Decency Act (CDA) was passed in 1996 in the US to tackle this problem.

[2]   The particular nature of the Internet adds to the dangers mentioned above. There has never been a more efficient mechanism for the mass distribution of the most pernicious material, which can be delivered while guaranteeing the anonymity of the viewer. Instructions on how to build bombs placed anonymously by a Finnish fanatic can be surfed by an 11-year-old in Scunthorpe. The potential for danger is huge if left uncontrolled.

[3]   Encryption, whereby information is encoded by the sender and can only be decoded by the intended recipient, is proving a handy tool for terrorist cells across the world. It is a right of governments to censor these encrypted transmissions in an effort to combat terrorism. Some countries, e.g. Pakistan and China, require citizens to submit passports or other ID in order to obtain 'clearance' to use the Internet.

[4]   The difficulty of doing something should not stop us trying. Although the dictatorial nature of many countries that censor successfully – e.g. China, Burma, censor our country's media, but the Internet is a different, genuinely worldwide phenomenon. The right to speak is valid only if someone else has the right to disagree – so if we allow a wealth of beneficial information to be transmitted, we must also allow a minority of immorality. An appeal against a section of the CDA was upheld by the US Supreme Court for this reason.

[2]   No school would allow an 11-year-old to wander on his own in an unknown town, and neither should it allow him unfettered access to the Internet. Adults are responsible for their own actions but must also be responsible for the young; that responsibility lies with parents and teachers rather than legislators. Parental control and restriction of the Internet (which can be done with software tools such as *SurfWatch* or *SafeSurf*) are not the same thing as censorship, just as the rating system for videos is not the same as banning films outright.

[3]   Encryption, by its nature, is also the tool for many advances in human rights – the only method that people under repressive regimes have to communicate with the outside world. It is also invaluable for safeguarding credit card details and other private information. If a government censors encrypted material, it has to censor it all – since it cannot see it to tell the difference!

[4]   The global nature of the Internet renders any individual country's efforts to censor it meaningless. If something is banned in Britain, then a computer user can access it by a different route in the Netherlands. China has had to relax

[3]   Problems of dysfunctional varieties that may arise are nothing to be alarmed about. They would equally have arisen from cross-breeding and simply illustrate that genetic engineering should be employed with as much care as any other cross-breeding technique.

[4]   Genetic engineering can be used in humans in two ways – either *germ line* therapy or *somatic* therapy. The former involves engineering genes in the sex cells of potential parents to alter the genetic material inherited by their offspring (e.g. seeking to remove the gene for Alzheimer's or MS) and thus has long-term repercussions. Somatic therapy deals only with the individual during his or her lifetime and is not inherited – e.g. giving a diabetic a gene to produce insulin internally. We should be more cautious with germ line therapy but both can be used for the medical benefit of humanity.

[5]   Cloning is an exciting new development – among other things, a way to provide children for childless couples. The opposition to cloning is almost entirely fantastical and hysterical. The medical profession will not allow people to believe that a clone will be a replica of themselves or a potential replacement for a deceased loved one. Identical twins, like clones, have identical genetic material, but we do not consider them replicas of each other – environment and experience make them into totally different people. The same will be the case with clones.

to resist frost, produced plants that never ripened.

[4]   Genes are complicated things related to each other in complex ways that we do not always understand. We know that some genes with negative effects (e.g. the gene for sickle cell anaemia) survive because of the positive benefits they also bring (immunity from malaria). We do not know what benefits and essential human traits we are playing with when we permanently alter genetic make-up at the germ-line level. We should err on the side of caution and have a moratorium on genetic engineering until our knowledge is better developed. The prejudices of the current age (in favour, perhaps, of very narrow sporting, economic or intellectual abilities) will be inscribed into our genetic heritage for centuries to come. This sort of mentality was behind the Nazi ideology that resulted in the Jewish holocaust.

[5]   Cloning is a procedure that is open to many of the same dangers and abuses as genetic engineering. It is, furthermore, worrying that people might be egotistical enough to clone themselves to make offspring. People like that are not fit to be parents. Clones will be used to replace deceased loved ones – disillusioning for the creator and demeaning for the clone. Clones of celebrities, scientists, the healthy, intelligent, athletic and so on will become commodities on a world market. Dictators will clone weak-willed and physically fit soldiers into armies. For these reasons human cloning is illegal in the UK, while a moratorium has been imposed on further research in the US.

Possible motions:
This House believes that the benefits of genetic engineering outweigh the dangers.
This House would send in the clones.

Related topics:
Abortion on Demand
Eugenics: IVF and Genetic Screening
Science: a Menace to Civilisation?

Global Warming, More Action on

Pros

[1]   The pollution we have pumped into our atmosphere since the industrial revolution threatens to cause long-term climate change. In particular, carbon dioxide from the burning of fossil fuels is thought to build up in the upper atmosphere and act like a 'greenhouse' – letting sunlight in but preventing heat from escaping. Projections show global temperatures rising by 3° Celsius in the next century, sufficient to melt the polar ice caps and cause widespread flooding. The four hottest years in recorded history have been in the last decade. Extreme weather phenomena have become more common, from droughts and floods in sub-Saharan Africa to water shortages in south-east England. Countries such as Bangladesh and some of the Pacific island states are in danger of being totally submerged in the near future if current levels of global warming continue. More limits on carbon dioxide emissions are essential – the progress made at the Kyoto summit was no more than a start.

[2]   Tighter controls on emissions must be introduced. Western countries should be allowed to 'buy' the emission quotas of developing countries that succeed in bringing their levels down. This will

Cons

[1]   The environmental lobbyists have been prophesying doom for decades, but the world still seems to continue with relative stability. There have always been natural climactic cycles – ever since the last Ice Age the world has been getting warmer. There is no conclusive evidence that man is responsible for the current change – in fact the earth's temperature fell between 1940 and 1970 despite a rapid injection of carbon dioxide into the atmosphere, and there has been no warming in the Arctic despite 'computer predictions'. But alarmism always makes better television than measured and sober scientific analysis.

[2]   The West has built its prosperity upon industrial growth. Pollution controls will have the effect of preventing such growth in the developing world – such controls amount to environmental imperialism. It is inevitable that at this economic stage emissions will be greater and it is hypocritical of the West to insist that developing countries do not do what they themselves have done for centuries. In the absence of hard evidence of the causes of global warming, emission limits should not be further reduced.

reduce total global emissions while also providing investment in, and financial incentives for, 'green' forms of industrial development in developing countries.

[3]   When the potential harm is so great, we cannot sit around waiting for 'certainty'. Putting economics ahead of the environment will mean that some countries cease to exist – presumably the worst economic scenario for any nation. The environment is fundamental to the flourishing of life from the most basic to the most prosperous and must be our number one priority. And pollution controls have many beneficial side effects – improving the quality of life for people choking in polluted cities and encouraging energy conservation rather than consumption.

[3]   Environmentalists wish to c jobs and reduce our nation's weal the basis of an unproven theory. scare-mongering and indoctrin (particularly of children) threaten very way of life. Energy conservatio pollution controls should be encou up to a point (as they already are) economic productivity and imp standards of living must remain number one priority.

Possible motions:
This House would take urgent action to global warming.
This House believes that global warmi the biggest danger facing the mo world.
This House would put the environn before economics.

Related topics:
Environment (Links to International Tr and Relations)
Nuclear Energy
Science: a Menace to Civilisation?

Internet, Censorship of

Since the 1960s, when the Internet was developed by the Pentagon as a military ne work capable of surviving nuclear war, the technology and number of users ha grown at an unthinkable rate. This explosion has brought with it all sorts of moral a practical questions.

The related topics, especially 'Censorship by the State', are crucial to this debate. will also be necessary to research the latest position on Internet control in vario countries, since this changes frequently.

Pros

[1]   We censor all of our media in the interests of society as a whole, and the

Cons

[1]   Censorship of any form is danger ous, and open to misuse. We can certainl

Indonesia and many Islamic states in the Gulf – may repel us, it shows that censorship can be successful. Web browsers could be adapted, for example, so as to be able to access only servers with an official stamp of approval.

[5]   If governments do not have the resources to monitor websites and control their contents, then they can force Internet Service Providers (ISPs) to vet the sites in their own domain and make them liable for indecent material transmitted. This procedure is being tested in Australia.

[6]   If a global solution is needed, it can be applied, based on the model of international treaties protecting intellectual property rights. The material we are discussing (e.g. racist propaganda) is considered undesirable everywhere.

its restrictions because of their ineffectiveness.

[5]   An ISP is a distribution medium, with no editorial control or input; it is bound by its contract to provide bandwidth and disk space to those who pay for it without having any involvement in the content. Also, if ISPs are threatened with severe penalties, they are likely to censor far too much in order to be safe – resulting in the loss of many harmless sites.

[6]   Not all countries share the same moral code and they cannot be forced to do so. Why should the US lose access to something because it is considered inappropriate in Singapore?

Possible motions:
This House would censor the Internet.
This House believes that the information super-highway needs traffic police.

Related topics:
Censorship by the State
Legislation v. Individual Freedom
Broadcasting (Ending Public Control of)
Privacy of Public Figures
Trials, Televised

Nuclear Energy

Pros

[1]   The world faces an energy crisis. Oil will be exhausted within fifty years, and coal will last less than half that time. It is hard to see how 'alternative' sources of energy will fulfil growing

Cons

[1]   The costs of nuclear power stations are enormous, especially considering the stringent safety regulations that must be installed to prevent disaster. Alternative energy, however, is only prohibitively

power needs. It is estimated, for example, that it would take a wind farm the size of Texas to provide for the power needs of Texas. The inefficiency of alternative energy technologies makes them impractical as solutions for large-scale energy needs. Only nuclear power can supply our energy needs, and the nuclear power stations we use at present (nuclear fission) will last for hundreds or even thousands of years. Though expensive to build, they are economic in the long run.

[2]   The Chernobyl disaster, widely cited as the reason not to build nuclear power plants, happened in the Soviet Union where safety standards were notoriously lax, and often sacrificed for the sake of greater productivity. In modern nuclear power stations the safety checks and procedures are strictly applied to ensure that there is never another Chernobyl.

[3]   Burning fossil fuels is highly polluting. In the lower atmosphere, the sulphur dioxide and other pollutants cause smog and can lead to acid rain. In the upper atmosphere, build-up of carbon dioxide is believed to accelerate the greenhouse effect, causing global climate change. So-called 'alternative' energy sources have their own environmental problems: for example river barriers and dams can devastate the eco-systems of wide areas (e.g. the Three Gorges Dam project in China, where an area of outstanding natural beauty was flooded in order to create a hydro-electric plant, leaving 2 million in need of new homes, destroying 30,000 hectares of farmland, thousands of fishermen without jobs and priceless historical sites submerged). By comparison

expensive because there is no economic imperative to develop it when oil and gas are so cheap. As fossil fuels become scarce, necessity will help us both reduce our energy usage and exploit new energy sources. Predictions of the end of oil are notoriously unreliable – we were told in the 1970s that fossil fuels would run out in twenty years. If governments were prepared to put the huge level of resources into research and development of alternative energy sources that have been into nuclear energy – as part of military research, with very little return – their efficiency and safety would increase massively.

[2]   It is simply not worth the risk. Nuclear power stations are lethal time-bombs, polluting our atmosphere today and leaving a radioactive legacy that will out-live us for generations. Chernobyl showed the potential for catastrophe; even twelve years later there were fields in Scotland that are considered dangerously contaminated, and wide swathes of Ukraine have terrifying cancer rates. Even when under 'control' in the UK, the leukemia clusters around our power stations and reprocessing centres for nuclear waste (e.g. Sellafield) show the inherent dangers.

[3]   Clearly the exhaustion of fossil fuels will bring many benefits by reducing pollution, but in the meantime they are the only cost-effective fuel we have. As for the claim that nuclear energy pollutants produce little pollutant – even after decades of well funded research, we have no way to dispose safely of high-level radioactive waste.

with these problems, nuclear power is positively benign, producing small amounts of pollutant that can be easily controlled.

[4] The problems of the nuclear energy programme have been a result of bureaucracy and obsessive secrecy resulting from nuclear energy's roots in military research. These are problems of the past. In the future we can improve on even this – the development of nuclear fusion in the next thirty years will provide a virtually limitless energy source with no pollution.

[4] In the 1950s we were promised that nuclear energy would be so cheap that it would be uneconomic to meter electricity. Today, nuclear energy is still subsidised by the taxpayer. Old power stations require decommissioning that will take 100 years and cost billions.

Possible motions:

This House says 'Yes, please' to nuclear power.

This House would extend the use of nuclear power.

Related topics:

Nuclear Weapons (Banning of)

Global Warming (More Action on)

Science: a Menace to Civilisation?

Science: a Menace to Civilisation?

Pros

[1] Science has to take a large measure of responsibility for providing the instruments of destruction (nuclear, chemical and biological weapons) used so often this century. Not only has it given us the means to destroy each other efficiently and ruthlessly, but we can also undermine the environment slowly and insidiously in times of peace, through the technological developments of the industrial revolution (c.1750-1850) such as the coal-fired steam engine, and more recently through fossil- and nuclear-fuelled power stations. Developments in genetic science have brought us to the brink of realising the nightmare scenarios of novels such as Aldous Huxley's *Brave New World* and George Orwell's *1984*.

Cons

[1] Science is like any other invention of mankind, and condemning the failures of science is as pointless as denouncing religion, democracy or philosophy for their failings. Science – the investigation, manipulation and prediction of natural phenomena – has been one of mankind's greatest endeavours for millennia and its benefits must be judged alongside its disasters. Discoveries in medical science have led to pasteurisation, vaccination, antibiotics, anaesthetics, the obliteration of smallpox, transplant surgery, genetic engineering and many more life-saving discoveries. Hysterical allusions to science fiction novels do not capture the reality of the tightly regulated practice of modern genetic engineering.

[2]   It is doubtful whether science has really improved our lives. Does today's technological society really make us happier and more fulfilled than the lifestyles of the pre-industrial age? It is far from obvious. Electronic entertainment technologies and information technologies threaten to numb the brains of each new generation, killing social skills and the art of conversation.

[3]   Science has also produced the underlying philosophies of modern times. The result has been a blank, atheistic vision − a vision of an impersonal and meaningless universe in which, in the words of Thomas Huxley, we are nothing more than 'specks of dust in the cosmic machine'. Despair, arbitrary cruelty, materialism and apathy prevail. Note that the two most destructive ideologies of the twentieth century were both inspired by science − Communism by Marx's 'scientific materialism' and Nazism by Darwin and eugenics.

[4]   Science has been responsible over the past 200 years for the systematic torture and exploitation of animals in medical research, cosmetics research, chemical research, and 'scientific' farming techniques. Only the uncivilised would allow this cruelty.

Possible motions:

This House believes that science is a menace to civilisation.

This House believes that the march of science has gone too far.

Related topics:

Nuclear Weapons (Banning of)

[2]   One can always criticise and the grass is always greener, but without the developments that science has brought in agriculture, sanitation, childcare and medicine, most of us would not be here − we would have been victims of the massive child mortality rates that prevailed in all previous centuries. Thanks to science, life expectancy has doubled in the past 200 years.

[3]   Science is not incompatible with a sense of meaning and wonder at the beauty of life and the universe. As Richard Dawkins has said, science can rival religion as a teacher of awe, of purpose and of morality. Marx's materialism had nothing really to do with science, and Darwin's theories can be used to argue many different ideological positions. In stark contrast to Nazi ideology, many (including Darwin himself) have interpreted Darwin's theory as demonstrating the equality of all races (and, indeed, all species) on the grounds of their shared ancestry. Science may have been used by some nihilistic or oppressive ideologies but belief in them is not required in order for science to be valid. Science, like religion, can be used for good or for evil.

[4]   On the contrary, the success of Darwin's theory of evolution by natural selection has been the driving force in civilising us in our attitudes to animals, by drawing attention to our shared ancestry. But, in any case, refusing to experiment on animals in developing cures for diseases of humans would not be a sign of civilisation but of lunacy.

Smoking, Banning of

Pros

[1]   Smoking tobacco is proved to cause emphysema, chronic bronchitis, heart disease and cancer of the mouth, throat, oesophagus and lungs. Half of the teenagers currently smoking will die from disease caused by tobacco if they continue to smoke, 25 per cent before they are 70. The nicotine in tobacco makes it extremely addictive. It is the responsibility of the state to protect citizens from themselves, which is why bareknuckle boxing and heroin are banned, and tobacco should be too.

[2]   In recent years more and more evidence has emerged of the effects of cigarette smoke on non-smokers – 'passive smoking'. Like drink-driving it greatly increases the risk of serious harm to self and to others. There are many conflicting studies on the risks of passive smoking – some saying it significantly increases the risk of cancer – but almost all agree that there are significant health risks involved.

[3]   At present millions of law-abiding citizens smoke, but 70 per cent of them say they want to give up. The banning of tobacco would be a severe but effective way of ensuring that these people *did* stop smoking. These people are not the sort

Cons

[1]   Tobacco does indeed increase the risk of contracting certain diseases, but the banning of smoking would be an unacceptable encroachment on individual freedom. We allow adults to choose how much fat to eat, how much exercise to take, how much alcohol to drink. All these decisions have far-reaching health implications, but we do not ban cream cakes, laziness or beer. The individual must be left to decide for herself if she wants to take the risk of smoking, rather than being dictated to by a nanny state.

[2]   Passive smoking has been a problem in the past, but this has been effectively addressed by the introduction of non-smoking sections in bars and restaurants and the banning of smoking in most workplaces, theatres, cinemas and public transport. The effects of passive smoking have, however, been greatly exaggerated. A recent WHO report stated that the risk of contracting cancer from second-hand smoke is less than the risk of cancer associated with eating citrus fruit or with having an abortion. We should also be aware that the massive air pollution caused by motor vehicles poses a significantly greater threat to everyone's health than do the relatively insignificant 'emissions' of cigarettes – surely cars should go first.

to get involved in underground drugs activities and so will simply stop smoking. Banning smoking is a form of 'tough love'.

[4] Unlike some other drugs, tobacco has *no* positive effects. Alcohol can make people relaxed and sociable and uninhibited in a positive way. Cigarettes give the illusion of relieving tension simply because of the relief of nicotine withdrawal; in fact smokers are the most tense, fidgety and anxious of all. Tobacco is particularly expensive and used more by the poor than the rich – but purchase of thirty cigarettes a day uses up most of unemployment benefit, for example. The present measure of ever increasing taxes on cigarettes does not make people stop smoking but just makes them poorer, more unhappy and more dependent on the drug.

[5] The economic cost of smoking to the NHS comes to hundreds of millions of pounds each year. Millions of working hours are lost annually to industry and commerce as a result of smoking-related illness. Those who smoke twenty cigarettes a day or more have twice as much time off work due to illness as do non-smokers. This is an unacceptable economic cost for something with no benefits.

Possible motions:

This House would ban tobacco smoking.
This House believes tobacco is a hard drug.

Related topics:

Legislation v. Individual Freedom
Drugs (Legalisation of)
Prohibition of Alcohol

[3] We must allow people to make their own decisions unless massive, certain and immediate dangers are involved (as with heroin, say, but not tobacco). People can become addicted to coffee, jogging, shopping and many other things. It is up to them to kick the habit if they want and are able to. Banning tobacco would immediately create a culture of millions of addicted criminals, forming a black market as did Prohibition in 1920s America.

[4] Smoking is relaxing. Even if the effect is the result of nicotine withdrawal or is mainly psychological, it does not alter the fact that for many people smoking is a genuine pleasure on which they choose to spend their money. It is true that to increase tobacco duty imposes a tax on the poor, which is why the duty should be reduced rather than increased – but that is not an argument for banning smoking. Banning smoking in some parts of public meeting places and forms of public transport is as far as the anti-smoking movement can reasonably go.

[5] Revenue from duty and VAT on cigarettes exceeds the cost to the NHS by more than 10 to 1 (estimated figures for 1997 put the annual cost to the health service at £610m while the revenue in duty and tax from cigarettes is over £10 billion). As for the question of lost working hours – how many hours of work are lost each year because of hangovers, or long corporate lunches?

Space Exploration

Pros

[1] Scientific understanding of the origins, nature and destiny of the universe we live in is one of the crowning achievements of human civilisation and a goal to be pursued for its own sake. The pictures of nebulae, black holes, distant galaxies, white dwarfs and other extraordinary phenomena produced by the Hubble space telescope may not be of immediate material use in terms of day-to-day economics but they are wonderful and fascinating achievements. It is also of great existential importance that we know where we came from and what our place is in the universe. The Big Bang theory and speculations about the future of the universe fulfil that existential need which used to be fulfilled by religion.

[2] Astronomy – the study of the stars – has always been used to understand and predict our own planet better. Ancient Egyptians used the stars to predict when the Nile would flood, and astronomy has always been used for navigation and meteorology as well. Studying the behaviour of light and chemical elements in conditions characterised by extremes of time, space, distance, heat and gravity tells us about the fundamental laws of nature and characteristics of matter – the same laws and matter that we seek to manipulate and predict here on earth. Space exploration may lead to the longed-for 'Theory of Everything' sought by scientists such as Stephen Hawking who are trying to unify general relativity and quantum mechanics.

Cons

[1] We cannot afford to spend billions on space telescopes, space shuttles, space probes, space stations and the like when poverty and starvation exist on earth. Quality of life for all must take priority over knowledge for its own sake. As for the existential dimension – scientific space research and cosmology has created a bleak and depressing worldview of an impersonal and purposeless universe condemned either to thermodynamic heat death or a 'big crunch' in which we are meaningless specks of cosmic dust.

[2] The earth itself provides ample testimony to the laws of nature and the nature of matter – testimony found in the discoveries of geologists, biologists, chemists and particle physicists. We will never encounter a black hole or a supernova or an object travelling at the speed of light and so do not need to understand them. Only scientists who are not content with everyday reality and earthly interactions seek comfort and escape in the speculative fantasies of cosmology and space research.

[3] Satellites are not really examples of space exploration technology. They would have been discovered without exploring space per se. They are essentially examples of terrestrial technology developed for purely terrestrial purposes.

[4] It is misleading to suggest that space exploration was a necessary prerequisite for all these discoveries. In the case of

[3]   Through space exploration and the need to construct probes and satellites, satellite technology has been developed which has provided us with massively increased and improved broadcasting, telecommunications and weather-predicting capabilities. This alone would justify the expenditure that has been put into space research.

[4]   Space research, especially experimentation done in zero-gravity conditions in space stations, has resulted in myriad scientific and technological spin-offs from super-conductors and miniaturised micro-chips to non-stick frying pans. We should continue to fund space research to allow more such breakthroughs to be made.

[5]   Investment in radio telescope technology and strategic space-based interceptors is imperative to foresee and avert comet and meteorite strikes. Outer space is filled with millions of meteorites (lumps of rock and metal) and comets (lumps of ice) travelling in orbits around stars such as our sun at huge velocities. One of these is bound to be on a collision course with Earth at some point in the future. Some scientists who studied Comet Swift-Tuttle when it passed by the earth in 1992, predicted that it would return to hit earth in 2126. The consequences of such an impact would be disastrous, causing massive 'greenhouse' effects, tidal waves, fires and earthquakes, and would shroud the earth in dust and water vapour. The death of the dinosaurs is believed to have resulted from such an impact.

[6]   The universe contains 100 billion

computer technology, as with so many technologies, the driving force was large-scale military investment in research and development. We should also look at the negative spin-offs – the Reagan administration's Strategic Defense Initiative or 'Star Wars' project which developed technology for space-based nuclear missile interceptors, and the escalation of the Cold War arms race.

[5]   Alarmist stories about the destruction of the earth make good television. In reality the chances of the earth being hit by a meteorite or comet are minimal, and in that eventuality the chances that we would have the time or power to do anything about it are minimal.

[6]   The size of the universe is the reason why there probably is intelligent life elsewhere and also, ironically, the reason why we will never get in touch with it. The distances involved are immense. The nearest major galaxy to ours is 2 million light years away, which means that even a message communicated at the speed of light from that galaxy to us would take 2 million years to arrive, and that could happen only if other life forms are communicative and located improbably close to our own galaxy. The search for extra-terrestrial intelligence is futile. Belief in aliens and UFOs is not a result of science but of popular superstition and hysteria whipped up by such cult TV shows as *Star Trek* and *The X Files*.

galaxies, each of which contains 100 billion stars like our sun. Since all galaxies and planets were formed through the same processes subsequent to the big bang 15 billion years ago, it is virtually certain that in some of these galaxies organic life and other intelligent life forms have also evolved. We should invest in space exploration to seek signs of extra-terrestrial life and use radio telescopes to listen for their communications to us.

Possible motions:

This House would increase funding for space exploration.

This House would boldly go where no House has gone before.

This House believes the truth is out there.

Related topics:

Tradition v. Innovation

Science: a Menace to Civilisation?